Policing, Ethics and Human Rights

Policing and Society Series

Series editors: Les Johnston, Frank Leishman, Tim Newburn

To Sarah and Diane
Looking forward to the return of weekends!

Policing, Ethics and Human Rights

Peter Neyroud
Alan Beckley

With contributions by
Paul Collier
Julia Clayton

WILLAN
PUBLISHING

Published by

Willan Publishing
Culmcott House
Mill Street, Uffculme
Cullompton, Devon
EX15 3AT, UK
Tel: +44(0)1884 840337
Fax: +44(0)1884 840251
e-mail: info@willanpublishing.co.uk

Published simultaneously in the USA and Canada by

Willan Publishing
c/o ISBS, 5824 N.E. Hassalo St,
Portland, Oregon 97213-3644, USA
Tel: +001(0)503 287 3093
Fax: +001(0)503 280 8832

First published 2001

ISBN 1-903240-16-6 (cased)
ISBN 1-903240-15-8 (paper)

British Library Cataloguing-in-Publication Data

A catalogue record for this book is available from the British Library.

Set in Palatino and Gill Sans

Printed by TJ International Ltd., Padstow, Cornwall, PL28 8RW

Table of Contents

List of figures   ix

About the authors and contributors   xi

Foreword by the Rt. Hon. Jack Straw, MP, Home Secretary   xiii

Part 1

**1 Ethics in context: policing and its environment in the
twenty-first century**   3
Policing, ethics and human rights?   3
A brief history of ethics and policing   5
Transition or crisis?   11
Summary and conclusions   17
Further reading   17

2 The purposes of policing: past, present and future   19
Introduction   19
Policing, government and the citizen   19
A history of the policing mission   22
The present: what do the police actually do?   26
Policing futures   29
The three 'futures'   30
The 'futures' at work   31
The lessons of the 'three futures'   34
Conclusion: which 'future'?   35
Further reading   36

3 From ethics to principles and practice   37
Introduction   37
Ethics and policing   37
Ethical theory   39
Duty, utility, virtue and care   41
The ethics of uncertainty   45
A new ethics for policing?   47
Principles in policing   50
Conclusions   51
Further reading   51

4 From ethics to rights   54
Introduction: human rights as a 'new agenda in policing'   54
Human rights: the history of an idea and its meaning   55
Human rights and international standards in policing   61
ECHR: articles and principles   61
Conclusions: rights and their impact on policing   68
Further reading   70

Part 2   71

5 Personal ethics   73
Introduction
The professional vocation of policing?   74
The cultures of policing   78
Discretion   82
Citizens in uniform   86
Conclusions   91
Further reading   92
Notes   93

6 Police performance management – an ethical dilemma?   94
Introduction   94
Governance of policing   96
Framework   98
Police performance management   105
Towards a new paradigm   117
Conclusions   120
Further reading   122
Notes   122

7 Operational ethics   124
Introduction   124
Covert policing   125

Contents

Ethical and human rights compliant covert policing?   131
Policing dangerousness   135
Police and the use of force   137
Conclusions: towards ethics in operational policing   143
Further reading   143

8 Organisational ethics   **145**
Introduction   145
'Operational accountability'   146
Complaints, misconduct and corruption   154
Policing diversity   159
Conclusions   164
Further reading   165
Notes   165

Part 3   167

9 Human resource solutions   **169**
Introduction   169
Recruitment of police officers   170
Training   175
Personnel investigations, operational controls and
    anti-corruption investigations and audits   181
Personal development of staff   183
Conclusions   186
Further reading   187
Notes   187

10 Decision making, codes and control systems   **189**
Introduction   189
Ethical codes   189
Decision making   198
Conclusions   202
Further reading   203

11 'Auditing' for compliance: a human rights case study **205**
Introduction   189
The UK police service's response to the Human Rights
    Act 1998
ACPO human rights programme: policy audits   207
Results and reality of policy analysis and evaluation   208
Making the link between ethics and human rights
    explicit   210
Can policy analysis and evaluation promote change?   211

Integrating human rights into performance management
and inspections 212
Observations from non-governmental organisations
and academics 213
Conclusions: a multiple-impact change programme 214
Further reading 214
Notes 214

12 Towards ethical policing 215

Bibliography 221

Index 236

List of figures

1.1   The 'vicious cycle'   10

2.1   The police role: 1962 Royal Commission   23
2.2   The Statement of Common Purpose and Values   24
2.3   The police role: 1993 White Paper   25
2.4   Overarching aims and objectives (HMIC, 1999)   27
2.5   The 'Four Tracks of Policing'   36

3.1   The 'Four Tracks of Ethics'   49
3.2   Comparisons of prisons   52

4.1   The principal rights of the UN Charter and European
Convention   57
4.2   Policing standards in the UN code of conduct for law
enforcement officials and the Council of Europe Declaration
on the Police   62
4.3   The five elements of proportionality   66
4.4   Flowchart showing the ECHR principles in decision-making
sequence   69

5.1   The police 'clinician'   79
5.2   Hierarchical value system of the Western Australia Police
Service   80

6.1   The vicious cycle of management control   95
6.2   Principal/agent relationship in policing   100
6.3   Control systems in the police   103
6.4   Stakeholder preference for control mechanisms   103
6.5   National key objectives for policing   108
6.6   Audit Commission performance indicators   109
6.7   Other performance indicators   110
6.8   Best Value performance indicators   111
6.9   Weighting for funding allocation to police forces   114

6.10   Analysis of criminal statistics   115
6.11   Trends in crime and detections per 100 police officers   116

7.1   Model of compliance with ethical and human rights
       principles   132
7.2   The continuum of force   139
7.3   Approaches to the use of force   142

8.1   The dimensions of police accountability in the UK   148
8.2   Levels of policing and their relationship to government   151
8.3   The Patten model of accountability (Patten, 1999)
8.4   Ekblom's model of community safety and crime reduction
       applied to Sherman's analysis of the causal factors in police
       corruption   157
8.5   SWOT analysis of the use of Stop and Search powers   162

9.1   PDR de-brief model of giving feedback   180
9.2   PDR action planning   180
9.3   Model of performance management   181

10.1   ACPO draft Statement of ethical principles (1992)   191
10.2   Existing ethical standards in the police service in England
       and Wales and Europe   192
10.3   The headings of the Police Code of Conduct (1999)   192
10.4   Decision making – ACPO in-force audit tool kit   201

12.1   The virtuous circle and its context   219

About the authors and contributors

Peter Neyroud

Peter Neyroud is the Deputy Chief Constable of West Mercia Constabulary. He is the Secretary of the National Committee on the Police Use of Firearms, Vice Chairman of the ACPO Committee on Human Rights and is leading the work on 'ethics in policing'. He is a Fellow of the Royal Society of Arts, a member of the Institute for Public Policy Research's 'Forum on Criminal Justice' and a council member of Justice, the human rights organisation.

Alan Beckley

Alan Beckley is the head of management development training in West Mercia Constabulary. He has written on the personal liability of police officers following major and critical incidents, and is the editor-in-chief of *Police Research and Management*, a quarterly management journal for police officers.

Paul Collier

Paul Collier is a lecturer in management accounting at Aston Business School, Aston University, and was formerly head of training and development at West Mercia Constabulary. He has particular responsibility for chapter 6, 'Police performance management – an ethical dilemma?'

Julia Clayton

Julia Clayton is an inspector in Cheshire Constabulary and was the chief architect of the ACPO audit of compliance. She is currently on secondment to the Audit Commission. She has particular responsibility for chapter 11, 'Auditing' for compliance: a human rights case study'.

Foreword by
the Rt. Hon. Jack Straw, MP, Home Secretary

My time as Home Secretary has strongly reinforced my belief in the high ethical standards which are the foundation of policing in the United Kingdom. Citizens expect and trust the police to do the right thing. That trust is rarely misplaced. The police service is rightly subject to the closest scrutiny. Its role at the sharp end of society frequently confronts officers with ethical dilemmas at personal, operational and organisational levels. These must be faced up to, not avoided. I am only too conscious of the hard decisions and choices which can be presented by issues such as the use of force, covert surveillance, community relations and the maintenance of public order.

The publication of this important book coincides with the implementation of the Human Rights Act, one of the most significant constitutional changes since the 1688 Bill of Rights. The Act is fundamentally about standing up for the values of fairness, respect for human dignity and inclusiveness to which the police service aspires. It emphasises the proper balance of rights and responsibilities between the citizen and the state which goes to the heart of policing.

The Act presents a challenge, but it is not a threat. It places a statutory duty on all public authorities, including the police, not to act incompatibly with the European Convention on Human Rights. However, the practice of policing in this country and the legislation governing it is already very substantially in line with the Convention rights and that has been confirmed by a detailed programme of work undertaken in partnership between the Home Office and the Association of Chief Police Officers. The Convention was largely British-inspired and reflects many principles that are long-standing features of our criminal justice system. In addition, milestone statutes such as the Police and Criminal Evidence Act 1984 have improved compliance further. The arrival of the Human Rights Act therefore confirms what everyone involved in policing already knows. This is that the privilege of providing a service to the public carries with it a special duty of care; a duty to deliver that service in a way which respects the fairness and dignity of the individual.

Striving to act in line with human rights involves the application of fundamental ethical principles which the police service has been standing up for since it came into being, but it can also present conflicts. Few rights are absolute. It is frequently the police who must take responsibility for guarding the boundaries where the actions of one individual have unacceptable consequences for others or for society at large. Long experience of acting in defence of the law is a strong basis for getting the critical choices right on the vast majority of occasions, but there is increasing recognition within policing that there is real value in analysing and understanding the ethical justification for decisions. Bringing ethics to the fore will help to build a culture where respect for human rights is a conscious factor in the whole range of police activity. Leadership at every level is essential to that process and all of us involved in or with a responsibility for policing must embrace and apply the ethical standards we want to see reflected throughout the service.

The issues raised in this book are complex and wide-ranging. I do not necessarily agree with all the views expressed! However, what I do endorse very strongly is the need to promote and strengthen the debate about ethics in policing. This timely book fills a gap by providing a framework for that debate and linking it to the developing agenda on human rights. It does so against a background of rapid change in the policing environment and offers a very helpful analysis of approaches to developing and ensuring an ethical policing culture. It benefits greatly from the authors' strong combination of operational and academic experience and their obvious commitment to the practical application of human rights.

Jack Straw

PART I

Chapter I

Ethics in context: policing and its environment in the twenty-first century

Policing, ethics and human rights?

The context of policing is changing and the challenges for policing with it. As we move into the twenty-first century, policing, both domestically and globally is in the midst of transition and crisis. There are a number of dimensions to this transition, which were neatly summed up by the questions posed by Patten (1999) in his report on policing for Northern Ireland:

> How can professional police officers best adapt to a world in which their own efforts are only a part of the overall policing of a modern society? … There is no perfect model for us, no example of a country that, to quote one European police officer, 'has yet finalised the total transformation from force to service'.
>
> (Paragraph 1.5)

It is no accident that the Patten Commission arrived at these dilemmas. They are the dilemmas of a transition which itself is driven by external change and internal turmoil, manifest in:

- Increasing globalisation (Bottoms and Wiles, 1996) and trans-nationalism (Horsman and Marshall, 1994)
- a 'New World Order' or 'Disorder' (Horsman and Marshall, 1994)
- rapid technological and social change (IPPR, 1993)
- the consequent pressure for 'security' (Bottoms and Wiles, 1996) and 'greying' or privatisation of policing (Newburn and Jones, 1997)
- national governments, under pressure themselves from a critical citizenry, seeking to squeeze more for less and, increasingly,

    questioning the traditional model of public policing (Leishman,
    Loveday and Savage, 1995)
- two decades or more of research which has, increasingly, questioned
  the effectiveness of public policing (Waddington, 1999)
- a series of 'cause celebres'

All of which have combined to create the context for a renewed debate
about the purposes, limits and ethics of 'public' policing. It is a debate that
has been intertwined with a debate about human rights. As the Patten
Commission report went on to say:

> It is a central proposition of this report that the fundamental purpose
> of policing should be … the protection and vindication of the human
> rights of all … policing means protecting human rights.
>
> (Patten, 1999: 18)

Similar words and sentiments have dominated the reforms of the police
forces of the former Soviet Eastern bloc countries, the responses of the
New Zealand and Canadian police forces to implementation of Charters of
Rights and now are permeating the language of British policing on the eve
of the commencement of the Human Rights Act 1998.

    This book has been written to help guide the thoughtful practitioner
and student of policing through these issues. We will argue, as the Patten
report argues, that securing and reconciling human rights – balancing the
rights of individuals and communities – provides a way forward for public policing that begins to address some of the questioning of its purposes
and functions. Moreover, it may provide a way out of the cycle of 'boom'
(such as crime-fighting, zero tolerance and proactive policing) and 'bust'
(corruption, miscarriages of justice and scandal), which have characterised recent policing history. This is particularly vital for a police service,
which, like the British system as it enters the twenty-first century, has
experienced a number of serious blows to its legitimacy and effectiveness.

    In this context, understanding 'ethical policing', with human rights at
its core, is vital for police leaders, police officers and those concerned with
the success of public policing. The final section of the book will, therefore,
seek to describe how ethical policing might be achieved. It will do so by
drawing on both the literature on this subject and the authors' experience
of introducing major strategic change in a British police force and, at a
national level, assisting with the preparations for the implementation of
the Human Rights Act 1998.

    This chapter will concentrate on setting the scene for the debate to
come, providing firstly a brief analysis of the previous writing on ethics,
human rights and policing, and secondly a discussion of the main
elements in the 'crisis' and the transition to 'ethical policing'.

A brief history of ethics and policing

There have been a number of similar watersheds in policing in the past and each has, in its turn, produced debates about the nature and purposes of policing and its ethical base. There has been a history of key books coinciding with such periods of change and challenge in policing domestically and internationally:

- O.W. Wilson was a police chief who sought to set out the agenda for the new police professionalism, at a time when US policing was seeking to set itself free from the dead hand of a fairly corrupt local democracy. Described as a 'moral administrator' (Elliston and Feldberg, 1985) or, less optimistically, a 'snappy bureaucrat' by Klockars (1985), Wilson's vision, which is still very relevant, was of a high-tech, highly trained corps of police officers operating to clear rules, independent of local politics and acting with impartiality and integrity.

- William Westley (1970) and Jerome Skolnick (1975) cast their sceptical eyes over the ability of the police to meet Wilson's professional agenda – observing the problems of corruption with sociologists' eyes at a time when the consensus in US politics was breaking down under the pressures of the Vietnam War and race riots. For Westley, who studied violence by officers, police failure to attain Wilson's vision was a product of a culture of isolation and mutually hostile relationships with the public. Westley argued for more open and accountable policing. For Skolnick it was the inherent tension within the police role that created the problem. Maintaining order and upholding the law he saw as potentially irreconcilable. How could an officer square the circle of a need to maintain order through coercive force and a requirement to respect the law and uphold individual rights? Skolnick's solution was that legality and upholding the law had to come first.

- W.K. Muir (1977) and Herman Goldstein (1977) were both writing against a backdrop of concern about the police use of discretion a decade on from a series of key Supreme Court judgments, such as *Miranda v. Arizona*, which had apparently limited that discretion. Goldstein felt the solutions lay with managers, who should be encouraged to 'formalise the informal' (Goldstein, 1977: 82) and ensure that officers were trained in the proper exercise of discretion. Muir, starting from the other end of the organisational hierarchy, through observation of police officers on the street, saw morality more as a product of police officers' views of human nature. Whilst managers and trainers could influence behaviours, individual officers had 'free will' to exercise choice about their style of policing. Crucially, both Goldstein

5

and Muir champion 'free will' and moral choice, whether it be of police managers or police officers, in contrast to Skolnick and Westley for whom the structural and social conditions of policing all but predetermined morality.

- For both Elliston and Feldberg (1985) and Gary Marx (1988) the backdrop was the growth of covert policing methods in the US. A series of high profile scandals had raised questions about the policing of privacy and the use of deceptive policing methods. Elliston and Feldberg tried to show that, in debating such issues, the standard approaches to moral philosophy such as utilitarianism were simplistic and flawed. A more complex approach that embraced other academic disciplines, such as law and sociology, needed to be brought to bear. In short, police ethics required 'joined up thinking'. Marx brought such thinking to bear on covert policing and the emerging 'surveillance culture' in society, which he felt was having a damaging impact on privacy, trust and freedom of expression. He argued a distinction between 'ethical deception' – authorised by the citizenry and controlled by law – and 'deceptive ethics', which he characterised as the state doing by stealth what it could not do lawfully. Judging the difference between the two was not just a matter of law, but also needed an awareness of the outcome, the threat and the collateral impacts.

- Edwin Delattre (1989) and Lawrence Sherman (1985) were both attempting to deal with seemingly endemic problems of corruption in policing in the mid 1980s. They returned to some of the themes identified by Muir and Skolnick – free will or the nature of policing and the system. For Delattre the solution was 'character': the way to achieve ethical policing was to recruit and develop people who had the habit of integrity. For Sherman, it was not the character of the recruit so much as the environment of temptation into which they were pitched that was the problem. A slippery slope from small gifts to major graft could only be prevented by police managers being intolerant of minor gratuities.

- Joycelyn Pollock (1998) and John Kleinig (1996a), stimulated by a decade of debate about the role of the police, police brutality (particularly the Rodney King beating), problems with covert policing methods and renewed corruption scandals in major US police forces, sought a solution in a broader definition of policing as 'public servants' rather than 'crime fighters' (Pollock) or 'social peacekeeping' (Kleinig), or a process of building trust and reconciliation in communities.

- Tom Barker (1996), who has had a long-standing focus on police corruption (Barker and Carter, 1986) was stimulated by the resurgence in corruption in the US and the issues arising from the O.J.Simpson trial. The resultant crisis of public confidence in policing was typified by adverse jury votes and national calls for investigations into policing, which parallel the UK developments around the death of Stephen Lawrence. Barker proposed a 'proactive' approach in order to re-establish the police reputation for integrity: opportunity reduction, undermining peer pressure for unethical activities, deterrence.

All the above authors have been American. This is not coincidental. The American constitutional tradition has viewed police, as agents of the executive, with some suspicion. 'The Police are among the most powerful agents of the state' according to Elliston and Feldberg (1985: 1), while Cohen and Feldberg have this to say:

> Furthermore, compared to their counterparts in many other nations, American police officers are more civilianised and heavily restrained by law, constitutional limitations, community expectations and traditions in their exercise of authority and power.
>
> (Cohen and Feldberg, 1991: xii)

In the United Kingdom, police ethics have rarely been treated as a subject for discussion on their own. Where ethics have been discussed it has been through a focus on law, constitution and accountability or culture and the 'canteen'.

- Robert Reiner (1978) first concentrated on culture – in the form of 'police unionism', which was on the ascendant in the 1970s as a result of poor pay and conditions. He next turned to politics and accountability (1985), which had, by then, become a heated national debate focused on the 'democratic deficit' in policing. Reiner's starting point tends to place him firmly in line with Skolnick – police culture and behaviour being a product of the role and external environment. Reiner's most direct treatment of police morality has been in his studies of police images in the media (Reiner, 1994). He drew out the dualism of policing in a similar way to Carl Klockar's use of the *Dirty Harry* filmscript to illustrate difficult choices in policing.

- Lord Scarman (1982), in his report into the Brixton disturbances, placed great emphasis on the importance of 'consent and balance'. The community, he argued relied on the police to have the skills and common sense to exercise discretion and to do so in a way which balanced maintaining order and upholding the law. The former should always be given a higher priority and, therefore, by implication 'hard policing', which overemphasized enforcement and failed to take

7

account of community support was not good policing. This approach, which is an apparent reversal of Skolnick's solution to the dilemma, was to become the dominant ideology in British policing by the end of the decade (Reiner, 1991: 120).

- John Alderson (1979 and 1984), who gave evidence to Scarman's Inquiry as a Chief Constable, developed the theory of 'community policing', which he grounded in the concept of contractual government. Implicit in this work was an idea of policing as an activity for the whole community, within which the police role was one of balancing competing rights. This became more explicit in Alderson's later work (1998) where securing and preserving human rights moves to centre stage.

- Andrew Rutherford (1993) concentrated on the values of the leaders in policing and criminal justice agencies at the end of a long period of right-wing government, which had produced an increasingly polarised debate about criminal justice. Rutherford divided them into three 'credos': punishment – believing in the punitive degradation of offenders; efficiency – committed to pragmatic, expedient management; caring – dedicated to the achievement of legality and humanity in society. The latter, whose approach he clearly supports and into which Alderson would no doubt have fitted, he saw being confronted by a constant dilemma caused by the lack of congruence between the formal mission and the informal practice - their challenge being to close that gap. Rutherford suggests that this is not just a simple street cops/management cops divide.

- Michael Zander (1994) was a member of the Royal Commission on Criminal Justice, which was appointed to look into the spate of miscarriages of justice, many of which arose from terrorist trials. Zander argued firmly that police officers should not blame the criminal justice system for 'noble cause corruption'. Actions so motivated could never be right, however 'justified' in the short-term outcome. They were, furthermore, actions of individual choice that should be controlled by better supervision and management.

- Ralph Crawshaw (Crawshaw, Devlin and Williamson, 1999) dealt with the issues of policing and its relationships with human rights at a time when British policing was becoming increasingly exposed to the case law of the European Convention on Human Rights, after a decade of losing cases in the European Court of Human Rights. The distinctively different theme of Crawshaw's work is that policing is to be viewed in a context of international human rights. Its purpose has become to secure and preserve those rights. Police leaders must be aware of and seek to change their organisations to meet those standards. There are, therefore, absolute standards in policing.

• Waddington (1999) sees policing in a complex relationship with the citizen and the marginalized underclass. Strong citizen rights restrain policing and force it to be more respectable. But policing is always waiting for the next scandal because it 'operates in a nether world just beyond the limits of respectability' (Waddington, 1999: 158). The solution must lie in strong and inclusive citizenship and transparency in policing.

Alongside the US and UK literature, there are also some important Commonwealth contributions from Canada (Ericson and Haggerty, 1998 and Brodeur, 1995), Australia (Miller, Blackeler and Alexandra, 1997 and Chan, 1997) and India (Raghavan, 1999). They share the common theme of transition, crisis and search for renewal. For Ericson and Haggerty policing has become a process of risk communication, blurring neat law enforcement boundaries and challenging concepts of policing as a public good. For Brodeur, like Marx (1988), the risk results from technology and policing creating a 'new surveillance', out of reach of effective democratic control. For both Canadians, therefore, controlling the police is critical. For Miller, Blackeler and Alexandra and Chan the challenge is to reconstruct ethical policing after a series of catastrophic scandals about corruption and racism. Raghavan reflects similar problems in an Indian system, which has failed to achieve independence from a corrupt political system, and has yet to create the professionalism that Wilson hankered after fifty years ago.

This brief analysis has drawn out a number of the issues which will be pursued in this book. Firstly, it suggests that policing has been round a series of 'vicious cycles' over the past decades. These cycles seem to consist of four broad phases (Figure 1.1)

An example of such a cycle can be seen in the events surrounding the Brixton disorders (Scarman, 1982): a heavy emphasis on fighting street robberies; a major community disorder and substantial national concern about police actions and relationships with the ethnic minority community; changes to the legal framework of policing, which produced new consultative arrangements, revisions to the police complaints system and the lay visitors scheme; a gradual return to crime-fighting, cemented by the combination of a Home Secretary determined to revive his party's flagging fortunes by getting tough on crime (Rose, 1996) and an Audit Commission that, disastrously (Neyroud, 1998), turned the accountants' simplistic gaze on covert policing (Audit Commission, 1993).

Each of the authors reviewed above have tended to look at these problems from one side, whether from the point of view of police

Figure 1.1   The 'vicious cycle'

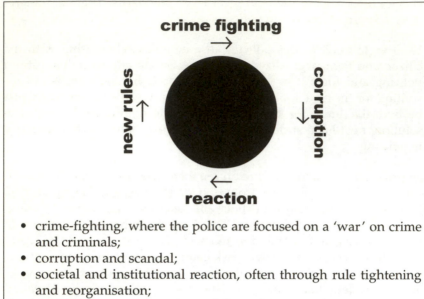

- crime-fighting, where the police are focused on a 'war' on crime and criminals;
- corruption and scandal;
- societal and institutional reaction, often through rule tightening and reorganisation;
- commitment to new norms, followed by a drift back to crime-fighting.

accountability, encouraging ethical standards, preventing corruption or, most recently, from the perspective of human rights (or in the US context, the constitution) and policing. Each have, in their own way, been just as reactive as policing to the crises. No one author has attempted to construct a model of the virtuous cycle, in which there is sufficient built-in correction for policing to avoid the roller coaster boom-and-bust ride.

Secondly, it is clear that the opportunities for reform only come at the bottom of the cycle. When the collective blood is up and moral panic about crime is high on the agenda, concerns about policing and its consequences tend not to be heeded. However, the major constitutional change in the United Kingdom to incorporate the European Convention on Human Rights in British law and the momentum in the emerging Eastern European democracies for a new contract of policing (ICJ, 1999) provide a unique opportunity. It heralds a major 'paradigm' shift for all police officers and practitioners in the criminal justice system (Starmer, 1999). The time is ripe, therefore, for fundamental change in thinking and actions.

So, thirdly, there is the question of how to construct the 'virtuous cycle'? It is certainly more difficult to construct a neat cycle, but it is possible to see some of the features that must be present. A good starting point would be to change the flawed conception that rights are necessarily antithetical to effective crime prevention and law enforcement. This dualistic approach, which finds favour with several of the authors reviewed, places police and the liberty of the citizen in opposition. This might be a reasonable argument if the only rights that are important and recognised in human rights jurisprudence are those of the citizen as suspect. But this is not the case. The European Court has been developing a far more complex view that encompasses rights for victims, witnesses and communities, as well as suspects and which provides the state with duties and obligations to protect them (Starmer, 1999). This allows us to begin to reconceive policing as the balancing mechanism between competing rights, rather than the problem.

The second element of the 'virtuous cycle' must be a better alignment of the formal mission and the informal and tacitly accepted practice in policing. This, in turn, requires a mission for policing which is broad enough to describe the whole of policing, from emergency service through to social assistance, rather than trying to focus on one or two politically favourable dimensions. Finally, there needs to be a legal and political framework, which supports such a broad mission and does not contradict it by measuring and focusing only on the traditional figures of crime and detection. Each of the elements needs to reinforce the other and need to be supported by a police service committed to the new mission and skilled in handling the dilemmas which it will present. These dilemmas and the 'virtuous cycle' will form an important part of the discussion to follow.

However, it is important to start by understanding where we are in the current cycle. As we have seen in reviewing the previous literature, the environment of policing plays a key part in shaping the terms of the debate about its ethics.

Transition or crisis?

Cause célèbres and causes for concern

There is substantial evidence for a crisis in the series of scandals and 'running sores' that have beset policing over the last few years. In the United States, as has been mentioned above, Barker (1996) has claimed that the American public has lost confidence in the police as a result of high-profile cases such as the O. J. Simpson trial. The effect of this, in Barker's eyes was to create an expectation that police would manufacture evidence and lie on oath – 'testilying'. Other commentators support Barker's analysis. The National Criminal Justice Commission registered concerns about corruption, abuse of force, over-policing and under-protection of minority communities (Donziger, 1996). There have also been the revelations around the handling of the Waco siege and, most recently, of serious allegations of misconduct by New York officers against members of the local black community.

In the UK, the most serious and obvious indications of crisis have been the events surrounding the inquiry into the death of Stephen Lawrence. Although much of the focus in the media was around the relationship between the police and the black community, the Macpherson report contained damning conclusions about police competence in investigating serious crime, the effectiveness of managerial structures, the use of stop and search powers and the adequacy of the complaints system. Macpherson on its own would have been damaging enough for the British police service, but it appeared at a point where a series of further problems were being revealed. Firstly, there was a growing focus on deaths in custody (Police Complaints Authority, 1999) and, particularly the disproportionate number of black suspects dying. Secondly and most notably, the Metropolitan Police Commissioner admitted to major corruption problems within the Metropolitan Police, corruption inquiries were commenced by outside forces in a number of other police forces and a series of chief officers – historically largely immune from such personal involvement – found themselves on the wrong end of very public discipline inquiries.

Such was the level of national concern that the Association of Police Authorities pushed the Home Secretary for an inquiry into the recruitment and appointment of senior officers and Her Majesty's Inspectorate of Constabulary conducted an inspection into 'Integrity', because

'of evidence that the public were becoming increasingly concerned about a suggested decline in the integrity of the police'

(HMIC, 1999a: 7)

Internationally, the tale is similar and can be told against the same themes:

Corruption
Perhaps the most notable corruption scandal was the one in Holland which lead to the parliamentary Van Traa Commission (Van Traa, 1996 and Justice, 1998). A high profile covert operation against drug dealing in North Holland ended in disaster as 'controlled delivery' methods produced a major increase in drug dealing, a corrupt conspiracy between informants and their police handlers and a complete failure of the managerial and political accountability systems. Marc Dutroux and his paedophile activities in Belgium dealt a similarly seismic shock to a national criminal justice system. Allegations of police incompetence and collusion led to mass demonstrations, the fall of the Minister of Justice and a loss of confidence in the institutions of government.

On the other side of the world, the Australian system is still recovering from the corruption problems in the New South Wales Police that led to the Wood Commission (1997). In India, there

'has been no perceptible improvement in integrity levels since the National Police Commission report (1977)'

(Raghavan, 1999: 227).

Covert policing and the 'fight against organised crime'
The extension and accountability of covert policing methods have raised widespread concerns (Justice, 1998). They were central to the Van Traa inquiry, and have been a source of major concern in the emerging democracies of Eastern Europe (ICJ, 1999).

Policing minority communities
Allegations of police mistreatment of minority communities are virtually universal and seem to have a set of stock characteristics: harassment; failure to take action against hate crimes; deaths in custody. The French police treatment of their North African community has become a current theme at the European Court. But one could equally easily cite German police and the Turkish community, the Czechs and Slovakians and the Romany community and any of the other Eastern European forces and the patchwork of minorities created by a post-cold War settlement which does not neatly match nationality to boundary. That this is not an exclusively European phenomenon can be supported by the example of the Australian police and the Aborigine community (Chan, 1997).

It might be argued that the examples set out above are simply that – examples, not a pattern, but a series of isolated events. Indeed, the HMIC 'Integrity' inspection does advance a version of the 'rotten apples' theory at one point, suggesting serious problems are confined to a small minority (HMIC, 1999a). However, the consistency of the themes across national and criminal justice system boundaries provides compelling evidence that the problems confronting policing are neither isolated nor simply 'events'.

Global, transnational and yet local

One of many reasons for drawing the conclusion that such events are not isolated is the increasingly globalised, international nature of policing and crime prevention. National boundaries are more and more irrelevant both in the commission of crime and, of necessity, its prevention and detection. Crimes such as drug dealing, money laundering, trafficking in human beings, sex tourism and cybercrime do not respect national boundaries: a single market in trade is increasingly a single market in crime. National governments and police agencies are confronting these problems with criminal justice and policing systems designed to police the citizen in a national context (Waddington, 1999). This approach on its own is proving more and more inadequate as the examples quoted above illustrate. National attempts to overcome these inadequacies vary from involving Security Services in policing (United Kingdom), extending the use of covert policing activities (almost universal), setting up bi-lateral agreements, deploying liaison officers and international teams (UK and USA) right through to creating multi-national agreements (such as Schengen). Each in these various ways extend policing outside the existing national framework of democratic control and accountability. As such this argues for the emergence of new international frameworks and standards in policing (Justice, 1998) – particularly in areas like covert policing, which might otherwise offer opportunities for the sort of problems seen at a national scale to be repeated on a wider stage.

Policing cannot be seen in isolation from developments in society and government. The internationalisation of policing reflects the wider transformation away from the nation state to a more complex and shifting 'New World Order'. The nation state has not ceased to be the main focus of identity, but its ability to control and influence change is reducing. The absence of an effective replacement has led Horsman and Marshall (1994) to describe this, less optimistically, as a 'New World Disorder', 'at once tribal and international in character' (p.xx), with local, national and international bodies striving simultaneously for legitimacy. Where the nation state once had the monopoly on legal violence, now a range of agencies, both public and private share and, sometimes, conflict. Horsman and Marshall suggest that citizens may find it easiest to engage at a very local level. Bottoms and Wiles (1996) also concur that globalisation at one level is being matched by 'localisation' at another and that policing and crime prevention are substantially affected by these twin pressures.

These arguments are not merely theoretical. As we shall stress below, legitimacy and authority, linked to democratic accountability, are crucial to any concept of ethical policing. Their attainment and their maintenance are becoming at once more complex and more difficult. Policing 'on thin air' (Leadbeater, 1999) demands new thinking and presents new ethical challenges. The original 'vicious cycle' may in the future be multi-layered – local, regional, national, transnational and global – each layer interacting the one with the other. Rather akin to the complexities of chaos theory, a scandal at one layer may ripple across all, with adverse consequences for policing internationally and domestically.

Risk and reassurance

Connected with these developments and the global state of uncertainty and change is the 'commodification of security'. Security, anxiety and its antidote, reassurance, have become part of a market into which the 'quiet revolution' of private security growth has gradually impacted (Shearing and Stenning, 1987). No longer can public policing lay claim to a monopoly on the use of force and no longer does it control the surveillance of public space. Private agencies are involved in running prisons, custody suites and detention centres, public space has become privatised (Hoddinott, 1994) and the public attracted into it by promises of a secure 'scanscape'. There is no longer a simple, indivisible concept of the 'public'.

The response of some police leaders has been to try to shift the public police from being monopoly providers to being the arbiters of the public interest, accrediting, licensing and controlling the boundaries of the 'public' and access to its legitimacy and authority (Blair, 1999). This is consistent with Ericson and Haggerty's observation that public policing is becoming a process of communicating risk (1998). An example of this is the role that police take in accrediting and checking information about criminal careers and acting as the gatekeepers of this information to other institutions. But the new concept of 'policing risk' extends far beyond information exchange. It includes the development of actuarial tools like risk assessment, the profiling of high-risk groups, the identification of high-risk locations (Johnston, 1997) and potentially, with DNA technology, the prediction of offending behaviour. Policing is becoming not just a process of communicating risk but is being increasingly expected to manage dangerousness and protect the public (Neyroud, 1999). This new role brings with it substantial burdens, as illustrated by the Osman case (see below in Chapter 7) (Starmer, 1999), new ethical dilemmas and new risks for public policing.

Technology, social change and trust

Changes in technology and social change are a key part of this new world in which policing strives to succeed. To say that technology has become of growing importance in our everyday lives is obvious. Its impact on policing, at the tactical level, is also obvious: computers and information technology; radio communication; new forensic science techniques. But there are two particular impacts of more strategic and social significance (Bottoms and Wiles, 1996):

> First and foremost, technology has changed the nature and potential of surveillance. As Marx (1988) has commented, the scope of the 'new surveillance' gives fresh meaning to the popular song, 'every move you make, every breath you take, I'll be watching you'. The implications for privacy are immense, the problems of trust and accountability substantial (Shipley and Leal, 1998).

Secondly, technology has made our world more visual, our news more instantaneous (and almost as instantly out of date) and the ability of organisations to manipulate both far greater. In the same way that surveillance can invade private space, so too, through the visual media can events, risks, and dangers, with an intimacy that can belie their global nature.

This leads on to a key aspect of social change: the change in the nature of 'trust'. Most famously this has been set out by Giddens in his discussion of the features of modernity (Giddens, 1990). He suggested that previous forms of trust relationship, such as kinship, local community of place, religion and tradition have been replaced by more abstract systems, notably those based on technology. Giddens' analysis has immense implications for policing and crime prevention. Public policing is still traditional and largely based on geographic communities. As such, it relies on the formal legitimacy of local or national community consent rather than the more individualised and disparate requirements of the new communities of risk (Johnston, 1997). Meeting these new needs and renewing the mandate of legitimacy has implications for crucial, traditional assumptions such as policing being an indivisible public good.

New public policing and new public management

Traditional though policing may be at the core, it has not been unaffected by the wave of managerialism and 'new public management' (Hood, 1995). Bottoms and Wiles (1996) have suggested that these are characterised by a number of key features: integrated policy; an emphasis on inter-agency cooperation, accompanied by a recognition that single agency missions overlap; strategic planning; performance management through development of 'indicators' and league tables. All of these and more – financial devolution, sponsorship, income generation and outsourcing – have now been followed, in the UK, by the regime of 'best value', based on a philosophy of continuous improvement.

Best value, 'new public management' with teeth, requires the organisation to challenge every activity, consult its community, compare its performance and compete – with other public and private agencies (DETR, 1999). It is likely to accelerate the processes of civilianisation and privatisation that have already significantly changed the shape of police forces. In combination with the new statutory requirements of partnership in the Crime and Disorder Act 1998, it may well break down the divisions between the public police and other agencies of social control and providers of policing and security. We shall return to these themes in the second part of the book.

Evidence-based policing

So far, we have seen change to the nation state, society, technology and, with 'best value', the organisation of policing. The last of our themes provides a challenge to the very professional knowledge and traditional assumptions about how policing is effectively performed. Two decades of significant research into policing and crime prevention are beginning to produce a new body of knowledge that could be called 'evidence-based policing' (Ekblom, 1999 and Home Office, 1998a). Policing is not alone in this respect, for all major areas of social policy are now debating evidence-based practice. Furthermore, this was a key theme running through the Labour government's Comprehensive Spending Review in 1998.

The logic of evidence-based policing is ineluctable and highly relevant for ethical policing. For if 'what works?' is the right way to undertake policing – and the yardstick against which the funding of public policing will be judged nationally – then logically, by implication, that which doesn't 'work', or perhaps, more significantly, can't be proved to work is not justified (and possibly not funded). Justification by faith alone – particularly relevant to patrol – is no longer a tenable argument: research or be damned!

Summary and conclusions

In this introduction, we have debated whether policing is in transition or crisis. The evidence would seem to suggest both. Indeed, the nature of the transition and the scale of change taking place as we enter the twenty-first century would, on their own, signal a crisis. Traditional nationally based public policing is trying to cope with a world joined together by trade, technology and, increasingly, crime. Its legitimacy, authority and knowledge base are being challenged. It is in a cycle of pressure for crime fighting and pressure about corruption, which we have suggested are self-reinforcing.

Nevertheless, there is an opportunity for change and renewal. We have argued that the negotiation of a new broader mission linked to human rights may offer policing a new basis for legitimacy and authority. Inevitably, this means that the next issue that we must turn to is the nature of the police role.

Further reading

Les Johnston's *Policing Britain: Risk, Security and Governance* (2000) is a good introduction to the issues debated in the concluding sections of this chapter. Francis, Davies and Jupp, *Policing Futures* (1997), Brodeur *How to Recognise Good*

Policing (1998), Morgan and Newburn, *The Future of Policing* (1997) and Bayley, *Police for the Future* (1994) provide excellent treatment of the issues of the future of policing.

Other key works for this opening section include:

- The Patten report (1999).
- The Inspectorate report on 'Integrity' (HMIC, 1999a).
- David Rose's book *In the Name of the Law* (1996) which provides a committed observer's viewpoint on 20 years of the vicious cycle.
- Tim Newburn's summary of the literature on corruption (Newburn, *Understanding and Preventing Police Corruption*, 1999), which was commissioned as part of a joint Home Office/Police Service initiative against corruption.

Policing and 'social control'

Our third dimension – policing and 'social control' – provides a more limited view of policing as 'an aspect of social control processes involving surveillance and sanctions intended to ensure the security of the social order' (Reiner, 1997: 1008). The role of policing is, therefore, an essentially conservative one. This view, the product of sociology, emphasises the fact that policing is not the exclusive province of the public police, but a much broader concept, embracing individual, collective, private and state policing. The public police as a specialised institution of social control are seen as a product of the division of labour in modern societies and can be distinguished from other types of policing by their ability to use legitimate force (Bittner, 1975). The public police, in this analysis, are neither inevitable in their current form nor uniquely responsible for social control. Good policing is, therefore, minimal policing – minimally intrusive and carefully controlled in its use of force.

Johnston provided a rather more developed version of this approach in his description of 'optimal policing':

> 'neither quantitatively excessive (to the detriment of alternative social values and objectives) nor qualitatively invasive (to the detriment of public freedoms) and which satisfies conditions of public accountability, effectiveness and justice for all'.
>
> (Johnston, 2000: 180)

'Optimal' policing has clear moral overtones embedded in the idea of good policing meaning balanced and diverse policing.

Policing, democracy and the citizen

The fourth dimension, which is critical for defining policing (Waddington, 1999), is the relationship between police and citizen. This relationship is a cornerstone of democracy. In the totalitarian states of the former Soviet eastern bloc, the prime purpose of the police was to protect the government from the population. In a modern democracy the police are both the symbolic 'shop front' of the state's authority and responsible for protecting individual and collective freedoms. Jones, Newburn and Smith's study of policing and democracy for the Policy Studies Institute suggested that this delicate balance requires a set of democratic principles to run through the police (Jones, Newburn and Smith, 1994). They identified these as: equity; appropriate service delivery; responsiveness; distributed power; openness of information; redress; participation. 'Good policing' maximises these principles and is a 'public good', which should be shared according to need.

The four dimensions are rather like the faces of a prism. Each provides a different view of the relationship of policing with government and the citizen, ranging from wary distrust (Locke) to encouraging participation and engagement. Each links with the discussion of ethical theory which follows in Chapter 3. Finally, each of these four dimensions has been reflected in the development of the policing mission.

A history of the policing mission

Dependence

It was the first dimension – the constrained and limited executive – that dominated the first enunciation of the police mission, with the founding of the Metropolitan Police in 1829. Concerned to avoid accusations of setting up a continental system of 'agents', Peel stressed instead that the police role was the prevention of crime.

It was no foregone conclusion that this mission and the new police would prove acceptable, particularly outside London, where the old constabulary had deep roots and was by no means dominated by incompetent village constables. It was the dislocating and disorderly pressures of post-war and industrialisation which hastened the change, together with an accommodation that brought the new police firmly under the control of the existing provincial ruling class (Storch, 1999).

Independence

It was, again, war and the threat of post-war disorder and industrial action, which stimulated a major step change away from local control towards a more independent, more national model of policing. The Desborough reforms pushed forward the principles of uniformity and national standards and enhanced national control through greater central budgetary provision (Emsley, 1991). The Willink Royal Commission provided the classic enunciation of the independent model, articulating a system of tripartite governance of the police that was, in conception, a careful balance of professional independence with local and national accountability (Critchley, 1978). Furthermore, the purposes of the police had broadened from Peel's original conception to a more interventionist model that included both the provision of emergency services and 'social services' (see Figure 2.1).

Scarman (1982) challenged the priorities within this multi-functional role by raising the 'maintenance of the Queen's Peace' above all others, but he also clearly stated that the 'independence of the police is the other principle of a free society' (p.104). Scarman and Alderson (1979 and 1984) suggested that the law and the duty to consult and listen to the community provided the balance. Despite this encouragement, by the end of the

Figure 2.1 The police role: 1962 Royal Commission

---

1 To maintain law and order and protect persons and property;

2 To prevent crime;

3 To detect criminals. In the course of interrogating suspected persons the police have a part to play in the early stages of the judicial process;

4 To control road traffic and advise local authorities on traffic questions;

5 To carry out certain duties for government departments;

6 The police have by long tradition a duty to befriend anyone who needs their help, and they may at any time be called upon to cope with major or minor emergencies.

(Willink, 1962, quoted in Critchley, 1978)

---

decade of repeated 'nothing works' messages (Young, 1999), Wolff Olins could describe the Metropolitan Police as 'defensive and isolated' and unclear 'about what it is there for' (Wolff Olins, 1988: 15). This crisis of purpose was felt across the service and resulted in the Operational Policing Review – a unique coming together of all levels of the service – which produced the 'Statement of Common Purpose and Values' (Figure 2.2). This was seen as Willink brought up to date: a new, balanced mandate.

However, in the minds of many commentators, the clearest statement of the policing mission during the 1980s was to be found not in the Scarman report, but in the actions of the police during the Miners' Strike. The message for many was that the police had moved, since Desborough, from dependence on local politicians to become the enforcement arm of central government (Waddington, 1999).

Emerging interdependence

Alongside Scarman and the Miners' Strike, a further feature of the 1980s was the emergence of the interdependent approach. The threads were there in Scarman's recommendations on consultation, which were developed in the Police and Criminal Evidence Act. They can be seen more strongly in the gathering impetus behind multi-agency approaches to crime prevention, child protection and racial harassment (Neyroud, 1993). The underlying message in all these approaches was that the police were not solely responsible for or capable of tackling these problems and that partnerships added value and were, by implication, 'better' than single

Figure 2.2   The Statement of Common Purpose and Values

The purpose of the police service is to uphold the law fairly and firmly; to prevent crime; to pursue and bring to justice those who break the law; to keep the Queen's Peace; to protect, help, and reassure the community; and to be seen to do all this with integrity, common sense and sound judgement.

We must be compassionate, courteous and patient, acting without fear or favour or prejudice to the rights of others. We need to be professional, calm, restrained in the face of violence and apply only that force which is necessary to accomplish our lawful duty.

We must strive to reduce the fears of the public and, so far as we can, reflect their priorities in the action we take. We must respond to well-founded criticism with a willingness to change.

(ACPO, 1990)

agency isolation. These arguments are at their strongest in the Morgan report (Home Office, 1991), where the police were moved from their traditional primacy on crime to a position of partnership with newly empowered local authorities.

Morgan's arguments stood in stark contrast to a narrower conception of policing which underpinned the so-called 'police reforms' of the mid 1990s. First, there was a White Paper, which, with the Audit Commission's support (Audit Commission, 1993), shunted the police into crime fighting (Home Office, 1993a) (Figure 2.3). Then there followed the Sheehy report which sought to apply the disciplines of the market to police pay and conditions (Sheehy, 1993). Finally, there was the attempt to reduce policing to a 'core', by identifying and removing 'ancillary' activities (Home Office, 1995). All three reviews were driven by the 'rising demand on the one hand, and affordability on the other' (Home Office, 1995: 5).

The reform programme had a limited impact on the formal mission of the police. Far more important were the growing privatisation of public space (Hoddinott, 1994), the growth of private policing (Newburn and Jones, 1997), the 'almost insatiable public appetite for visible patrol' (Audit Commission, 1996: 5) and security (Police Foundation/Policy Studies Institute, 1996) and a blurring of the boundaries of public policing. The latter was the result of several processes: the privatisation of functions such as court escorting; new police powers to deal with trespass and offences in private space; the increased mandate for the security services to 'trespass' into previously police only areas of serious crime. The police were both being challenged in their key role of visible patrol (Morgan and Newburn, 1997; ACPO, 1996a and Audit Commission, 1996) and were finding themselves in controversial, confrontational roles with committed

Figure 2.3   The police role: 1993 White Paper

> 1   To fight and prevent crime;
> 2   To uphold the law;
> 3   To bring to justice those who break the law;
> 4   To protect, help and reassure the community;
> 5   In meeting those aims, to provide value for money and must maintain
> their traditional role of policing by consent.
>
>   (Home Office, 1993a)

protestors, who often had widespread public support. The policing of road protests, such as Twyford Down[1] and Newbury, encapsulated the difficulties. Sandwiched between protesters with local and wider public support and private policing, hired by the government, protecting the private space of the road, as well as intense media coverage, the police role evolved uneasily into a mixture of neutrality, mediation, order maintenance and enforcement of the new public order legislation.[2] Lockean and democratic approaches had become difficult and increasingly complex, particularly as the 'community' being policed had become so diverse and disparate.

A much clearer role for the police was being advocated by those attracted by the siren call of 'zero tolerance' policing. This late twentieth century 'moral backlash' had its origins in the 'Broken Windows' philosophy of Wilson and Kelling (1982) and achieved momentum through its perceived success in the New York's 'miraculous' crime reductions. Public policing seemed to have found a new and exclusionary mission – 'social peacekeeping' with an intolerant edge – in cracking down on anti-social behaviour and anti-social people. Zero tolerance, whilst a good campaign slogan, was limited by its pretence that crime could be severed from its context – the growing inequalities and diversity of the late twentieth century – and could be solved by a single agency employing a single method.

Interdependence

In contrast, Blair's Labour government, seized with a belief in cross cutting and tackling 'wicked issues' (Richards, 1998), adopted a more radical approach, which pushed the police firmly in the direction of interdependence. The Crime and Disorder Act removed any doubt about the exclusivity of the police role in dealing with crime, by providing Local Authorities with the duty to tackle crime and disorder. New arrangements for shared audits, strategies and targets were supplemented by extending the ability of the police to share information with their partners. With the new strategies and the creation of Youth Offending Teams, the police became pivotal to a new and evolving network of agencies, public, private and voluntary.

Three further changes altered the police mission: the creation of new 'Overarching Aims and Objectives' (OAO); the Human Rights Act; the implementation of the 'Best Value' regime. The first of these, the product of the 'Comprehensive Spending Review', provided the most complete statement of the police role since Willink. It significantly enhanced the theme of interdependence, because it was consciously drafted to complement similar statements for other agencies and for the criminal justice system as a whole. This was re-emphasised by the government's 'Crime Reduction Strategy' which stated that the 'key to delivering reductions in crime on the ground is through the police and local Crime and Disorder Partnerships' (Home Office, 1999a: 10). That strategy also made a clear link between funding, best value and OAO. This link was designed so as to ensure that this was not a cosmetic change. An examination of the statement shows how fundamentally the formal mission has changed:

> Importantly, OAO envisages a mission which is multi-layered, clearly linked to values, has a strong emphasis on partnership and aims, which stresses not 'crime fighting' but 'safety and justice'. However, although the mission stated is a broader one, the tenor of the Government's crime reduction strategy still emphasised the 'crime-fighting role' within it, describing funds for additional police officers as a 'crime-fighting fund'
>
> (Home Office, 1999a: 14)

The distinction between 'crime fighting' and an 'interdependent' mission for policing is an important one, with a moral dimension. A force that is fighting part of the community cannot truly be 'of the community' (Braithwaite, 1989). Crime fighting, rather than an interdependent, enabling role, implies the domination of an 'enemy', not the 'public service' or 'social peacekeeping' role suggested by Pollock (1998) and Kleinig (1996a). Furthermore, as Glover (1999) has argued in discussing the morality of war in the twentieth century, moral identity is important for moral choice. A police force that regards its mission as fighting sections of the community is one that will find it easier to focus on the ends of 'victory' rather than the means of battle. It will also be a police force that finds it difficult to 'move away from repressive social control to moralising social control' (Braithwaite, 1989: 184).

The present: what do the police actually do?

One hundred and fifty years on from Peel, therefore, the formal police mission has grown progressively more complex. However, as we have seen, the connection in public, government and police officers' eyes

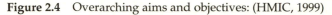

Figure 2.4 Overarching aims and objectives: (HMIC, 1999)

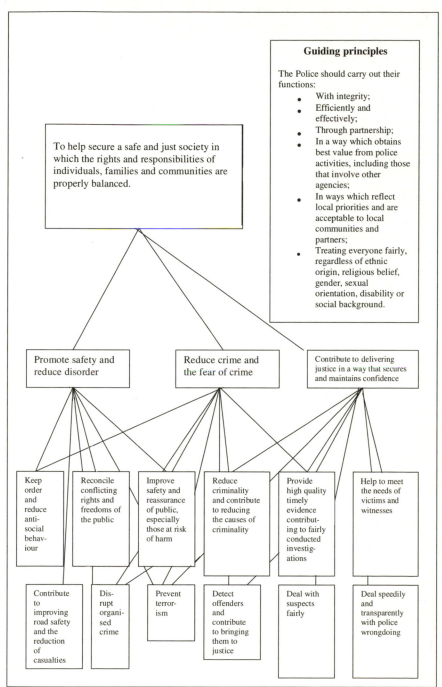

between the police and crime fighting has, with the exception of Scarman's attempt at reprioritisation, remained central to the police role. This is despite the fact that a major body of research and many prominent commentators on policing have argued that the police are not an effective means of controlling crime; that, in any case, dealing with crime is not the major part of what the police actually do and, furthermore, it is neither solely nor distinctively the role of the police (Morgan and Newburn, 1997 and Home Office, 1998a). In contrast, the distinctive roles of the police have been described variously as the 'legitimate use of force' (Bittner, 1975), 'authoritative intervention' (Waddington, 1999) or 'managing and communicating risk' (Ericson and Haggerty, 1998).

These arguments are important. The lack of congruence between the formal mission and the activity of policing is a major issue that has been widely debated. However, we should not overemphasise the dissonance. Firstly, Bittner argued that the 'specific competence of the police is targeted on the handling of all sorts of problems in which force may have to be used to bring an untoward development under control' (Bittner, 1975: xi). As Bittner clearly identified, the 'authority to proceed coercively in every conceivable crisis' (Bittner, 1975: xi) is a competence, or a means, to the ends of policing, which can more properly be described by the sorts of formal mission statement which we have debated above.

Secondly, the police can be effective in delivering local crime reduction strategies, but it seems very unlikely that they alone can deliver long-term reductions without wider partnership approaches which deal with the 'distil' or long-term factors in the environment, economy and society (Ekblom, 1999). Furthermore, a factor which is highly significant in the context of ethics, is that for every police action there are 'subtle consequences', such as displacement (Young, 1999), which need to be carefully taken into account.

Thirdly, it is clear that, as the OAO sets out, what the police actually do is much broader than 'crime fighting'. There are a number of ways of showing this:

1 Expenditure

An analysis of the approximate percentage of an average UK police budget[3] spent on each of the headings of the OAO and the force's support functions shows that 'reducing criminal activity', disrupting organised crime and providing quality evidence – those components that could be said to be most specifically devoted to 'crime' – are only £23 million of the £99 million budget. Even allowing for a percentage of the support budget contributing to the 'crime' function, the latter is budgeted for less than 40 per cent of the force's effort. Functions to do with maintaining order, reassurance and service to victims and witnesses are equally important. These ratios do not vary much in other jurisdictions. Bayley (1996) showed that on average 15 per cent of police forces' assignments were devoted exclusively to crime investigation. Patrol (59 per cent) – most of which involved symbolic, public reassurance and the maintenance of order– was by far the largest area.

2 Activity and demand

In a similar way, analysis of the calls to the police from the public shows that crime is at most, including 'potential crime', 50 per cent of the public's demand of the police (Shapland and Vagg, 1988).

3 Public priorities

Key surveys, such as the Operational Policing Review (Joint Consultative Committee, 1990) have identified a broad range of public priorities, not always well matched to the realities. They showed the high priority the public accorded reassurance in the form of response to emergencies and foot patrol, higher even than the investigation of crime.

Our analysis of both the formal mission, the activity of policing and the public demand on policing indicate that simple descriptions of policing are likely to be either misleading or merely one aspect of the purposes of policing. Whether we look at how a police budget is divided, why the public contact the police or what the public's priorities for the police are, the tale is not a simple one. It is certainly not summed up as 'crime fighting', since various forms of 'reassurance' and public service take up a large percentage of police activity and public demand. Equally, whilst Bittner's focus on the legitimate use of force is an important description of a key aspect of the police role, it is not a sufficient or completely convincing one. Ericson and Haggerty's research has identified how the police role is evolving and increasingly encompassing the policing of 'risk'. This does not always, or, indeed, ordinarily, involve force: it does require trust, information, analysis and a network of contacts and partners. It also, critically, involves choices. The importance of choice between different styles and approaches to policing is a key part of the final section of this chapter.

Policing futures

With the pace of change in society, organisations must reflect on their past, actively learn from the present and seek to influence the future. This last section of the discussion of the purposes of policing is, therefore, future focused. We have drawn on the issues that we identified in the first chapter and those set out above in this chapter. We have then developed them through three 'scenarios' to provide a view of the future of policing in the early twenty-first century. There are two very obvious links between this process and the ethics of policing. Firstly, ethics are about choices, their consequences and their outcomes. These scenarios set out some of the possible choices facing policing and their probable outcomes. Secondly, we will argue that ethical police leadership requires a clearer focus on the future. 'It is time to become anticipatory' (Beckley, 1997a: 3), to influence the shape of the future and the future shape of policing.

The three 'futures'

First of all, there is no one future, just as we have seen there is no one past or present in policing. The three scenarios for the future are extrapolations of the past and present, oversimplifying existing approaches in much the same way as the Commission for Social Justice did in creating their three models: the investors; the deregulators; the levellers (Commission on Social Justice, 1994). Instead of these three, we will develop the enablers, crime fighters and the social engineers. Although there is no police force which is pursuing any one of these roads exclusively, we believe that these are identifiable styles that are predominant in certain organisations, just as Reiner (1991) and Rutherford (1993) were able to distinguish styles amongst practitioners.

1 The 'enabling' police force

The enabling police force has learnt from the 'internal market' and seized the opportunities presented by 'best value'. Building on global trends towards 'steering' rather than 'rowing' in government (Osborne and Gaebler, 1992), the enabling police force accepts that 'public policing' has no exclusive monopoly on policing and that it can have a new role in collaborating with, regulating and managing other forms of policing. It seeks to combine the ethics and equity of public policing with the dynamics of the 'social market' and community-based provision. It provides a core of basic services – national crime service, call handling, serious crime management and intelligence – and manages and collaborates with a series of locally provided private and community patrol forces through 'intelligent regulation'. Its performance management is based on outcome measures which are themselves coordinated with other agencies involved in crime reduction and criminal justice, its legitimacy on regional and local (often very local) democratic mechanisms.

2 The 'crime fighters'

The crime fighters are waging war on crime. Theirs is a police force which is a lean, professional machine whose real business is fighting crime or 'efficient law enforcement' (Bayley, 1994). Ancillary aspects of policing which do not support or form part of 'crime fighting' are increasingly privatised or outsourced. Community policing is valued only as a function of intelligence gathering and enforcement of the law in a 'zero tolerance' approach. The force is highly specialised into investigators and intelligence staff split into teams. Its uniform staff is used primarily to conduct systematic and targeted 'crackdowns' in high crime areas, using stop search, vehicle searches and warrants. It has invested heavily in high technology surveillance, tracking, tagging and intelligence systems. Performance is geared to detection and disruption of crime.

3 The 'social engineers'

The 'social engineers' are pursuing 'determined crime prevention' (Bayley, 1994). The aim is to create stable communities and the police take the lead in defining the solutions to arrive at such communities. Problem-oriented policing is the style of delivery supported by 'community policing'. There is an extensive commitment to community crime prevention and diversion through restorative approaches. The professional police officer is perceived as a 'social mediator' in uniform whose core skills are those of problem solving and negotiation. Intelligence systems and investment in technology are important, but only as a means to identify problems and provide information with which to arrive at solutions through multi-agency approaches. The massive resources that the 'crime fighters' have directed at surveillance and offender targeting have been invested in long-term education and youth work. Performance is assessed by long-term measures of social outcome and crime reduction.

The 'futures' at work

In Chapter 1 we identified that policing was in the midst of transition. Key aspects of this were: a cycle of crises, corruption and reform; social and technological change; globalisation; political and constitutional change; fiscal restraint, but rising expectations. Arising from these issues, there are two key strategic choices for each of the 'futures': firstly how does public policing sustain and develop the quality and values of its services within a context of *fiscal restraint* and rising demand; secondly, how does it deal with *constitutional, social and political change*?

1 The enabling police force

The enabling force sets out to cope with *fiscal restraint and competition from the private sector* by providing high value professional services at the core, whilst low cost, private, community or volunteering are encouraged to fulfill a number of general functions, particularly patrol and public reassurance. The strategy is pursued by building on experimentation with local patrol services (Wiles, 1996) and through responding to increasing requests from a resurgent local government, for whom patrolling services are an essential part of meeting local crime reduction strategies. It is supported by a government committed to a greater role for local government, the 'social market' (Kay, 1997) and local voluntary action (Blair, 1996). Moreover, as *constitutional change* brings a gradual shift to more regional government, the enabling force becomes a regional 'purchaser' (Faulkner, 1996) of local policing services, some provided by more entrepreneurial unitary and elected mayoral authorities, some by private companies and some by consortia formed by police forces themselves. In order to support these developments the enabling force uses all the instruments of the 'new governance' (Stoker, 1997) – citizen's panels, budget-making initiatives, extensive information sharing and involvement of local communities in implementation of new local initiatives.

The enabling force may sound far-fetched and a radical shift from current structures. However, in the success of Sedgefield, the tentative move towards 'horizontal integration' by some police forces (such as the formation of trusts to provide private policing services), the increasing use by local councils of legal provisions to provide additional police patrols and the global development of complementary patrols, there are more than straws in the wind. Diversity, as Johnston outlines in describing 'optimal policing', has become an increasingly important feature of the 'market', public and private, in security and policing services.

The challenges for the 'enabling' approach are many. Too rapid a change to policing would threaten its legitimacy. Symbolism is a key part of policing. The delicate balance between delivering patrol and other services locally in a more diverse way could easily be broken by a public perception that the quantity of service was not being matched by quality. The 'social capital' of policing may be very vulnerable to such obvious gaps between expectations and delivery. The sheer complexity of managing, regulating and negotiating so many different partnerships would be a major obstacle. All the evidence on partnerships and multi-agency approaches suggests that increasing the complexity and 'decision points' increases the chances of paralysis (Neyroud, 1992). Finally, the challenge of maintaining the professional core would be immense. As the shift towards more diversified local forces accelerated, the current single tier force would have to change. The 'professional core' would have to accept, as most police forces internationally have, a variety of entry points, perhaps linked to national vocational, professional or degree qualifications. The public police would have to become a more flexible and open organisation. The cultural changes need to be transformational and, would, therefore, probably be the biggest challenge of all.

2 The crime fighters

The crime fighters' principal strategy is the development of the force into high value, 'leading edge' crime management. In order to create room for such a focus, other activities have to be carefully managed. Hence, a call-handling strategy which seeks to resolve problems by telephone without deployment, a community and media approach which manages down public expectations of patrol, partnerships which get CCTV installed in town centres and at crime 'hot spots' and a managerial approach which uses outsourcing and private capital financing extensively in an effort both to squeeze short- and medium-term costs and fund vital IT and infrastructure investments. Finally, the core of the crime fighting force is intelligence and a new set of skills both for the workplace and managers in analysis and deploying its results. The human resources approach seeks to develop these skills by specialisation and a performance management structure, which drives hard at 'intelligent' crime detection and disruption.

The crime fighters are recognisably developing the 'National Crime Management Model' (ACPO, 1995 and 1996a). They face a number of challenges. First and foremost, the 'crime-fighting model' sits uncomfortably with public demands for reassurance through high visibility patrol (Bucke, 1995). The reluctance of the crime-fighting force to fill this gap on the grounds that it is not effective in dealing with crime means that private, local and voluntary provision may expand uncontrolled with long-term consequences for the legitimacy and presence of the public police. Second, the pressure for short- and medium-term cost savings may be at the cost of long-term viability. The evidence, for instance, of the long-term cost benefits of many out-sourced and privatised functions is not rosy, particularly when the full costs of managing the process are included. Moreover, the erosion of trust and commitment within the organisation may be difficult to reverse. Third, the reliance on technical equipment, surveillance and informants in the drive for detection and disruption carries a high risk of corruption or unethical behaviour. Such methods are likely to attract increasing challenge unless they are used sensitively and within a firm democratic and legal framework (see chapter 7). Finally, there must be questions about the sustainability of the crime fighting approach. Whilst, as we have said above, the police have a key role to play in tackling crime, the evidence is that social factors are much more significant (Young, 1999). A strategy, which can only deal with the symptoms of the problem and must do so under tight fiscal restraint, does not look sustainable.

3 The social engineers

The 'social engineers' build their approach around the omni-competent patrol officer, supported by small teams of specialists and high quality IT systems for crime and incident handling. Policing is seen as a series of clusters of problems that demand skills of mediation and negotiation linked to problem analysis (Goldstein, 1990) and, therefore, performance management is geared to their long-term resolution.

However, just as the crime fighters have problems with public expectations of patrol, the social engineers have difficulty meeting the expectations for crime detection and rapid response to incidents. Moreover, the 'problem solving approach' with its emphasis on analysis sits uneasily with the experience- and action-based cultures of policing. Furthermore, the social engineers may have difficulty managing their costs – omni-competent patrol officers are an expensive resource – and problems coping with rising demand. For, although their approach relies on solving problems by identifying clusters, the demand payback is balanced by the effort of achieving solutions to complex problems, most of which require a multi-agency approach in which negotiating the solutions is time consuming and uncertain (Neyroud, 1992). Research has also suggested that there are limitations on the effectiveness of deploying police officers into the sort of social and educational work that social engineering advocates (O'Connor, Evans and Coggans, 1999). Finally, social engineering raises democratic concerns about the role of the police in defining solutions for the community.

The lessons of the 'three futures'

The 'three futures' have clear lessons for the choices facing public policing. Firstly, all three share a number of common threads that are crucial:

- *Demand management:* all need to manage demand very carefully.
- *Diversity:* all three, by moving to a very local structure as the key building block in policing, recognise that social changes over the last two decades mean that policing has to cope with segmented and diverse communities.
- *Developing knowledge:* analysis and new skills in problem solving are critical in all three futures. Effective public policing has to invest in the skills, technology and management that will deliver a front-line which is information and knowledge led.
- *Development:* moreover such an investment is a continuous one and requires the development of an organisational approach that has been described as the 'learning organisation: an active, flexible, organisation that uses information in a focused way to achieve its clearly articulated outcomes'.
- *Declaring clear priorities and managing to them:* following on from the

concept of the 'learning organisation', the success of public policing is going to be closely linked to the ability to negotiate and then manage clear priorities. The policing plan, best value plan and community safety strategy, which look increasingly like 'contracts' with the community (Leishman, Loveday and Savage, 1995) will be both legally and politically critical to this, making the police accountable for 'customer outcomes'.

These are the common threads and we return to them in the chapters to follow. But it is also clear that there are stark differences between the 'three futures':

- The 'enabling force' could be more flexible and responsive to change, better able to develop the type of open and transparent organisation that may inhibit corruption and discourage professional isolation.
- The 'crime fighting' force would be less flexible. It is wedded to one view of the world. How would it respond to a local authority demanding more emphasis on patrol as part of a statutory crime reduction plan? After all, diverting more resources into patrol would be at the 'expense' of the organisation's core crime-fighting capability.
- The 'social engineers', whilst adopting an open and problem-solving approach based on front-line patrol officers are going to find problems negotiating their view that 'the problems are too many demands on the police' (Goldstein, 1990) with local authorities who take an holistic view of local resources to tackling crime and, after the Crime and Disorder Act, want greater control of them. For the social engineer, partnerships are instrumental in accomplishing the ends of policing not essential as the cornerstone of a new way of policing.

Conclusion: which 'future'?

In the way we have presented them the three futures appear to be contradictory. Taken to extremes, none of them is likely to be sustainable. As we have already suggested and as is supported by the concept of 'optimal policing' (Johnston, 2000), balance is a key component of the policing mission. We have argued that the 'enabling' approach is a better fit with the challenges that public policing faces. However, an effective enabling force needs to incorporate the best of all three. Such balanced approaches do exist. The 'Four Tracks' approach (West Mercia Constabulary, 1999 and 2000a) is one such model. It incorporates the key elements of the 'social engineers' (problem-solving policing and beat managers as the spearhead of such an approach) and 'crime-fighting' (targeted policing is a much broader concept which includes disorder and quality of life issues as well as 'crime'). It has a strong emphasis on demand management (responsive policing). Finally, in 'partnership' policing it has the beginnings of the enabling approach.

As 'Four Tracks' illustrates, to try to deploy only one of the 'futures' and treat it, or other approaches such as 'zero tolerance' (Dennis, 1997) as an exclusive solution to the problems of policing is unconvincing. The public, as survey after survey has demonstrated, has a sophisticated view of what they want from policing (Morgan and Newburn, 1997). Overarching Aims and Objectives are a fair reflection of the spread of services that the public expect from their police. They emphasise the increasingly interdependent nature of policing by stressing that the police must 'carry out their functions through partnerships'.

Figure 2.5   The 'Four Tracks of Policing'*

*West Mercia Police, 2000a.

Further reading

Good introductions to the debate about the purposes of policing include:

- Reiner's short chapter for the *Oxford Handbook of Criminology* (Reiner, 1997).
- The report of the *Independent Inquiry into the Roles and Responsibilities of the Police* (Police Foundation/Policy Studies Institute, 1996) is readable and wide-ranging.
- For more extended reading there are Bayley, *Police for the Future* (1994), Waddington, *Policing Citizens* (1999) and Johnston, *Policing Britain: risk, security and governance* (2000).

Notes

1 One of the authors was a ground commander for the Twyford Down demonstrations in 1993.
2 Cf *Steel and others v UK* (1999) EHRR on the human rights dimension of the protests
3 Figures drawn from the West Mercia Constabulary budget

Chapter 3

From ethics to principles and practice

Introduction

In the first two chapters we have debated the challenges facing policing and some of the choices which face police leaders. In this chapter we move on to examine the ethics and principles which can and must assist with those choices. In doing so we are primarily concerned with two things: firstly, how the theory of ethics can be applied in practice in policing; secondly, building a workable framework of principles, which we will test against the key ethical issues in policing that are the subject of the second part of the book.

There are, therefore, five parts to this chapter:

- Ethics, their meaning and why they are important in policing.
- The major ethical theories with particular relevance to policing and their strengths and weaknesses.
- The impact of the challenges we discussed in Chapters 1 and 2, particularly of 'post-modernism' and 'globalisation', on 'classical' theories of ethics.
- A 'best fit' framework combining several approaches.
- The principles for policing which we can draw out of our analysis.

Ethics and policing

We are concerned in this book with how police officers and police leaders make the right judgements and do the right things, for the right reasons. In order to do so they must have an appropriate ethical system and there should be a clear relationship between that ethical system, individual and organisational moral values, judgement and decision-making (Pollock, 1998). The clarity of that relationship is important because ethics are the theoretical basis for the 'principles of moral behaviour' (Honderich, 1995) and provide both the boundaries for morality and the pathways for proper thinking about real life choices. Both ethics and morality – often used interchangeably – are concerned with the distinction between right and wrong. The difference between the terms is similar to the difference between thought and action: ethics are concerned with analysis and reflection on the problems of human conduct; morality is more about the nature of the conduct itself (Lawton, 1998).

We have discussed the police role in the last chapter. Central to that role is a need to make judgements about right and wrong: between crime and non-crime; between order and disorder; between different methods of investigation; whether to use force or not; whether to act or intervene or not. Pollock argues that the study of ethics is particularly important for criminal justice practitioners in general and the police in particular because:

• They have discretion to make decisions which affect the life, liberty and property of other citizens;
• They have a duty to enforce the law;
• They have a duty to protect the rights of citizens;
• They are public servants and, therefore, as the appointed guardians of the public's interests, they must show high standards of integrity (meaning, literally, a commitment to a moral life) (Pollock, 1998: 3-4).

To Pollock's list it would be possible to add several more specific points:

• The police have the power to use intrusive, covert and deceptive methods. Such methods have both become more important to policing and, as a result of technological advance, have greater potential to intrude, disrupt and deceive.
• The police have a crucial role in protecting hard-to-reach minority groups – they are the gatekeepers of citizenship and respectability.
• The integrity of the police worldwide has suffered a series of shocks, whether it be as a result of corruption, incompetence or racism (Chapter 1).

For the International Association of Chief Police Officers, 'ethics is our greatest training and leadership need today and into the next century: nothing is more devastating to individual departments and our entire profession than uncovered scandals or discovered acts of officer misconduct and unethical behaviour' (IACP, 1999: 1). Lawton (1998) suggests that this message applies more broadly to public service management. He endorses Pollock's view in stating 'it is assumed that managing public services must, by definition, be ethical'. The stewardship of the 'public interest' that lies at the heart of policing demands ethical standards and practitioners of high moral character (Delattre, 1989). Furthermore, the study of ethics helps to develop practitioners' grasp of those standards, their ability to think critically, weigh up the consequences of their decisions and understand their personal responsibility.

These are particularly important points when they are held up against the way in which most police training is conducted. Even with the recent shift in the UK to competency based training, the emphasis is on training officers and leaders *to do things right, rather than to do the right things* (Mackenzie, 1999). The focus is on skills, knowledge and procedure, rather than on the reasons lying behind them. This is very much a reflection of the underlying organisational culture. Much as British law is obsessively precedent driven, so equally British policing relies on procedures developed in response to problems. Whilst this is a strength in many contexts – it provides for stability and certainty combined with a measure of adaptability – the level of change confronting the organisation and the nature of the challenges they present requires a less reactive, but more reflective, analytical, ethical and value-driven approach. More and more, police officers and police forces are being asked to account not just for the decisions they take but also for the way they take them (Beckley, 1997b). A grasp of ethics and an ability to relate theory to practice are, therefore, an essential, but underdeveloped part of the police officer's portfolio.

Ethical theory

Although this section is primarily a discussion of the theory of ethics we are anxious to relate the theory to practical examples. We will, therefore, test the theory at each stage against a number of key examples:

Case study 1
Smith has kidnapped Gemma and secured her inside a concrete drain. He has left her with only very limited food and water. He demands a large ransom from her millionaire father who promises not to contact the police in return for his daughter's life. Despite this, the father contacts the police. They persuade the father to let them control the handover of the money. In the handover Smith is arrested. He is removed to a police station where he is questioned but refuses to disclose Gemma's location, other than to tell police that she

must now be starving to death. Police are unable to locate Gemma and are running out of custody time. They discuss whether they should exclude the solicitor from the interview and use some 'stronger' tactics.

Case study 2
Jones is a serious sex offender, who commits offences against children. Police are desperate to catch him and his network before they kill a child. They are contacted by Jones' daughter, aged 15, who offers to provide information to the police covertly. The police debate whether to use the daughter as an informant in view of her age, the family relationship to their suspect and the possible dangers to her.

Case study 3
Thomas is a local community constable. He is dealing with a series of complaints about an 11-year-old boy, who is racially harassing and abusing elderly residents. They demand that Thomas takes some action and suggest a 'good clip round the ear'. The boy, when spoken to is rude, abusive and spits at Thomas. Thomas, angry and convinced that the boy will not respond to reason, slaps him hard. The boy and his parents complain about the officer. The local residents and the local media strongly support his actions. Managers have to decide what action to take against him.

This is an approach that we will use more extensively in the next sections of the book. We have constructed these examples carefully using real cases – but they are not completely based on any one such case. We have designed them not only to support our text but also for wider use in training and discussion. There is a long-running debate about using such scenarios in developing an understanding of ethics. For Delattre (1989), ethics cannot be taught: individuals without character cannot be made virtuous through instruction. Jackson (1993) is more optimistic, suggesting that people's ability to think critically can be substantially enhanced by a combination of approaches including both theoretical knowledge and discussion of 'naïve' scenarios. We have, therefore, sought to keep our scenarios simple and realistic.

The discussion of ethical theory, which follows concentrates on those theories – duty, utility, virtue and care – which are more 'universal' and which more closely meet Gensler's three rules. Gensler (1998) used these three rules to distinguish between low and high levels of development in ethical theories. The first group, includes relativism, subjectivism and egoism. The second group of theories is characterised by: *consistency* (such as between ends and means); *congruity with the 'golden rule'* (or the moral imperative to treat others as you would be treated yourself); *moral rationality*, or a requirement for the individual to think critically and make a genuine exercise of personal discretion (Gensler, 1998).

Unsurprisingly, it is this second group that we will then use to try and formulate a set of principles that could underpin policing. For an organisation whose mission includes concepts of community and public interest, relativism, subjectivism and egoism are flawed approaches. Even if they were acceptable standards in wider society, the 'role morality' of policing requires a higher standard. As Miller, Blackeler and Alexandra (1997) have argued, in certain occupations, such as policing, the nature of the mission demands a 'role morality', which is distinctly different from 'ordinary morality'. The mission of policing, including as it does the upholding of the law, demands a role morality, which excludes torture and includes integrity. Whilst tolerance is important for policing, any ethical standard that could provide an easy justification for torture and assault by police officers is not a standard to which policing should aspire.

Duty, utility, virtue and care

In contrast, the ethics of duty, utility, virtue and care provide, in their contrasting ways, standards that are appropriate to policing. We shall set out their main points before discussing their application to the case studies.

Duty

We have used 'duty' as a shorthand for 'deontological' ethics or 'non-consequentialism', the ethics of exceptionless rules and universal rights, which is dominated by the work of Immanuel Kant. The latter started from the presumption that there is a universal law of right and wrong and that morality is product of man's rationality. Central to his thinking were:

- The 'categorical imperative' that 'I ought never to act in such a way except that my maxim should become a universal law' (Kant, 1949) or put simply, we must not act in any way unless we agree that the same behaviour would be universally acceptable.
- Moral actions must stem from duty not self-interest. Motivation is more important than outcome.
- The concept of personal autonomy and the requirement that no person should be treated as a means to an end.
- That people should be treated with dignity and respect.
- That, because we can only control our actions and not their consequences, we must act in a moral fashion without regard to the consequences.

The ethics of duty have a clear consistency with the police mission, particularly the concept of a universal rule, the requirement to act from a sense of duty and the exhortation to treat people with dignity and respect. The use of the child in Case Study 2 as an informant – effectively both using her as a means to the end of catching her father and encouraging her to deceive her father – would be inconsistent with the ethics of duty. However, by providing exceptionless obligations, the same ethics face a challenge when two sets of principles conflict: covert policing may be vital to prevent serious crime, but may be argued to be unethical because of the use of deception to accomplish its aims (Bok, 1989). Likewise, in Case Study 1, the duty of the father not to lie should have persuaded him against telling the police. This would have left him little alternative but to pay the ransom. However, this, in itself, might be deemed immoral, in which case, because he must not consider the consequences of his actions, he must wait and hope that his daughter's life is spared. Such an absolutist position does not seem to accord with common sense and, in any case, seems to ignore the right to life of the daughter. Seen from a utilitarian position, failure to tell the police and then to detect the crime provides no deterrence to more kidnaps and, in the short term provides little opportunity for a beneficial outcome for the father, the daughter or the wider community.

In seeking to overcome such dilemmas, Ross proposed that, rather than exceptionless duties, there should be *'prima facie* duties' (Ross, 1930). He suggested seven basic *prima facie* duties: fidelity; reparation, or making up for any harm caused; gratitude; justice; beneficence or doing good to others; self-improvement; non-maleficence or not harming others. An individual would be obliged to do that which had the greatest weight of *prima facie* duties. This approach would produce a significantly different outcome for Case Study 1. The father's duty of fidelity would be outweighed by his duty of non-maleficence and beneficence towards his daughter, which would probably encourage contacting the police. However, Ross would provide no easy resolution for the officers to the dilemma as to whether to move outside strict legal procedures to try and rescue the daughter. This dilemma is very similar to the 'Dirty Harry' example discussed by Klockars (1985: 70), where 'dirty means' were employed to achieve a good and 'compellingly moral outcome'.

Utility

Consequentialist or 'teleological' ethics are often contrasted with the ethics of duty because of their concern with positive outcomes. There are a number of different strands of 'utilitarian' theory: classical, 'act' or 'direct' utilitarianism, which is usually associated with the nineteenth century British philosophers Bentham, Mill and Sidgwick; rule utilitarianism; utilitarianism of interests, which runs through Singer's work on 'applied ethics' (Singer, 1993). All start from the same presumption, that the rightness or goodness of any action or organisation depends solely on the goodness of its results. An action becomes obligatory and right if, and only if, its consequences would be better – producing a better balance of pleasure over pain – than any available alternative. This simple formula of utility is complex to implement. It requires, like the rational comprehensive model of planning, the ability to perceive all the possible alternatives and to weigh them against each other. At its most literal it could be argued that it might permit a wrongful conviction if the deterrent effect was a better consequence. It could certainly be deployed to support the actions of the officers in Case Study 1, if, after weighing up the consequences of using some more coercive tactics, they concluded that such tactics were most likely to save the girl's life and that this was a 'better' outcome.

In order to overcome the perceived arbitrariness of this approach, rule utilitarianism introduces a set of rules – such as not convicting the innocent or torturing suspects – into the utility equation. Instead of weighing solely the utility of each action, it is necessary to weigh the precedent it sets and the longer-term outcome of that precedent as a general rule. For example, rule utilitarianism would require the precedent of using a child as an informant in the circumstances of Case Study 2 to be weighed against the consequences of the long-term 'rule' in favour of child informants. In contrast, act utilitarianism would weigh only the consequences of the particular actions. Rule utilitarianism can, therefore, be criticised for being too concerned with the process and not concerned enough with the outcome.

In the third variation, having dismissed the ethics of duty and challenged 'simple' utility, Singer proposed a utilitarianism, which 'requires me to weigh up all those interests and adopt the course of action most likely to maximise the interests of those affected' (Singer, 1993: 13). Singer's approach, by considering 'interests' rather than 'pleasure and pain', pushes the individual to consider decisions from the point of the impartial spectator, rather than through the filter of self-interest. Singer was concerned with practical judgements or, in the title of his main work, 'Applied Ethics'. Singer's version of utilitarianism would take a more balanced view of Case Study 1 and add the longer-term interests of society. These would probably include the need to have a law-abiding police force that did not torture suspects. For Singer also placed a high value on critical thinking 'if people cannot put forward any justification for what they are doing, we may reject their claim to be living according to ethical standards'.

A further difficulty for utility – indeed for most of the theories discussed here – is that the common way of considering each set of circumstances as a discrete problem can prove unhelpful and produce results which defy common sense. Singer proposed that it is far better to 'think along the lines of some broad principles' (Singer, 1993) and deploy what Hare (1981) called 'intuitive' thinking. Hare contrasted this 'everyday' thinking with 'critical' thinking, which was more properly reserved for major new issues. 'Intuitive' thinking includes the idea of following the course which 'will pay off most of the time'(Singer, 1993). This adds an important layer to utilitarian thinking. Instead of thinking about the weighing of benefits on an individual basis, this allows the professional to bring in experience and everyday common sense to judge whether a particular decision matches a wider framework of knowledge. This connects the ethics of utility with the concept of risk, which has become integral to modern policing (Neyroud, 1999).

The most important objection to the ethics of utility is that they take no account of principles or rights and that the utility equation places a high value on 'hedonism'. However, as Smart has argued and as our discussion of Singer's approach suggests, their strength lies in their simplicity and generality, which seem to bring them close to the 'common sense' of everyday (Smart and Williams, 1973). Thus, in each of the case studies, the ethics of utility would allow the police officers to weigh up all the factors, consider the past experience of similar situations, take into account the long term factors and the risks and make a clear decision.

Virtue

The ethics of virtue focus on the intrinsic qualities of the good person rather than the goodness of their actions. Starting out from Aristotle's Nicomachean ethics, a series of authors, most notably MacIntyre (1981) and Baier (1985) have argued that virtue, always the mean between extremes of character, will lead to happiness. For Aristotle, virtue was a combination of intellectual and moral traits. All men have, by nature, the capacity for virtue, but not all learn the habit. This was very much the position taken by Delattre in his study *Character and Cops* (1989): inner goodness of character will produce good ends. Both MacIntyre and Baier have gone to describe the types of virtue – courage, honesty and justice – which will produce good practices.

The challenge for a virtue approach is to distinguish between choices. Although its proponents, such as Delattre, might argue that, with good character, the right choices will naturally follow, this does not appear to assist the police officer wrestling with ambiguity. MacIntyre's solution to these sorts of dilemmas was closer to the ethics of duty than utility, in that he disregarded external consequences and focused on the internal qualities. This would encourage the officers in Case Study 1 to stick with their sense of honesty and justice and avoid ill-treating the prisoner, would discourage the potential exploitation of the young informant in

Case Study 2 and would certainly condemn the lack of virtue demonstrated by the officer in Case Study 3.

Care

The last of our four, the ethics of 'care', derive from the works of feminist authors such as Gilligan (1982), Baier (1995) and Held (1995). Gilligan argued that women favour an ethic of love and caring in contrast to the ethic of obligation favoured by men. Held suggested that this difference has much to do with women relying on emotion, while men prefer reason. The resultant care perspective provides an approach which emphasises relationships and needs rather than rights and universal laws. There are important connections between 'care' and the restorative and peacemaking justice approaches, which several authors have advanced as alternatives to the traditional justice system (Braithwaite, 1989 and Braswell and Gold, 1996). Furthermore, 'care', by placing a value on relationships, fits well with the 'enabling' approach we set out above and the 'connexity' of the modern globalised world, which Mulgan (1997) has described. In each of the case study examples the ethics of care would focus on the nature of relationships and needs, both individually and in terms of police with the community. The father's relationship with his daughter and her needs would predominate in the first case study, in the second the impact of betrayal of her father on the child would weigh heavily against using her as an informant; and in the last example a reparatory solution, a sort of community group conferencing (Braithwaite, 1989), involving all the actors – residents, young man and constable – would probably provide the best way to 'reintegrate' broken relationships.

The ethics of uncertainty

The ethics of duty, utility, virtue and care provide, or rather are claimed to provide, solutions to our moral dilemmas and guidance on ethical standards. However, the case studies we discussed placed the actors in very individual, personal relationships. They were able to perceive the consequences of their actions directly. One of the features of the changing world that we described in Chapter 1 is that such moral 'proximity' is diminishing. More and more of the decisions we take either have consequences beyond our knowledge or the decisions themselves are difficult to disentangle from the decisions of others. One small-scale example would be the growth of multi-agency approaches to tackling crime. It is frequently difficult to distinguish cause and effect and individual responsibilities. Another similar example might be the issue of discrimination in the British criminal justice system. Research by Roger

Hood has demonstrated quite clearly that the outcome of the system is discriminatory (Hood, 1992). Yet, because so many different actors are involved in different roles, with separate accountabilities, individual agencies have been reluctant to accept responsibility for their part (Macpherson, 1999). Glover demonstrated this more dramatically in his study of the moral history of the twentieth century (Glover, 1999). In particular, he discussed how, as warfare has become technological and politicians, strategists and major combatants have become distant from the results of their decisions, so they have been disconnected and have disconnected themselves from the moral responsibility for them.

Bauman has argued that these challenges of 'postmodernity' create dilemmas that the 'classical' theories cannot resolve: an 'aporia', or contradiction that cannot be overcome (Bauman, 1993). The separation of deeds and outcomes by distance, time and space produces moral uncertainty. The further separation of each individual's actions from outcomes by the intervention of team actions and role actions (such as the actions of a police officer when acting in that role) enhance that confusion. In short, our moral identity has become divided and separated from our moral self (Glover, 1999). The attempt to find universal philosophies, which resolve the tension between the individual and common interests, cannot, in such circumstances, succeed. Furthermore, the pace of change has accelerated and with it the interdependence of changes, adding complexity to ethical dilemmas (Toffler, 1999). Bauman, in response goes on to set out the features of 'postmodern ethics':

- Human beings are neither 'good' nor 'bad': they are morally ambivalent. No single, logically coherent code will fit this.
- Moral phenomena are inherently non-rational and do not fit utility or rules, which presume *one* right choice.
- Most moral choices are ambiguous and any 'moral' approach taken to extremes will produce an immoral result. A most startling example of this was the use by Adolf Eichmann, at his trial for holocaust crimes, of Kant's ethics of duty to justify his obedience to orders (Glover, 1999). In contrast, Bauman stated, 'One can recognise the moral self by its uncertainty, whether all that should have been done, has been.' (p.12).
- Morality is not universalizable: one single imposed moral code is immoral.
- Morality is irrational and he cited the conflict between personal autonomy and community as a key example of this (Bauman, 1993).

Bauman's pessimism is not complete. He refuted the suggestion that he was proposing moral relativism. He was seeking a living ethics, realistic, responsive and flexible enough a morality to cope with what Mulgan has described as 'a moral republic, with no absolute authorities and no divine rights, but rather a continuous conversation' (Mulgan, 1997: 147). Mulgan himself was much more optimistic. He suggested that the very 'connexity' of the modern world 'makes the universal potential of morality practical for the first time' (Mulgan, 1997: 167). A new ethics was now possible incorporating some old principles – he cited truth-telling as particularly important in a world saturated with 'second-hand information' – and some new ones. Of the latter the most important would be personal responsibility and stewardship.

Traditional ethics of universal moral laws, based around concepts of authority and state power, are no longer sufficient. They are inadequate to cope with the demands of the twenty-first century. That is not to say that existing approaches must be jettisoned. 'What I would like to do is to hold on to the rights that we have, but expand them to take account of the new ones' (Toffler, 1999: 2). Glover, in addition, suggested that a new humanised ethics, drawing on people's sense of moral identity and innate human responses such as respect, provide a base for the future.

A new ethics for policing?

Building forward from the arguments above and seeking to construct an approach to ethics in policing, which takes account of them, is not easy. There are, however, some common threads that provide a starting point. Singer, Bauman, Mulgan and Glover all favour an applied approach, which emphasises the responsibility on each individual to exercise personal judgement. Singer would favour relying on weighing interests; the others would see a role for key principles, as long as they were not applied indiscriminately.

This suggests that we should look for the 'best fit' between the mission of policing, the 'virtues' of good police officers and the ethical framework outlining good policing practice. Lawton represented this as a chain, linking 'VALUE-VIRTUES-PRINCIPLE-PRACTICE' (Lawton, 1998). Implicitly, this model suggests that there must be congruity between these four. An example of an ethical framework fitted to a public service – medical practice – is to be found in Gillon (1994). The latter suggested, a little like Ross, that we could all commit ourselves to four *prima facie* principles:

1 **The respect for personal autonomy**: This is derived from the ethics of duty. In policing this would include respecting the rights of citizens, showing dignity and respect to them and to colleagues and not using either as a means to an end;
2 **Beneficence**, and
3 **Non-maleficence:** These are taken from Ross, but their interpretation – a

balancing of interests – must be from the ethics of utility. Taken together, beneficence and non-maleficence require police officers to help people without harming others.

4 **Justice:** Gillon drew on three approaches to justice: Rawls' distributive justice; respect for people's human rights; and respect for morally respectable laws, which finds support in Singer (1993). These three would ensure that public policing was a public good, delivered according to need, with a high value on human rights and legality.

Gillon's framework draws primarily on the ethics of duty and utility. It is missing the additional dimension of the ethics of virtue and care. Drawing on the discussion above, we would argue for the addition of a further set of principles:

5 **Responsibility:** This concept, which Mulgan (1997) placed great store by, would require police officers to justify their actions and take personal ownership of them.

6 **Care:** As we set out above, this approach to ethics is an important complement to 'justice' and emphasises what Glover has described as the natural human responses of care toward each other (Glover, 1999). It emphasises 'interdependence' which we have argued above is an increasingly important concept in the policing mission.

7 **Honesty:** For Mulgan and MacIntyre (1981) this was a key virtue. It is central to policing and to the authority and legitimacy of police officers. It includes not just honesty with and towards others but also honesty in self-reflection.

8 **Stewardship:** Mulgan (1997) stated that this was a complex idea, which incorporated the idea of trusteeship over the powerless and over police powers. It implies obligations to use the latter carefully and with discretion. It links with the important issue of police accountability.

This set of principles does not provide a clear and unambiguous answer to every moral dilemma facing police officers. Bauman has, rightly in our view, argued that this is not possible. We have already established that the police mission is contradictory and, like the approach to ethics we have outlined, necessarily, contingent. However, it is important that contingency is not mistaken for relativism or we end up with the approach of Arthur Nebe, the Nazi Gestapo chief, who said 'there are no such things as principles only circumstances' (quoted in Alderson, 1998). The eight principles reconcile key features of the ethics of utility, duty, virtue and care. Up to this point we have tended to emphasise the differences between these four, in order to explain them. However, the practical differences between alternative ethical perspectives can be over-emphasised. All four provide a strong prohibition against killing, a presumption against lying and encouragement for integrity – the commitment to a moral life – because each has regard to Gensler's three maxims of the 'golden rule', consistency and moral rationality.

It is, moreover, possible to envisage how the four ethical approaches could be modelled, along with the principles we have derived from them. In the previous chapter we set out the 'Four Tracks of Policing', which provides a balanced way of thinking about policing. It is possible to apply a similar 'Four Tracks' approach to the four ethics (Figure 3.1).

What the model illustrates, using the same philosophy as Four Tracks of Policing, is the need to consider problems using all the approaches. Thus, to take the case studies as an example, rather than just looking at the problems as a Kantian or a utilitarian, the Four Tracks model would force consideration of a wider set of arguments, placing duty alongside care, utility alongside virtue. The method of distinguishing between choices would still be largely utilitarian – very similar to Singer's balancing of interests – but reasoning through four paths, not one, should satisfy Bauman's objections about simple, single choices. Furthermore, as we see in the next chapter, such balancing in decision-making can be considerably assisted by the addition of the principles that underpin human rights: legality; proportionality; necessity; accountability. Together, the human rights principles and the principles in this framework can help to guide and channel reasoning and subsequent decisions.

Figure 3.1 The 'Four Tracks of Ethics'

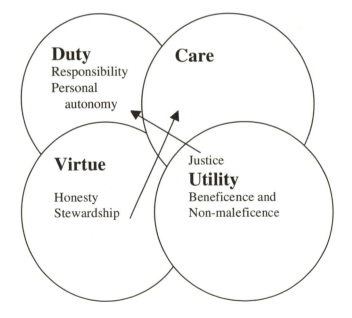

We will test the model and the principles further against four major dimensions of police ethics – personal, performance, operational and organisational – in the second part of the book. First of all, we will compare them to the sets of principles outlined by a number of authors, research bodies and government reports.

Principles in policing

During the 1990s, there was a rash of publications advancing proposals for 'principles' in policing. The major ones were as follows:

- Cohen and Feldberg (1991), who based their principles around the Lockean social contract and the American Constitution;
- Lord Nolan (1995), whose report on *Standards in Public Life* generally has major lessons for the police;
- Jones, Newburn and Smith's (1994) research on 'Democracy in Policing' for the Policy Studies Institute;
- The 'Integrity' Inspection report from the Inspectorate (HMIC, 1999a);
- Sir William Macpherson's report on the death on Stephen Lawrence (1999);
- Alderson (1998), whose book was actually entitled *Principled Policing*;
- The *Patten Report* (1999) on policing in N. Ireland.

It is possible to place their principles side by side and compare them with the eight principles set out above (Figure 3.2). There appears to be a strong correlation between our set of eight principles derived from a discussion of the major ethical theories and the approach of the six authors. The differences lie in emphasis and balance. Thus, for example, Cohen and Feldberg (1991), take as their starting point the US Constitution and a Lockean, contractual view of the relationship between police and citizen. In contrast, Alderson, whilst still endorsing Locke, also espouses the more interventionist utilitarianism of Popper. Nevertheless, there is a remarkable synergy between the six versions in their support for principles such as accountability, representativeness and equitable service delivery, which fit within the principles we have set out.

The difference between our approach and these others is that none of them are comprehensive. Each, because of their starting points, is missing some part of the framework. The more comprehensive approach provided by the Four Tracks – drawing on four sets of ethical theory – and the eight principles is significantly fuller. It has the added advantage of encouraging decision-making with the widest possible consideration of different standpoints – almost a definition of the sort of decision-making police officers are having to make more and more in the twenty-first century of 'diversity'.

Conclusions

We seem to have a substantial amount of consensus about the sort of principles that must underpin policing and, now, better understanding of how these principles can be derived from ethical theory. With the Over-arching Aims and Objectives, it is also much clearer how the principles link with the mission of policing. They are quite clearly, in the model of OAO, the filters through which the mission is perceived, or, seen from another angle, the way the mission is carried out. This raises the question as to how the principles should be used. There are four areas that we will be concerned with:

- Most obviously, as we have suggested above, they must be a part of decision-making. Whether they are applied 'critically' or intuitively will depend on the nature of the decision and the environment and circumstances in which the decision is being taken.
- Secondly, the principles must necessarily be a part of training and the standards – such as ethical codes – which are being trained and which could support professional standards in policing.
- Thirdly, the standards could be used to audit policing and its policies, challenging existing systems and culture.
- Finally, the principles could form the centrepiece of a commitment to value-driven policing.

These four elements – decision-making, training and professional standards, auditing compliance and value-driven policing are central to the third part of the book, where we will seek to develop a workable approach to 'ethical policing'.

Before we do so, however, there is a major element of our ethical framework, which we need to develop further. We have alluded to human rights in the discussion above. We now need to expand on the theory, history, principles and implications for policing of human rights.

Further reading

For a good basic overview of ethical theory the *Oxford Companion to Philosophy* (Honderich, 1995) is invaluable. Gensler, *Ethics: a contemporary introduction* (1998) is a readable introduction with a good use of case studies. More specifically related to the police, Pollock, *Ethics in Crime and Justice* (1998), Kleinig, *The Ethics of Policing* (1996a) and Delattre, *Character and Cops: ethics in policing* (1989) have good treatment of the main ethical theories. Lawton, *Ethical Management for the Public Services* (1998) provides this from a broader public service viewpoint.

Figure 3.2 Comparison of principles

Summary and links to the 8 principles	Cohen and Feldberg	Alderson	Jones, Newburn and Smith	Nolan	HMIC and Macpherson	Patten
Effective and appropriate service delivery: (Beneficence and non-maleficence)	Deliver safety and security	A sense of justice (derived from Rawls)	Appropriate service delivery and responsiveness			Effectiveness and efficiency
Objectivity and impartiality: (Responsibility and honesty)	Non-partisan objectivity			Selflessness and objectivity		Impartiality
Accountability and redress: (Responsibility and stewardship)		Vigorous civil society as a counter-balance	Redress and participation	Accountability	Acceptable local priorities	Accountability
Representative and fair access to service: (Justice)	Fair access to their services	Obligations to protect those in need (derived from Popper)	Distributed power and equity		Representative and recognising the needs of minorities	Representativeness

*Commitment to human rights: (**Respect for personal autonomy and Justice**)*		Commitment to human rights				Respect for human rights
*Trust and Integrity: (**Honesty**)*	Public trust			Honesty and integrity	Integrity	
*Partnership and leadership: (**Care**)*	Teamwork cooperation, communication and coordination with other agencies			Leadership	Partnership	Partnership
*Openness: (**Responsibility**)*		Open, liberal democracy	Openness of information	Openness		

Chapter 4

From ethics to rights

Introduction: human rights as a 'new agenda in policing'

Human rights have replaced capitalism and socialism, the sparring partners of the second half of the twentieth century, as the 'big idea' for the new millennium. In the vacuum created by the sudden collapse of the Berlin Wall and all that it symbolised in both East and West, those, like New Labour, searching for a unifying doctrine in the centre left have turned increasingly to human rights. The scramble to subscribe conceals some quite serious differences of emphasis. For, as we shall see, human rights do not provide a complete and unified model for morality or for national or international law.

However, the accelerating international movement in the direction of human rights has been quite startling. The Council of Europe, the ministerial body responsible for the European Convention on Human Rights, had by 2000 some 41 countries as members, a good half of whom have only joined in the last decade. There has been a major investment of governmental and non-governmental organisation time and effort in developing rights in the new democracies of eastern Europe, a movement enhanced by the desire of many to enter the EU, which has itself been making a major drive towards human rights. Outside Europe, within the last decade of the twentieth century a number of national states such as Canada, New Zealand and South Africa have adopted new human rights charters or bills. More than 100 national constitutions now explicitly protect human rights.

Alongside the broader movement to develop human rights internationally and within states, there has been a particular drive to provide international standards for policing. Not only has the United Nations followed up the International Covenant for Civil and Political Rights with a Standard for Law Enforcement Officials, but also the Council of Europe has been seeking to develop a detailed human rights based ethical code for policing. In addition, the International Commission of Jurists, the United Nations-affiliated body of human rights lawyers, has been seeking to develop standards in the more controversial areas such as covert policing (ICJ, 1999).

The reasons for this shift to a human rights agenda are complex. One aspect is almost certainly the discrediting of socialism and the search for an alternative, inclusive, political philosophy in the centre left (Gearty and Tomkins, 1996). Secondly, the globalisation of late twentieth century trade, politics and crime has increased the need for an internationally recognised body of law (Mulgan, 1997). Developing that theme, Bellamy suggests that the attraction of adopting human rights is that the common standards that they purport to provide 'allow space for a large degree of diversity', so permitting both globalisation and localisation – a plurality of pluralities (Bellamy, 1999: 167). Thirdly, as we have discussed in Chapter 1, some authors (Giddens, 1990) have argued that the shifts inherent in the 'post-modern' or 'late-modern' world have encouraged an increased reliance on 'abstract' systems, as against traditional forms of belief. One part of the explanation for the rise of human rights may be that they seem to provide just such an abstract system. However, as with the ethical theories that we set out in the last chapter, we should not allow that to lull us into assuming that human rights provides a single, clear body of theory.

This chapter will, therefore, seek to provide an overview of human rights in theory and practice, which can be applied in the second part of the book. The chapter is in four parts:

- Firstly, we will set out the key points in the development of human rights, their meaning and their specific relevance to policing.
- Secondly, we will discuss the main elements of a particular human rights convention – the European Convention – and compare these to the other major international conventions.
- Thirdly we seek to draw out of ECHR the principles that underpin it and connect these with the principles we discussed in the last chapter.
- Finally, we will debate the implications of these for policing.

Human rights: the history of an idea and its meaning

Human rights have a complex origin and a controversial past and present, which can be summarised in the following key stages:

- The eighteenth-century enlightenment saw a shift from the divine state to a state and a theory of state revolving around man and the rights of man. The state became a contract between individuals to guarantee collectively their individual rights to life, liberty and the pursuit of happiness. The individual claimed these rights or 'liberties' *against* the state.

- The nineteenth and twentieth centuries saw the development of claim rights *upon* the state, creating a duty on the state to intervene to secure the rights. Hence, whilst a citizen might have a right to freedom from discrimination, a corresponding claim right might oblige the state to redress the balance in pre-existing discrimination.

- The post-war era brought a step change and a determination to prevent the mass abuse of human rights that had taken place under the Third Reich. The establishment of the Council of Europe and the European Convention on Human Rights quickly followed the United Nations Universal Declaration on Human Rights. The former was supported by a court and, by the 1960s, by a right of individual petition to the court.

- The post-cold war era has seen a further rapid expansion of human rights jurisprudence. In Europe, membership of the Council of Europe has become an essential step to statehood and recognition. The European Court has seen a burgeoning caseload brought by citizens from both developed and emerging democracies to enforce their rights.

This growing momentum by individuals and their representatives to assert 'human rights' raises important questions about the rights and the way in which they apply. At the most obvious it suggests that the enthusiasm for rights is not just governmental, but has also become a key aspect of the relationship of modern Europeans with their states. In particular, for policing and the criminal justice system, whence many of the cases arise, it suggests a willingness to challenge the exercise of discretion and use of powers. It is, therefore, important in considering the impact of human rights on policing to understand the nature of the rights that are being deployed. We shall do this under four headings: the rights themselves; the elements that make up each right; the way in which the rights apply; the relationship of rights to law and democracy.

The rights themselves

Producing a definitive list of 'human rights' is difficult. There is substantial and problematic disagreement about the boundaries of human rights (Bellamy, 1999). We can divide them into two groups: civil and political rights, which, in the Lockean tradition, protect the citizen from intervention by the state; economic, social and cultural rights, which, as we have suggested above, require more positive intervention by the state. Using those two broad definitions, an examination of two major human rights instruments across the world suggests that the lists includes the following, as set out in Figure 4.1.

However, these are 'unfinished' lists, because work continues within bodies such as the Council of Europe to develop new rights, such as a freestanding right to equality. This continuing development of what are billed as fundamental human rights might give us pause for thought as to whether they are 'fundamental' or merely contingent on perceived social and political needs. It is important, therefore to look inside the rights and see how they are constructed.

Figure 4.1 The principal rights in the UN Charter and European Convention

The Rights	UN Charter	European Convention
Political and Civil Rights		
Rights of life	Article 3	Article 2
Freedom from torture, inhumane degrading treatment	Article 5	Article 3
Freedom from slavery or forced labour	Article 4	Article 4
Rights to liberty and security	Article 9	Article 5
Right to fair trial	Article 10 and 11	Article 6
Right to private and family life	Article 12	Article 8
Freedom of thought and conscience	Article 18	Article 9
Freedom of expression	Article 19	Article 10
Freedom of assembly and association	Article 20	Article 11
Freedom from discrimination	Article 2 and 7	Article 12 and 14
Right to enjoyment of property	Article 17	Protocol 1, Article 1
Right to political participation	Article 21	
Right to a proper remedy for breach of rights		Article 13
Freedom of movement	Article 13	
Right to education	Article 26	Protocol 1, Article 2
Social and cultural rights		
Right to social security	Article 22	
Right to work and free choice in employment	Article 23	
Right to rest and leisure	Article 24	
Right to standard of living adequate for health and well-being of himself and family	Article 25	
Right to free participation in cultural life	Article 27	

The elements of rights

Wellman has defined human rights as 'a cluster of ethical liberties, claims, powers and immunities that together constitute a system of ethical autonomy possessed by an individual as a human being vis a vis the state' (Kamenka and Erh-Soon-Tay, 1978: 56). He broke down the cluster into four component parts:

- *'Ethical liberty'*: a freedom to perform some action, provided that there is no duty not to do it. An example would be the freedom to attend a church.
- *'Ethical claim'*: creates a corresponding duty, such as the duty to protect life or not to cause injury.
- *'An ethical power'*: the freedom to waive one's rights, such as to consent to a search of one's property.
- *'An ethical immunity'* against having rights removed, such as by an arbitrary action of the state. This immunity emphasises the personal autonomy and choice that rights provide.

Wellman's approach is useful in that it illustrates that 'human rights', as set out in the major conventions such as ECHR, are not simple 'one way' rights. They create not just rights, but also corresponding duties on the state, the individuals and communities. We will examine this in more depth below when we turn to look at the Articles and underpinning principles of ECHR.

Another more straightforward way of unpicking the elements that characterise rights has been set out by the United Nations in their training material for police officers (UN, 2000). They cite the key characteristics as:

- 'Internationally guaranteed
- Legally protected
- Focus on dignity of the human being
- Protect the individual and the group
- Oblige states and state actors
- Cannot be waived or taken away
- Equal and interdependent
- Universal' (UN, 2000: 20)

Despite the seemingly authoritative stamp of the United Nations, some of these statements, such as 'cannot be waived', are, as we have already seen from Wellman's approach, challengeable. Furthermore, it is difficult to maintain that the rights are 'equal', even if they are interdependent. Within ECHR, for instance, there is a clear hierarchy of rights: absolute rights, rights from which states can derogate in emergencies, and conditional rights.

The application of rights, 'up, across and sideways'

Both the UN and Wellman saw 'a human right' as being 'a right that any individual has as a human being in the face of the state' (Kamenka and Erh-Soon-Tay, 1978: 56). Rights in this conception are perceived as part of the 'vertical' relationship between the citizen and the state. In the case of the European Convention as brought into British law, this relationship starts from the assumption that it is unlawful for public authorities to act in a way that is incompatible with Convention rights. Public authorities are defined as courts and tribunals and any person who performs functions of a public nature, which clearly includes police officers. Where the rights of a victim or an aggrieved person have been infringed, they can bring an action against a public authority in two ways. Firstly by bringing proceedings in an appropriate court or tribunal or by relying on convention rights as a defence in any legal proceedings. The only persons who can bring proceedings are those who are actually affected by the act or omission of the public authority or persons being at risk of suffering. Victims under this legislation can be natural (actual) persons, legal persons such as companies, non-governmental organisations (NGOs) and groups of people. This emphasises the existence of 'corporate' and 'group' citizens. Courts can award damages to victims whose rights have been infringed or apply any other remedies that court has available to it such as orders of injunction. The objective of ECHR in this 'vertical' relationship is to afford 'just satisfaction' to victims and therefore the judgment should be 'just and appropriate'.

However, there are strong arguments for rethinking this as the sole way in which human rights should have effect. The first of these relates back to our earlier point about the distinction between rights and claim rights and the position of children and vulnerable adults. For a small, but growing, number of cases in the European Court have explored the 'diagonal' application of rights. The most obvious examples of this are the cases being taken on behalf of children who have either been assaulted or abused by their parents (*A. v UK* [1999] and *Z. v UK* [1999]). In these cases it has been established that where actions between two individuals breach a fundamental human right – such as the right to physical integrity or to freedom from torture or inhuman of degrading treatment – the state can be held responsible for failing to protect the injured parties either by failing to legislate effectively or by failing to intervene. These types of cases have become increasingly important for law enforcement as they have been applied to areas like child protection.

With the contraction of the state, the out-sourcing of key, former state functions and the growth of private policing (Johnston, 2000), there is a growing debate about the 'horizontal' – or interpersonal – effect of rights (ICJ, 1999). This can best be illustrated by comparing the example of an interference of rights inside a police force, which is clearly caught by the 'vertical' effect, and the same interference – for instance intrusive surveillance in the workplace – within a private security agency. The latter would seem to be just as much a breach of fundamental rights – the right to a private life – as the former. It seems highly probable that horizontal rights will become more and more important, raising intriguing questions as to whether public policing will be seen as the key arbitrator in horizontal rights disputes.

Rights, consumers, democracy and the rule of law

The third aspect of human rights that is important for policing is the relationship between the rights and law and then, in turn, rights, the rule of law and democracy. The former is neatly summed up by Kamenka's definition of human rights as 'a proposal concerning the morally appropriate way of treating men and organising society' (Kamenka and Erh-Soon-Tay, 1978: 12). This places human rights not as a system of law but as an ethical framework. This distinction between 'natural rights' and positive law has been particularly important in Britain, where legislated, enforceable rights, rather than natural rights derived from a Bill of Rights or Convention have been central to the legal tradition (Feldman, 1993). The incorporation of the European Convention into British law (and similar approaches in Canada and New Zealand) to some degree turned that argument on its head by providing citizens – in itself a novel concept in a legal tradition based on the 'subject' – with a means of enforcing their rights and courts with a duty to support them. Furthermore, the change has added strength to the important tension between subjects, citizens and consumers. Each of these has importance for the relationship between police and the public. Whilst the consumerist agenda has become increasingly dominant (Johnston, 2000), rights provide a new emphasis on citizenship, duties and responsibilities.

Democracy cannot exist without certain rights, such as freedom of speech, and rights cannot exist without democratic freedoms and an effective legal system, which provides access to justice (Feldman, 1993). However, this relationship is also, as is the experience in Canada and New Zealand, one with inherent tensions. Notably, the shift from political mechanisms to the unelected judiciary as the arbiters of the balance between conflicting rights can be seen as anti-democratic (Bellamy, 1999). It remains to be seen whether this shift will produce a greater resort to direct action. It is possible that the decisions in controversial cases will be seen as less legitimate because they have not been debated in the democratic arena. In turn, this has implications for policing as both the guarantor of those rights and, as it seeks to enforce the law and balance the rights of victims, offenders and community, the agency most directly exposed to their effect.

Human rights and international standards in policing

It is unsurprising, therefore, that, as human rights have become more and more central to the relationship of the citizen to the state, so policing has moved centre stage as an area for development of international protocols and guidance. Not only has the United Nations agreed the code of conduct for law enforcement officials, the basic principles on the use of force and firearms, standard minimum rules for treatment of prisoners, but also rules affecting children, juvenile justice and treatment of victims. Likewise the Council of Europe has developed its own 'Declaration on the Police' and has been seeking to develop standards on ethics in policing and covert policing.

In Figure 4.2 we have added a column to show the clear connection between the code and Declaration and the set of principles that we derived from our discussion of ethics in the last chapter. This is a very significant connection. One of the reasons why the code and Declaration have not had a major impact may well be the 'so what?' factor. By this we mean that it is not clear from either instrument how police officers should use them. They appear as declaratory statements, rather like the oath of office. It could be argued that they provide a context and boundaries on behaviour. However, we will argue below – in Chapter 10 in particular – that ethical policing relies on ethical decision-making at strategic, operational and tactical levels. It is in decisions, the decision-making process and in the daily exercise of operational discretion that the key to change lies. The code and Declaration do not provide a flexible, balanced model to help and support officers and leaders convert declaratory statements into real life ethical judgements. The Four Track approach to ethics that we have set out above potentially does.

These codes and conventions have had a limited impact until fairly recently. However, the growing international shift to human rights has been gradually encouraging their incorporation as the basis for national standards (Crawshaw, Devlin and Williamson, 1998). The UN has sought to accelerate this progress by requiring national reporting back every five years. In Europe it is much more the combination of pressure from the jurisprudence of the European Court of Human Rights and the rapidly growing need for European law enforcement agencies to work together to counteract organised crime that has driven ever-closer standards.

ECHR: articles and principles

In the United Kingdom the incorporation of the European Convention on Human Rights into British law has pushed that process rapidly. The British government has made a commitment to creating a 'true human

Figure 4.2 Policing standards in the UN code of conduct for law enforcement officials and the Council of Europe Declaration on the Police

Policing Standards	UN code of conduct for law enforcement officials	Council of Europe Declaration on the Police	Linkages with the 'Principles of policing'
To fulfil the duties imposed on them by the law	Article 1	Article 1 (also requires protection of citizens from violent acts)	Duty Responsibility Justice
To respect human dignity and uphold human rights	Article 2		Respect for personal autonomy and justice
To act with integrity, dignity and impartiality		Article 2	Honesty
To use force only when strictly necessary and and then proportionately	Article 3	Article 12 and Article 13 (requires training and guidance on the use of firearms)	Stewardship
To maintain confidentiality	Article 4	Article 15	Stewardship
Not to use torture or ill-treatment	Article 5 (and that 'obedience to orders' is no defence)	Article 3 (police officers are under an obligation to disobey orders in breach of this duty) and Article 4	Beneficence and Non-maleficence
To protect the health of those in their custody	Article 6	Article 14	Care
Not to commit any act of corruption	Article 7	Article 2 (and to oppose all acts of corruption	Honesty
To respect the law and the code of conduct and oppose violations of them	Article 8	Article 5	Justice
To be personally liable for their acts		Article 9 and Article 10 (which specifies a a clear chain of command)	Responsibility

rights culture' (Straw, 1999). In Northern Ireland, the Patten report placed human rights at the centre of its proposals for a re-formed Northern Ireland police force (Patten, 1999). In the rest of Britain, the government sought to prepare the public sector for the new culture. The police service recognised the challenge presented by the change and, in England and Wales, embarked on a major audit of policing policy and practice against ECHR (ACPO, 1999a), to which we will return at greater length in Chapter 11.

Before considering some of the implications of human rights in general and ECHR in particular for policing, it is important to understand the way in which the rights operate and the principles that underpin them. The latter need to be linked up with the debate we have already had in the last chapter about ethics and the principles of policing.

Firstly, although our concentration is primarily on ECHR, one of the common features of human rights jurisprudence is the ability of courts to draw down examples from other jurisdictions and read across. This comparative approach challenges the historical, precedent-based approaches of common law jurisdictions. It seems likely, as it has done in New Zealand and Canada, to create considerable uncertainty and change at the boundaries of state intervention in the lives of citizens.

There are five further key features of ECHR which are critical to its operation:

1 A Hierarchy of rights
At the highest level are the 'absolute rights' of life, freedom from torture and slavery. These always apply and states cannot derogate from them, unlike the next tier of rights, the 'derogable' rights, where there is scope for variation in 'emergencies'. The British government has used the latter provision to extend detention times in terrorist cases. The final tier of rights is the 'qualified rights' of private and family life, thought, expression and assembly and property. For these the convention provides the state with an ability to intervene provided certain principles and conditions apply. We will deal with these below.

2 Linked rights
The rights cannot be seen in isolation. A fair trial may be impeded by a breach of privacy rights; the right to freedom from detention may be affected by the discriminatory way in which discretion is exercised.

3 Living rights
The case law of the Convention interprets it as a 'living instrument', responsive to changing values in society. The Court has also stressed that the 'Convention is intended to guarantee ... rights that are practical and effective' (*Artico v Italy*, 1980). It is also the case that the Council of Europe

is constantly adding to the Convention. For example, new freestanding rights of equal treatment and non-discrimination are in draft.

4 *Conflicting and overlapping rights*

As well as the rights being linked, they are also conflicting and overlapping. Sometimes it may seem simple to resolve the conflict by reference to the hierarchy – placing the right to life before the private and family life. However, the conflicts are rarely so simple and straight-forward. They are particularly difficult to resolve when they involve the newer social and cultural rights and will frequently involve balancing individual, group and wider community interests. This balancing act is complicated by one of the frequently quoted difficulties with the ECHR approach. This is that the right of individual petition means that the starting point is the individual asserting their position rather than a fuller democratic debate (Bellamy, 1999). This means that the individual or group's challenge drives the debate, rather than the democratic process.

5 *Balancing the rights of victims and suspects*

For policing, the most complex aspect of the conflict between the rights is the growing debate about the rights of victims and the balance with suspect rights. The European Court has increasingly recognised the importance of the victim's position, according rights to effective investigation (*Aksoy v Turkey, 1997*), protection from intimidation in court (*Doorson v Netherlands*, 1996) and protection from risk (*Osman v UK*, 1999).

From a police officer's perspective it is easy to feel that the complex, conflictual and interdependent structure of the Convention provides an unwieldy tool for law enforcement. However, lying behind the detail of the Articles and incorporating legislation are a set of principles that can be linked with the ethical principles we set out above. These principles are, for police officers, the real building blocks of a human rights approach to policing.

The four key principles are as follows:

1 *Legality*

We have already seen that the UN Code and European Declaration lay great stress on police officers complying with their obligations under the law and upholding the rule of law. ECHR adds some important clarification to the concept of 'legality'. For the law that police are obliged to comply with and uphold must be clear and transparent. Legality requires law that is accessible and available to the citizen. Furthermore, it also requires law that has been properly created – primary or secondary legislation – rather than secret or undisclosed administrative guidelines. A good example of this was the European Court's adverse reaction to the

Home Office Circular that used to provide the authorising process for telephone interception in the UK prior to the case of *Malone v UK* (1984). The guidelines were not accessible to the citizen. Legality, therefore, emphasises openness and due process. It requires police officers to intervene only where they have powers that are clearly articulated, 'in accordance with the law' (ECHR, Articles 8, 9, 10 and 11). In this sense, 'legality' applies a clear restriction on discretion and a substantial change from the common law position where a police officer could interpret the boundaries of practice as much by relying on the spirit of the law as its detailed substance.

2 *Proportionality*
This second principle, on the other hand, firmly requires the active exercise of discretion. Proportionality introduces a form of utilitarian calculus into human rights. As Starmer comments, the principle of proportionality is about the 'need to find a fair balance between the protection of individual rights and the interests of the community at large' (Starmer, 1999: 169). It requires a police officer to balance the means proposed against the outcome intended, or in the words of the judgement in *Handyside v. UK* (1976) to ensure that any action is 'proportionate to the legitimate aim pursued'. For example, in *Steel and others v UK* (1999) the Court found that the arrest and detention of non-violent protesters against the arms trade outside a conference had been 'disproportionate to the aim of preventing disorder and protecting the rights of others'. Starmer (1999) suggests that it is possible to break proportionality down into five elements. We would suggest that it is also possible to draw parallels between the elements of proportionality and the principles we have set out in Chapter 3.

All of these elements are relevant in considering whether a decision is 'proportionate'. The five elements draw on a balance of means tests – procedural fairness and safeguards – and ends tests – justifying reasons and alternative courses – to determine whether an outcome is compliant. The final judgement is arrived at by weighing these issues against the interests of the affected parties: typically the individual whose rights are affected, potential victims (such as those attending the conference picketed by demonstrators in *Steel and others v UK*) and the wider community. This balancing of interests, very much akin to Singer's utilitarianism of interests, is particularly well matched to the realities of a police mission, which is ambiguous and inherently conflicting. Cohen, who focused on the 'ends-means' dilemmas in policing argued that the process of reasoning or 'justification' involved in ranking 'priorities' 'shed much light on the moral consequences of policing' (Cohen, 1991: 95)

Figure 4.3 The five elements of proportionality (based on Starmer, 1999)

5 elements of proportionality	Comparison with the principles of policing
Whether relevant or sufficient reasons have been advanced	Honesty (good faith and an acceptable assessment of the facts: *Buckley v. UK*), Care, beneficence and non-maleficence
Whether a less restrictive alternative was available	Stewardship (careful use of powers)
Whether there was procedural fairness in decision-making	Justice
Whether safeguards against abuse exist or external authority for exercise of	Responsibility (answerability to a judge power)
Whether the restriction destroys the 'very essence' of a right	Justice and respect for personal autonomy

3 *Necessity*

Proportionality links closely with the third principle of the Convention, 'necessity'. This principle has two distinct threads: 'absolute necessity', which is the test the Convention demands when lethal force is used by the state (Article 2, ECHR); 'necessary in a democratic society', or more precisely, 'pressing social need', which is the added layer of justification that the Court has required of the state when interfering with conditional rights. The first thread of necessity is a more demanding requirement than the 'reasonableness' test that British law has applied to police powers such as the use of force. Even more than proportionality it requires that alternatives have been considered and either tried and failed or have been rationally discarded. In firearms situations it has been extended to include a need for planning that minimises the risk of harm (*Andronicou and Constantinou v. Cyprus*, 1997). The second thread emphasises the democratic context of the Convention and the clear limits on state intervention. Although the state may have a legitimate reason for intervention, such as the prevention of crime, it may still not be able to justify action where it cannot show a 'pressing social need'. The latter requires the state and, therefore the police, to be pluralist, tolerant and broadminded (*Handyside v UK*, 1979–80). Necessity, like legality, provides a substantial discipline on discretion. It also provides a link between policing and the values of democracy.

4 *Accountability*

The fourth and final principle is accountability. Most obviously, this principle is articulated in the requirement in Article 13 for the citizen to have an effective remedy for breaches of rights. In the context of policing this principle is particularly important. It suggests a need for an independent system of dealing with serious complaints (*Govell v UK*, 1998), for independent investigation of the circumstances leading to deaths caused by the police (such as deaths in custody) (*Aksoy v Turkey*, 1997) and the independent oversight of key powers such as intrusive surveillance (*Malone v UK*, 1984).

In summary, we can see that the European Convention provides a complex framework of overlapping rights, which are underpinned by a set of principles. There are several ways to look at these four human rights principles. Firstly, we can represent them as a sequential decision-making process (see Figure 4.4). In this model, the principles stand on their own as a filter through which decision criteria can pass. This is helpful and we will seek to develop this approach in considering ethical decision-making in Chapter 10.

A second way of using the principles is as a template against which to lay policy and practice in policing. It is this approach that we will discuss in Chapter 11, where we consider the use of the human rights principles as the basis of an ethical audit tool. This, we will suggest, is a powerful methodology, which is capable of challenging existing practice.

Thirdly, we can link them with the 'four tracks' of ethics and the principles of policing, which we set out in the previous chapter, in order to locate human rights within a wider moral framework. This is relatively straightforward with the first and last of the four human rights principles – legality and accountability – which fit inside 'justice' and 'responsibility'. Proportionality and necessity, however, provide a significant additional dimension. As we have suggested above, they can be seen as adding the balancing mechanism, which might allow us to weigh up the different interests, or in the 'four tracks' model, the different arguments. For we have suggested that the most helpful way to see the principles of policing is as a *prima facie* ethical framework. Proportionality and necessity provide a potential means of judging the extent to which each principle should inform our 'everyday' judgements in a given set of circumstances.

Thus, to return to the examples in Chapter 3, the police officers in Case Study 1 were confronted with difficult choices between respect for the suspect's rights and saving the life of the girl. On the one hand respect for life is an absolute right and the police have a positive duty to protect life, on the other hand they have a duty not to harm or torture the suspect. Proportionality would demand that they consider carefully the sufficiency and logic of their arguments, the possible less harmful alternatives, the fairness, the safeguards and whether 'stronger tactics' might destroy the very essence of the rights of the suspect. Necessity would require the justification of a very pressing social need and consideration of the wider impact of police officers harming those in their custody. The two tests allow the balancing of the duties and interests of each party. In a similar way, the four tracks and the principles provide a means of identifying and informing the debate about what those duties and interests might be. This approach we will seek to develop in the next four chapters, looking at four dimensions of police ethics: individual; organisational; performance and best value; societal.

Conclusion: rights and their impact on policing

By looking at human rights in these three ways – decision-making, audit and a mechanism for ethical calculus – we can begin to see how the principles that underpin them have the potential to alter dramatically the way policing is carried out and the way in which practitioners and leaders think about their role. The implications for policing are profound, as Patten (1999) recognised. Indeed, he went so far as to completely redefine policing as 'protecting of human rights' (p.18). This, as we have seen, does not help us provide clarity in the policing role because the very nature of human rights, like the very nature of policing, is ambiguous and conflictual.

It is, however, possible to identify some key impacts on policing of placing human rights in the centre of democracy in the way that the UK and a number of other western nations have done in the late twentieth and early twenty-first century. The list is daunting, but certainly includes the following:

- *Use of police powers* – the requirements for clear justification of necessity and proportionality in the use of basic powers such as arrest, search, detention, interrogation, seizure of property, covert policing, intrusive surveillance, and stop and search.
- *Use of force* – the 'absolute necessity' threshold as justification for use of force, potentially degrading treatment such strip searches and any life-threatening actions.
- *Decision making* – must be 'reasonable' and compatible with convention rights.
- *Duty of care* – the positive duties to uphold convention rights and protect life and other rights such as private and family life and freedom of speech.
- *The rules of natural justice* – openness, transparency, fairness in investigations and hearings, decision-making and 'audit trails' for decisions.

Figure 4.4 Flowchart showing the ECHR principles in decision-making sequence

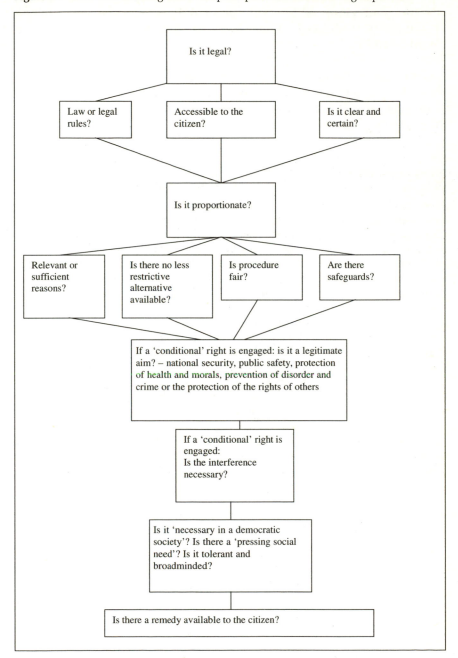

- *Accountability* – personal and organisational responsibility for human rights compliance and the emphasis on independent oversight provide significant additional dimensions to the framework of police accountability.

It is our intention to return to this list in future chapters. We shall try to show how practitioners and managers can comply with the rigorous criteria outlined above and perform their duty ethically and with respect for human rights.

Further reading

There is a growing number of texts on human rights law in general and the European Convention in particular. Keir Starmer's guide to the European Convention and its practical application is readable and accessible (Starmer, *European Human Rights Law: the Human Rights Act 1998 and the European Convention on Human Rights*, 1999). Gearty and Tomkins collection of essays provide a wide-ranging treatment of the theory and practice of human rights (Gearty and Tomkins, *Understanding Human Rights*, 1996). The United Nations have produced a hand-book *Teaching Human Rights to Police Officers* (UN, 2000), which provides a comprehensive list of the existing international human rights instruments which affect policing and criminal justice. The handbook and a range of other human rights documentation is available through the UN website at www.itu.int/unions. The European Convention and its case law is readily accessible through the Council of Europe website at www.echr.coe.int. Kamenka and Erh-Soon-Tay (*Human Rights*, 1978) provide a series of articles on the development of human rights, while Feldman (*Civil Liberties and Human Rights in England and Wales*, 1993) places international rights in British legal context. Bellamy (*Liberalism and Pluralism: towards a politics of compromise*, 1999) in his chapter on 'Trimming democracy' sets out the major critiques of human rights as the basis for resolving disputes in democratic societies.

PART 2

In this second part of the book we develop the discussion in Part 1 by examining four areas of policing ethics:

- Personal ethics
- Best value and performance ethics
- Operational ethics
- Organisational ethics

Chapter 5

Personal ethics

Introduction

In this chapter we are interested in the 'personal ethics' of policing. Our starting point for this discussion is the much-debated question of whether police officers are 'professionals' and, if they are in some way, what the implications of this are for the ethics of policing. As we shall see, there are no simple answers to that question and what answers there are touch upon our second area of concern – the culture of policing. This has been a major area in the literature on policing, often with a concern about the rather unhelpful epithet 'canteen culture'. It remains, however, an important issue, not least because for some authors (Reiner, 1985 and Holdaway, 1996) the culture of policing (usually perceived as a 'bad thing') is a more important determinant of the way policing is carried out than the professional will of individual officers.

The culture of policing has been seen as particularly important in the way that our third area, discretion, is exercised. Discretion – or the scope for choice – is highly significant in policing and police discretion is highly significant for the whole criminal justice system (Bayley, 1994). Furthermore, the active, evidenced deployment of discretion is central to the operation of human rights in policing (Starmer, 1999).

In exercising discretion police officers must be seen to be acting fairly and impartially (HMIC, 1999a), in short, with integrity. The last area we shall deal with is, therefore, the relationship between police officers in their occupational role and police officers as private citizens. We shall seek to link this with the discussion about corruption in the next chapter.

The professional vocation of policing?

The development of the 'new police' in nineteenth-century Britain and the late nineteenth-century US and Canada brought with it a shift from an 'amateur' system of policing to a 'professional' force of constables (Storch, 1999, Reiner, 1985). However, it took a number of years for police work to develop a distinctive identity. It was not until the third quarter of the nineteenth century that a specific ideology of public service, a distinct professional identity and a recognisable body of policing skills emerged. Reiner (1985) has argued that securing support for this new 'professional police' rested on seven main foundations:

- The creation of a bureaucratic organisation, with clear rules and command structure.
- The adherence to the rule of law.
- A strategy of minimal force.
- Non-partisanship.
- A clear commitment to a 'service' role.
- An emphasis on preventive policing.
- Effectiveness in controlling crime and maintaining order.

Although these foundations did not make policing a 'profession', they do show how policing was becoming an increasingly specialised discipline. In the twentieth century police officers have had a constant aspiration to go beyond that and to be regarded as professionals in their own right. In the 1930s Vollmeyer and Wilson had sought to provide a vision of a police force which was composed of independent professionals working to high ethical standards and deploying scientific methods, in contrast to a working-class occupation whose members were often in compromising relationships with local politicians (Kleinig, 1996a). More recently, in internal debates about the role of the Association of Chief Police Officers in England and Wales, the concept of a professional institute of policing and an ethical code to support that professionalism have been key themes (Savage and Charman, 1995).

The nature of the occupation of policing and its professional status are important, not only for the signals that they give the public that policing serves, but also for the identity and ethos of policing. On a strict taxonomic approach – either trait or functional – policing falls short of all the elements necessary to qualify for full professional status (Friedson, 1983). If we take the six areas identified by Kleinig (1996a) we can set policing against them as follows:

Provision of a public service
Whilst many would argue that policing is and should be a public service,

the coercive core of policing means that policing is a not a 'simple' public service. Indeed, some have argued that the coercive core is more about the exercise of state power than the provision of 'service' to the citizen (Waddington, 1999).

Educational qualifications
Entry to the 'profession' in the UK is by assessment centre and the Police Initial Recruitment test. This provides a significant difference between the police and many other semi-professions and a clear difference between the police and other emergency services, such as the fire brigade. However, PIR is not a graduate qualification and whilst there are qualifying examinations for promotion, there is only a limited culture of lifelong learning and reaccreditation. However, this situation is changing with the linking of degree courses to the probationary training, the introduction of a National Training Organisation and occupational competencies and moves to establish mandatory requalification at senior and middle management (Home Office, 1999b). In many other countries, the management ranks of the service are filled from direct entrants, who are usually graduates. This approach emphasises a division between a 'professional' group of managers and a 'blue collar' majority of police officers.

Code of ethics
In the USA the IACP code of ethics has provided a basis for unifying policing into a single community of practitioners (Kleinig, 1996a). In the UK attempts to introduce a code encountered stiff opposition from rank and file concerned about the overlap between the code and new discipline regulations (Lawton, 1998).

Self-regulation
The very nature of policing and the powers police officers wield mean that no police force is or, under human rights legislation, can be self regulating. However, as increasing pressure for public accountability has come upon even the established professions, so self-regulation has come under increasing fire.

Autonomy and discretion
Whilst police officers have considerable discretion within the law, the 'para-military' structures of the organisation, the legal framework of accountability and the police framework substantially restrict its exercise (Mastrofski, 1998).

Expert knowledge
As Turner (1987) has shown, knowledge is crucial to a profession and central to the struggle by professionals to resist 'routinisation' of their

work and its fragmentation to groups of para-professionals. In the case of the police the competition from private providers has grown substantially (Johnston, 2000). Secondly, within the organisation, key skills such as analysis and intelligence gathering have been 'in-sourced' to non-attested 'civilian' specialists. Thirdly, the main skills of policing have been described as 'craft skills', not based on theory, but on the 'dirty work' of managing the boundaries of respectability (Waddington, 1999). Furthermore, much of that craft remains unvalidated (Bayley and Bittner, 1994). At the same time the effectiveness of police investigative skills have come under critical examination from the Lawrence report (Macpherson, 1999) and reviews of unsolved murders (HMIC, 2000). Yet, on the other hand, there has been the codification of major crime investigative skills into 'expert' systems, a greater emphasis on those skills and those of operational command by the creation of National Crime and Operational Faculties at the National Police Staff College and some serious attempts to provide a theoretical underpinning for serious crime investigation (ACPO, 1999b).

The picture this analysis presents is equivocal. The attempts to develop ethical codes, to increase the education of entrants and managers and the work to develop and codify expert knowledge suggest a process of 'professionalisation' in the UK that is incomplete and aspirational. To this picture could be added the partial reform of working conditions which followed the Sheehy report (Sheehy, 1994) that saw many overtime and allowance payments disappear in favour of a more 'professional' structure.

This partial professionalisation raises the question of whether in the context of ethical policing, police officers and managers should be striving more vigorously to achieve full professional status. From the 'virtue' perspective, the professional ideal of a commitment to public service and ethical standards has much to commend it. Equally, in the functionalist approach to professions the benefits accruing to professionals are viewed as part of a contract with society for investing their skills and knowledge in the public interest. This seems to accord well with the contractual notions of policing which we have set out in earlier chapters.

There are, however, some serious challenges to the idea that professions are beneficent and these are directly relevant to the police. Firstly, these come from authors who see the professions as part of a strategy of control and 'social closure' or from a New Right perspective creating a monopoly in the marketplace, from which professionals seek to secure benefits for themselves (Parry, Rustin and Satyamurti, 1979 and Anderson, Lait and Marsland, 1981). The exclusive state powers accorded to the police or the 'police monopoly' has been cited by some as evidence of this, providing police with powers to be used against the working class from one perspective and an ability to exclude effective competitors from the other (Hoddinott, 1994). In these two views the police officer as professional is either an oppressive representative of the ruling class or a member of an inefficient cartel – neither of which would sit easily with 'ethical policing'.

A second and connected feminist critique has identified the professions as being an extension of the patriarchal system and sought to document the ways in which predominantly male professionals reinforce patriarchal values through their relationships with clients and subordinate semi-professions (Dale and Foster, 1986 and Garmarnikow, 1978). This critique can be extended in western society to seeing the professions as an ex-tension of the predominant white culture. There is an extensive literature that identifies how on the one hand the police have failed to deal with issues like domestic violence and racist attacks effectively (Edwards, 1989, Bowling, 1999), whilst on the other many women and ethnic minority police officers have been marginalized and subjected to harassment (Brown, 1997). We shall return to the issue of discrimination in chapter 8.

The third challenge to the police professional is the rise of mana-gerialism. Waddington has argued that management strategies, such as policing by objectives and the development of the performance culture, contradict the drive for professional status by substituting a new command structure in the form of the policy cycle and performance indicators (Waddington, 1999). The accelerating impetus of this regime, the desire to compare units at a very local level and the 'naming and shaming' culture underpinning them question the status of the independent professional practitioner.

Whilst these three perspectives on the police officer as professional raise serious questions, each provides only a description of one aspect of the profession of policing, not a prescription for what policing should be. Critiques based on social closure or monopoly fail to take account of the burgeoning growth of private provision and new forms of public patrolling (Johnston, 2000). The feminist and race critiques are more powerful, but are essentially arguments for a more inclusive and non-discriminatory policing. Managerialism, as we will see in Chapter 6, has some serious shortcomings in the complex and ambiguous context of police performance.

In short, none of these perspectives seem to offer a convincing alternative to greater professionalism, although they do highlight the fact that professionalisation is not a panacea. However, given that the frenzy of rule-making which follows each turn of the vicious circle we set out in Chapter 1 does not seem to have produced a virtuous circle yet, the case for a more professional self-imposed discipline through an ethical code and ethical approaches to decision-making seems stronger. Wiles has phrased this as 'accountability by a system of professional ethics supported by contractual obligations' (Wiles, 1993: 56). His arguments and those of the advocates of 'community policing' (Rosenbaum 1994 and Skogan and Hartnett, 1997) present a vision of a police professional whose 'Discretionary powers are no longer ignored or disavowed, but are celebrated as essential to the practice of a profession, just as a physician is expected to exercise discretion in diagnosing and treating patients' (Mastrofski, 1998).

This police 'clinician' solving problems by diagnosis, acting with greater autonomy and working within a framework of values fits well within the 'enabling' approach we set out in Chapter 2. The diagram below (Figure 5.1) seeks to compare this sort of professional with a general practitioner, who diagnoses problems and is able to call on specialist interventions, both acute and long term, to tackle problems. The shift to such an approach is not an easy one, given the political environment of instantaneous success and shaming for failure and the culture of the police organisation. But the shift is important in order to develop a 'new professionalism' of highly skilled, evidence-based practice and operational autonomy. This in turn needs to be balanced by personal accountability and greater openness and transparency in decision-making and performance outcome. This 'new professionalism' we would contrast with the 'old professionalism' of incident-driven response and paramilitarism, which is strongly rooted in the culture of the organisation. It is this aspect of policing to which we turn next.

The cultures of policing

Culture has been an increasingly important theme of both organisational theory and studies of policing since the 1960s. Schein (1984: 3) neatly described culture as 'the pattern of basic assumptions that a group has developed to cope with its problems of external adaptation and internal integration' and Robbins (1990) put it even more succinctly as 'the way things are done round here'. Culture is, therefore, both extremely important in understanding an organisation and very complex. It is a key determinant of how work – in this case police work – is interpreted and performed. It is through the processes of recruitment, induction, sociali- sation and training that it affects individual members of the organisation (Schein, 1984).

Reiner's influential analysis of the police occupational culture (Reiner, 1985) drew on earlier work by Skolnick (1975), Muir (1977) and Manning (1977) to provide a description of what he called the 'core characteristics of cop culture'. These were:

- A sense of mission, which is primarily seen as 'action' led.
- Cynicism/pessimism about the world and those they deal with.
- Suspicion, which is partly a product of the need to categorise and discriminate those they confront, but is also encouraged by the training and socialisation process.
- Isolation and solidarity: a combination of social isolation and solidarity and loyalty to colleagues in the face of danger or external threat.
- Conservatism, which was seen as partly a product of the role – upholding the status quo – and partly related to the stability of the organisation and its enforced neutrality.
- Machismo, which was evidenced by the hard drinking and aggressive sexuality of many male officers.
- Racial prejudice, some of which Reiner links to the dominant attitude of the majority towards minorities, some to the transactional relationships between police officers and the minorities they police against.
- Pragmatism.

Many of these aspects of police culture appear to conflict with the formal values of the police mission. Indeed, the analysis paints an almost universally negative picture. This was counterbalanced by Reiner's sug-

Figure 5.1 The police 'clinician'

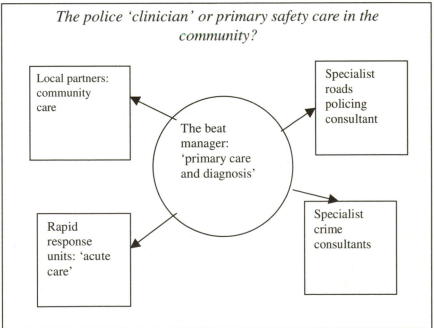

gestions that there were different cultural types ranging from the 'bobby' and 'new centurion' to the 'uniform carrier' and 'professional', which he related to the different departmental subcultures within the organisation.

Small and Watson (1999) took a slightly different approach, which has considerable significance for ethical policing. Instead of concentrating, as Reiner appears to do, on the 'manifest' level of the rituals, stories and behaviours of the street and canteen, they have sought to interpret the police value system at the 'core level'. This must treated with some caution, because their sample was small and, as Schein (1984) has argued, interpreting the core level is difficult. However, their conclusions are interesting in that they outline a value system where Reiner's largely negative qualities are balanced by positives. Small and Watson (1999) have also suggested a hierarchy of values:

Figure 5.2 Hierarchical value system of the Western Australia Police Service*

*From Small and Watson (1999)

Taking each of these values in turn:

Risk avoidance
This was seen as the dominant value of policing and related both to the reduction of danger and the avoidance of the risks associated with misconduct. Moreover, Small and Watson suggested that police officers' views of the ethics of misconduct were directly related to their views of its risk. Low risk misconduct being regarded as unnecessary rather than unethical.

Comradeship
This was closely related to risk avoidance and could be a risk-reducing

mechanism in considering misconduct. Although 'proper' conduct that achieved positive policing outcomes was always preferred, the absence of 'honesty' and 'integrity' from the value system meant 'there were no other competing values to prevent misconduct' (Small and Watson, 1999: 229). Kleinig also highlighted the link between 'loyalty' and misconduct (Kleinig, 1996a).

Outcome
Police officers were interested in positive policing outcomes without regard to the legality or objective ethics of the conduct in question. In relation to our earlier discussion of ethics, this suggests, as Cohen has argued (Cohen, 1991) a strong leaning towards the ethics of utility and a concern with ends rather than the ethics of duty and the importance of means. A similar argument was made by Zander (1994) in his discussion of 'noble cause corruption' – a typology reinterpreted by Small and Watson as 'outcome misconduct'.

Professionalism
This was a relatively low tier value, which had a limited impact on comradeship and outcome and competed with masculinity ('male' be-haviour and a preference for the physical option to resolve disputes).

Opportunism
A low tier value, which was defined as a tendency to take advantage of the opportunities that policing offered the individual officer. It ranged from the acceptance of low-level gifts up to more serious and improper graft.

Community standing
Although universally valued, this 'played a minor normative role in policing' (Small and Watson, 1999: 232).

The way in which the elements of Small and Watson's hierarchy are balanced and interrelated is crucial. What their analysis starts to indicate is that crude attempts to tinker with one element of the value system by rule-tightening or cultural change may not have the impact desired. On the contrary, we can begin to perceive a more sophisticated approach which seeks to support the positive values by enhancing officer safety, increasing the risks of misconduct, emphasising the rewards associated with pro-fessionalism, changing the gender balance in the organisation, increasing the transparency of the organisation to community inspection and, above all, seeking to develop the virtues of honesty and the ethics of integrity. Furthermore, the four track approach to ethics would seem to be par-ticularly well adapted to provide a more balanced ethical approach than the utility dominated approach Small and Watson identified.

The debate on determining the strategies for changing the police organisation has been heavily influenced by views on the nature of police culture. In an important study that has challenged many previous approaches, Chan (1997) has argued that most studies of police culture, Reiner included, tend to be underpinned by three assumptions: that police culture and the nature of police work are interrelated; that the culture is fairly stable over time and fairly uniform; that the culture has a negative impact on policing, in particular in police relationships with minority communities. As we have seen, Small and Watson challenge the wholly negative conception of police culture. Chan has further challenged the conception of police culture as immutable, monolithic and isolated from external influence. She has argued 'police practice is to be understood in terms of the interaction between specific structural conditions of police work (the field) and the cultural knowledge accumulated by police officers which integrates past experiences (habitus)' (Chan, 1997: 225). The linkage between the two means that attempts to break out of the vicious cycle we have described must involve both changes to the internal and external environment – such as legal and accountability reforms – as well as a commitment to effective training and education. One is unlikely to be successful without the support and congruity of the other.

Chan's arguments are doubly significant in the light of the shift to a new human rights culture and accountability in policing in a number of Western nations, including the UK. As we have started to suggest in Chapter 4, this provides precisely the shift in the structural conditions of policing which Chan concludes by advocating as a necessary precondition of change. In particular, the thrust towards open and justified decision-making and greater personal and organisational accountability lead to a fundamental change in the cultural assumptions of secret, unaccountable pragmatism. However, following Chan's logic, changing the structural conditions alone will not produce a long-term change in the culture. That will only happen if the structural change is accompanied by an equally significant shift towards ethical values underpinning the leadership, recruitment, education, training and decision-making processes of the police.

Discretion

It is to decision-making, particularly discretion, that we now turn. For discretion is a critical part of policing. It is also a controversial aspect. In America, the 'discovery' of the true extent of police discretion provoked a heated debate about whether police officers were usurping quasi-judicial functions (Davis, 1975). Although there have been attempts in the US to limit discretion by legal provisions requiring strict enforcement, such provisions are in Waddington's view doomed to failure:

> Because of the uncertainties that inevitably accompany rules it is virtually unimaginable that police action could be anything other than discretionary … the police do not enforce the law because they cannot. Laws must be interpreted and that interpretation is always context specific. Therefore, discretion is unavoidable …
>
> (Waddington, 1999: 38–9)

If discretion is inevitable, then it is important to understand its meaning, impact and, in the context of ethical policing and human rights, to begin to see how it might be made to operate fairly and effectively. Turning first to the meaning of discretion, one of the more helpful metaphors to understand it was set out by Dworkin (1977). He described discretion as the 'hole in the doughnut'. The hole cannot exist without the ring of the doughnut, which symbolises the standards both societal and organisational within which discretion operates. In the case of the police, the ring represents the mission of the police, which we described in Chapter 2. As we have seen and as the quotation from Waddington suggests, the police mission is not precise and, therefore, discretion in policing requires the exercise of judgement.

It is possible to break that judgement down into types of discretion. Kleinig, in describing 'ethical issues in police decision-making' (Kleinig, 1996b), provided four types:

- Scope decisions
- Interpretative decisions
- Decisions about priority
- Tactical decisions

It might be helpful to illustrate these four dimensions by four case studies. In Case Study 1 the point at issue is whether the matter falls within the police role or whether it can be ignored or handed on to another agency. Scope discretion has been highly controversial in areas like the policing of domestic violence, where many police officers, using the typology 'domestic dispute', sought to move it out of the scope of policing and into the civil arena of inter-familial disputes (Edwards, 1989).

In interpretative discretion the issue is not whether the police should be dealing with the incident, but rather how to resolve it – formally by using legal powers or informally through negotiation. Domestic violence has also been significantly affected by 'interpretative' discretion. Even where police officers were prepared to accept responsibility for the case, the resolution was too often by negotiation rather than arrest for assault.

Case Studies 3 and 4 make the important point that discretion is not just

Case study 1: Scope discretion
Police officers are called to a house where the tenant is complaining that his landlord is trying to evict him and has made 'veiled threats'. Police officers have to decide whether this is a police matter, a 'civil dispute' or the responsibility of another agency.

Case study 2: Interpretative discretion
The same officers attend the same premises for a second time. This time the landlord is present and both he and the tenant are agitated. The tenant demands that the police arrest the landlord for 'breaking in without permission'; the landlord states he has a perfect right to enter his own premises and refuses to leave. The officers have to decide whether they are dealing with criminal offences and if so whether enforcement or negotiation is the best – most proper and most effective – option.

Case study 3: Discretion about priority
A police inspector responsible for a rural area attends a local consultation meeting. Residents demand that the police do more to deal with local quality of life issues – local youths hanging around the shops, litter, dog fouling, noisy motorbikes. None of these issues have been prioritised by the crime audit compiled for the whole area, nor do they feature in the national priorities set by central government. The police force espouses 'community policing', with a strong emphasis on meeting public priorities. The inspector has to decide whether to concentrate on existing priorities and explain this to the residents or consider diverting resources to meet their demands at the expense of other priorities.

Case study 4: Tactical discretion
An extreme political grouping applies to march through the main town of the police area. Their presence seems likely to provoke violent counterdemonstrations and fear in the community. The police commander has to decide whether to permit the march or seek to ban it. In doing so he/she must balance the rights of the marchers and the local community and set the right tactics to achieve that balance.

a street issue. As Bossard (1981) has pointed out, managers have their own type of dilemmas. In these case studies, the dilemmas are over the balancing of resources against priorities and the balancing of rights and the decisions over exercising intrusive powers in a potential public disorder. The difference between the street and management dilemmas lies in the complexity and the number of actors and the decision-making environment and time frame. Street decisions tend to involve relatively fewer choices, a smaller number of actors, but a short time frame and potentially an environment of danger. For managers the choices are many, the actors many and multi-layered, but the time frame and environment may be less problematic.

The common theme that runs through all four case studies is that the boundaries of the 'doughnut ring' are not clear. Indeed, as societal priorities have changed so the boundaries of expected police intervention have changed. Domestic violence is a prime example of this, where a combination of changing attitudes and research indicating the effectiveness of arrest as an intervention (Sherman and Berk, 1984) has driven greater police proactivity and public expectations. A second example would be the shift to human rights based jurisprudence. As we have seen, this brings a transformation from implicit pragmatism (well summed up by the police slang 'the Ways and Means Act') to explicit legality and decision-making principles.

If the 'doughnut ring' is unclear and evolving, what is the impact of the exercise of police discretion? It is quickly apparent that any verdict depends heavily on the framework of analysis applied to it. For there are a wide variety of perspectives:

- Davis' influential studies of discretion (Davis, 1975) saw discretion through the eyes of a student of the law and constitution and concluded that it could be described in terms of individuals misappropriating judicial power. His work was devoted to structuring and confining discretion through rule-tightening and accountability mechanisms. For Davis, the police officer must not be allowed too much 'free will', he/she is an agent of the law, not its interpreter.

- In contrast to Davis a second group of authors have seen discretion as substantially beneficial, either 'a necessary element in tempering law with humanity' (Pollock, 1998: 157), a question of balancing law for the individual with law for the group (Cohen, 1991) or as the 'selective exclusion' of people from the criminal justice system (Bayley, 1994). This group of authors tend to use the idea of the social contract as a starting point (Reiman, 1996). Implicit in their model is an active civil society prepared to challenge police when their discretion breaches the contract. As long as police stay within the contract, they have the free will to make choices. Indeed, they are trusted to act ethically and use their judgement.

- A third approach is to describe it as a process of discrimination

(Kappeler, Sluder and Alpert, 1984). This approach has tended to focus on interpreting the results of discretion, such as the disproportionate use of the stop and search powers against minority ethnic communities (Fitzgerald, 1999). This approach moves beyond the legalistic one taken by Davis and sees the exercise of discretion as something undertaken by an individual officer constrained by 'operational ideologies' or 'cultures' (Lacey, 1992). As we suggested in the discussion of culture above, in this model, the officer has little free will. His/her actions are largely determined by the culture. Suggested solutions to the 'problem' of discretion include a combination of rule-tightening, intrusive accountability and training-led change.

- The most positive view of all was taken by Davis (1996), who saw discretion as the essence of informed professionalism in policing. He argued strongly against those who would bind the police 'professional' with more and more detailed rules, 'intrusive supervision' (HMIC, 1999a) and 'command and control' hierarchies. Instead, like our 'police clinician', he advocated more freedom for professional judgement, within recognised and clearly articulated professional standards. Such standards are not without their problems, but they are not impossible to develop. Research has gradually begun to suggest the outlines of effective, evidence-based practice (Home Office, 1998a). Davis suggested that these standards could be further developed through a combination of training, particularly in ethics, constant debriefing and reflection on practice and sharing of good practice.

Looking at the four approaches together and putting them into the context of twenty-first century policing and, above all, human rights, it is the professional clinician model of discretion that appears to offer the best future. Human rights policing demands that police officers become adept at balancing competing rights, demonstrating clear and justified decision-making and keeping this under constant review. A rigid, rule-bound bureaucracy would simply be unable to create and sustain an operating culture flexible enough to cope with this challenge. Increased professional autonomy and a more reflective practitioner are essential for the development of public policing.

Citizens in uniform

The greater the professional autonomy that police officers are accorded, the more intense will be the focus on their integrity. Two important aspects of this, which are potentially in conflict, are the perceived independence from partiality of the individual officer and the organisation on the one hand and the rights of the police officer as an individual citizen on the other. We have already stressed the significance of honesty, personal responsibility and stewardship in Chapter 3. But it is also important to recognise that police officers have both responsibilities and rights – to be protected, to private and family life and to freedom of expression and assembly to name but three – and the balance between them and the rights of other citizens provides an additional complexity to the dilemmas of police managers. There are a number of dimensions to this issue: the membership of groups and associations; involvement in politics; the acceptance of gifts, gratuities and sponsorship.

In the UK an area of major controversy in respect of the first issue has been the question of police officers' membership of Freemasonry. Highlighted in the corruption scandals of the 1960s, associated with (but never proven to have been a key factor in) the allegations of misconduct in the West Midlands Regional Crime Squads and claimed as a link between the suspects identified by the North Wales inquiry into institutional abuse, freemasonry in the police has had a bad press. The reasons for this go deeper than the often speculative associations made by some authors (Knight, 1983). At the heart of much public concern is the perception of partiality and secrecy.

At issue for senior managers, as the first case study suggests (Figure 5.5), is whether that perception is sufficiently serious to intervene. The Home Affairs Select Committee (1998) argued that it was and agreed with Knight's call for a register of membership for police officers. Such an approach is entirely consistent with the Nolan Committee (1995). The latter called for public servants to avoid real or apparent conflicts of interest. This would also extend to cover the very obvious conflict set out in the second case study, where the officer's freedom of expression seems inconsistent with his impartial performance of duty and the officer who wants to drive a taxi in Case Study 3. The European Court has accepted that police officers are fundamentally different from the citizen and cannot expect the same rights in employment or to freedom of expression.[1] The police officer, like the civil servant[2] has a relationship with the state and state power that means that his or her own rights must be more restricted when performing their duty than those of the ordinary citizen. This restriction might not deny them the right to be a Freemason, but it might allow the state to require them to register their interest.

The membership of groups becomes more controversial and difficult when the groups concerned are based on religion. In examining the Royal Ulster Constabulary, Patten (1999) needed to deal with the representation of different religious communities within the force. He identified that a force split 92 per cent Protestant and 8 per cent Catholic was a serious problem. He concluded that, in view of the serious historical policing problems related to the religious divide, the police must be representative of communities if they were not to be perceived as partial. More Catholics needed to be recruited 'as a matter of the efficiency and effectiveness of policing: it is not just a matter of fairness' (Patten, 1999: 81). In the circumstances of Northern Ireland, therefore, he argued that the state could justify actions based on the religion of the officer and, implicitly, require the officer to disclose his religion.

Patten then debated whether these arguments necessarily extended to include sexuality and was reluctant to agree that this was so, on the grounds that the requirement would be too intrusive. Patten's argument rightly identifies that each intrusion on the private lives of officers must be properly justified. On this reasoning, management intervention against the officer in Case Study 5 would be very difficult to justify on the facts presented alone. Given that the officer was a consenting adult and the

Private Lives: case study 1
A police officer announces to his Chief Constable that he is proposing to set up a Freemasons Lodge exclusively for police officers and retired police officers. The Chief Constable responds by thanking him for his openness and asking him to encourage his fellow freemasons to register their membership with the force. He also states that, despite this openness, he, as a Chief Constable, regards freemasonry as incompatible with police duties because it conflicts with the impartiality that he regards as essential for a police officer.

Private Lives: case study 2
A police officer who is passionate about animals becomes aware, through his duties, of plans for a cull of badgers as part of a national trial. On the first day of the cull he is on duty as one of the police officers protecting the team carrying out the cull. On the following day, his day off, he attends the demonstration himself and protests peacefully against the cull. Both police officers and protestors identify him. His line manager instructs him not to attend any future demonstrations.

Private Lives: case study 3
A police officer applies to his Chief Constable to become a taxi-driver when he is off-duty. He states that his salary is insufficient to support his family and he is being forced to supplement his income with state benefits. The Chief Constable refuses his application in the grounds that being a taxi-driver was incompatible with being a police officer, because the police were involved in the licensing and enforcement of the taxi licence regulations.

Private Lives: case study 5
During the course of a routine raid on a sex shop photographs are discovered at the premises showing an officer from the local station involved in sado-masochistic group sex. The officer is unmarried and when confronted by his line manager candidly admits that he regularly takes part in such events. He states that what he does in his private life is 'no business of the job' and has no effect on his duties.

Private Lives: case study 6
A police officer who is very involved in her local community is invited to stand for the local town council as an independent. The council is 'non-political' – none of the members have overt political affiliations – and has very limited responsibilities for the upkeep of play areas, local tourism, footpaths and the town hall. They are anxious to have the officer involved to secure her commitment to local initiatives. The Chief Constable seeks to prevent her involvement on the grounds that even such limited semi-political involvement is incompatible with her role.

Private Lives: case study 7
A police officer who is a keen footballer player in his local community accepts sponsorship for his sports kit from the local brewery who own most of the public houses in the area. The officer's line manager requests him to cease the sponsoring relationship because it is creating an impression of partiality in enforcing the licensing laws locally.

sexual activity was not *per se* illegal, there would not seem to be proportionality or necessity grounds to interfere. However, some authors have argued that public perceptions of the officer's moral authority and, therefore, judgement might well be affected and this could justify interference (Kleinig, 1996a). Such an approach has found some favour in the US Supreme Court[3] and is reflected in the IACP Code of Ethics, which admonishes officers to 'keep my private life unsullied as an example to all …honest in thought and deed in both my public and private life' (IACP, 1999). The latter seems a rather onerous commandment and difficult to justify, even by Kleinig's argument about the need for credibility in court. It presumes a high level of consensus and clarity about morality and seems to sit uneasily with a liberal democratic tradition which, according to the European Court of Human Rights, is underpinned by the values of 'pluralism, tolerance and broadmindedness'.[4]

In reality, there are many shades of grey in the restrictions on officers' private lives. For example, in the UK there has been a substantial debate about whether officers can be members of their local parish councils, which are essentially apolitical bodies, much like the example set in Case Study 6. Central government has sought to limit the right, but their justification seems to fall some way short of the test proposed by the European Court (*Rekvenyi v Hungary*, 1999).

The grey edges at the boundaries of virtue and professional integrity are particularly hotly debated when we move to the issue of gifts, gratuities and sponsorship. For some, there should be a clear line – usually described in very absolute terms including admonitions against even a cup of coffee (Goldstein, 1975). For others, this is an unrealistic stance that indicates a lack of trust in officers. Kleinig (1996a) and Kania (1988) carefully argued through both sides of this argument. Combining their analysis produces ten points that demonstrate the shades of grey well:

Arguments for accepting gifts and benefits
- True gifts or rewards for good service: for Kleinig, these are freely given in appreciation and create no obligation.
- Insignificant: and, therefore, create no obligation.
- Officially offered: not to an individual but as a wider discount, thus creating no sense of individual obligation.
- Community links: Kania called this a 'true gratuity' for a 'continuing reciprocal obligation.
- Police culture: that it is an accepted part of police work and would cause more harm than good to stop it. This seems the least persuasive of Kleinig's points.
- Trust and discretion: that it is important in seeking to develop a 'professional' culture of autonomy and empowerment not to bind officers with intricate rules.

Arguments against
- Obligation: or in Kania's terms 'uncalled debt', which creates credit for future legal or illegal favours.
- 'Slippery Slope': Sherman (1985) suggested that gratuities were the beginning of a psychological process that would gradually lead the officer to self-identify as someone who was morally and then actually corrupt.
- Temptation.
- Preferential treatment: this is a powerful argument, which was developed by Feldberg (1985). He points out that the intent of many gratuities, such as free meals, is to attract police to pay more attention to certain premises. Policing thereby ceases to become a public good

provided in response to need and becomes a service more available to those 'sponsoring' officers.

The arguments of Kleinig and Kania indicate some of the dimensions of the problem, but not the outlines of the boundaries. We can begin to flesh these out by applying the four tracks of ethics to the issue:

- Duty: gratuities could only be justified if the gift could be argued to be appropriate for all officers from any source. Moreover, as soon as the gift becomes a means for the giver to achieve something that he would not otherwise have got, then the giver is treating the officer not as an individual, but as a means for gain (Pollock, 1998).

- Utility: the focus is now on the outcome of accepting gifts. Where this is part of cementing good relationships in the community, it may be appropriate. As soon as the outcome is a diminution in trust or respect for the police, then it would not. A major aspect of the utilitarian calculus would be the impact on the perceived impartiality of the organisation and the officer.

- Care: here the key question is 'what does the act of giving and receiving tell us about the relationship between the officer and the giver?' Where the relationship has been a close one and based on respect the act of giving could be seen as part of the relationship and not improper. Where it was an early part of a new relationship, much more searching questions might need to be applied.

- Virtue: in the last of the tracks, it is the impact of the act of receiving on the officer's honesty and integrity that would be at issue.

The four tracks would seem to suggest a fairly restrictive test for the acceptance of gifts, gratuities or sponsorship. Motivation and impact on the receiver are extremely important. It is clear in the same way that officers must avoid real or potential conflicts of interest, so they must also avoid a real or potential impression of obligation. The question then arises as to whether this judgement is one for each officer as an individual professional acting within an ethical code or one that for which a detailed rulebook and rigorous discipline code is deployed.

Conclusions

This last question brings this chapter full circle. We started off by looking at the police officer as a professional. We concluded that police officers were striving for professional status. This had not yet happened: partly because of the role itself and partly because some issues such as an ethical code and evidence-based practice are not well advanced (in the UK at least). However, we argued that it is becoming increasingly important for policing to progress further down this road. Human rights policing demands some greater urgency, because the personal responsibility of the practitioner to make, evidence and be held accountable for complex ethical judgements will increase. Of the many possible responses to human rights a more rule-centred, bureaucratic model seems the least likely to succeed. Moreover, as imaginative approaches to policing such as problem solving gain credibility alongside community-based models, it will also become operationally advantageous to develop the 'police officer as clinician'.

This presents a substantial challenge to the deep-rooted operating culture of the organisation (West Mercia Constabulary, 2000b). However, as Chan has convincingly demonstrated, the coincidence of internal and external pressures can help to change that culture. That, in turn, helps to influence the operational and ethical judgements that police officers make. In the section on discretion and on citizens in uniform we saw that there was little to support the rigid rule-bound hierarchy as an effective future for policing organisations. The judgements in policing are too complex, too multi-layered and the enabling model that we have argued for in earlier chapters demands a more flexible and adaptive police officer: professional, not paramilitary, ethical rather than merely outcome oriented.

Further reading

Kleinig's study, *The Ethics of Policing* (1996a) is unquestionably the most comprehensive discussion of the issues in this chapter. His companion volume of essays, *Ethical issues in police decision-making* (1996b) is also very strong in its treatment of discretion, as is Reiner's chapter in the *Oxford Handbook of Criminology* (Reiner, 1997). On professionalism in policing Reiner (*The Politics of the Police*, 1985), Waddington (*Policing Citizens*, 1999) and the essays in Brodeur (*How to Recognise Good Policing*, 1998) provide a good introduction, whilst Lawton (*Ethical Management for the Public Services*, 1988) offers a broader treatment of public services. It is also important to look at the Code of Ethics produced by the International Association of Chiefs of Police (IACP, 1999) which can be found on their website at www.iacp.org along with information about training ethics. The report of Her Majesty's Inspectorate of Constabulary on Integrity (HMIC, 1999a) is also available on the Internet through the Home Office site www.homeoffice.gov.uk. Pollock (*Ethics in Crime and Justice*, 1996), Kania ('Police acceptance of gratuities', 1988), Sherman ('Becoming bent', 1985) and Feldberg ('Gratuities, corruption and the democratic ethos in policing', 1985) provide good coverage of the debate about gifts and gratuities.

Notes

1 The key case is *Rekvenyi v Hungary* (1999) where it was held that a police officer could be denied the right to be a member of a political party, because of the need to be seen to be impartial.
2 *Ahmed and other v UK* (1995), *Lombardo v France* (1992) and *Pellegrin v France* (1999) all comment on the different status of the public servant who exercises the powers of the state. Such officials (and the police are specifically included in the Pellegrin judgement) do not get the full protection of the Convention, particularly in employment rights. However, the state must still justify interferences with rights.
3 *Shawgo v Spradlin* (1983) where a sergeant and an officer were disciplined for off-duty dating and inter-rank cohabitation. The Court held that the Department only had to show that the case could have resulted in 'unfavourable criticism' or have been prejudicial to public order (Kleinig, 1996a).
4 *Handyside v UK* (1977).

Chapter 6

Police performance management – an ethical dilemma?

Introduction

Previous chapters of this book have developed the argument that ethics and human rights are concerned with how police officers and police leaders make the right judgements and take the right actions for the right reasons. We have suggested that an enabling model – involving increased professional autonomy and a more reflective practitioner – is essential for the development of policing. The professional clinician model proposed in Chapter 5 involves discretion, diagnosis and problem solving and an orientation to ethics, rather than to outcomes alone. However, this does not fit well with the existing managerialism and performance culture in the police service.

A wide variety of performance indicators are published so stakeholders may make judgements about police performance. However, judging police performance is a complex matter, because of the absence of a clear purpose and clear expectations about what police services should deliver. Despite the publication of 'league tables' by the Audit Commission, press attention is concentrated more on levels of crime and detection. The Home Office believes that 'performance measures and comparisons act as a powerful incentive to improve performance and demonstrates how the expectations and needs of national and local communities are met' (Home Office, 1999c). This 'new public management' (Hood, 1995) emphasises the rhetoric of control at the expense of discretion. Yet the renewed emphasis on ethics and human rights in the police service suggests that we need to reverse the rise of managerialism that has taken place at the expense of professional autonomy. This chapter aims to understand the complexity of police performance management[1] and its impact on police officers and police officers-as-managers for issues of ethics and human rights.

The vicious cycle described in Chapter 1 defined the boom and bust of the shifting focus on crime fighting and reform. The managerial reforms of the 1990s have provided the appearance of rationality through multiple methods of control. These managerial reforms encompass the introduction of cash-limited budgets, recommendations on best practice published routinely by HMIC and the Audit Commission and a diverse and ever changing suite of performance indicators. They culminate in the introduction of best value and proposals for an efficiency index. A perspective on this vicious cycle is shown in Figure 6.1 below, as it relates to control.

In this chapter, we will suggest that:

1 A 'policy networks' approach may yield better results in defining purpose and performance management than a contractually-based agency approach;
2 The existing systems of performance control are founded on the assumption of rational decision making. This is contrasted with an approach that is based on culturally-dependent values and rituals; and
3 A shift from a control paradigm to a learning paradigm that values risk-taking and experimentation may result in long-term solutions to problems that equip police officers to face emerging ethical and human rights issues.

The second section of this chapter describes the governance of policing. In the third section, a brief overview of agency theory and different types of control systems provides the scheme to understand the different and competing expectations of external stakeholders. The fourth section describes

Figure 6.1   The vicious cycle of management control

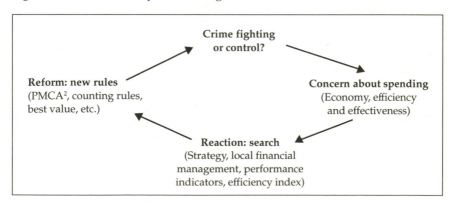

those expectations in terms of police performance indicators, the reporting of crime, police funding and how judgements are made about police performance. In the fifth section, we suggest a new paradigm to improve on the current system within a human rights framework. In the final section, we draw some conclusions.

Governance of policing

Policing in the United Kingdom is organised through 52 separate police forces. With the exception of the 8 Scottish forces and the Royal Ulster Constabulary, there are 43 forces comprising 129,000 police officers and 53,000 civilian support staff in England and Wales. These are the 'Home Office' forces. There are additional non-Home Office forces that carry out special purposes, the largest being the Ministry of Defence Police and the British Transport Police.

The governance of public policing is through a tripartite structure. The Police and Magistrates' Courts Act came into operation in 1995 and introduced reforms to police governance and accountability as a consequence of the Sheehy Inquiry (Sheehy, 1993), and a Police Reform White Paper (Home Office, 1993a).

1 The Chief Constable (or the Commissioner in the Metropolitan Police) is the professional head of the police force in each geographic area, with responsibility for the 'direction and control' (Police and Magistrates' Courts Act, 1994) of the force. There is no national police force in the United Kingdom, and each Chief Constable has constitutional independence (*Fisher v. Oldham Corporation*, 1930: 2 KB 364) for operational matters in their force area. Chief officers work closely together through the Association of Chief Police Officers (ACPO), which exercises a considerable influence over the activities of individual forces through national standards and policies (Reiner, 1991; Savage and Charman, 1995). Despite their operational autonomy, chief constables are accountable both locally and to central government.

2 The Police Authority, as the second tripartite member, has responsibility to maintain an 'efficient and effective' (Police and Magistrates' Courts Act, 1994) force for its area. Its members are drawn from local authorities and magistrates' courts, together with 'independent' members appointed by the Home Secretary. On the basis of local consultation, the Police Authority establishes and reviews objectives and targets in conjunction with the Chief Constable, and issues a policing plan for its area. Using the targets contained in the policing plan, the Authority has considerable influence in its role of monitoring force performance. Police authorities

exert national pressure through the Association of Police Authorities (APA: Jones and Newburn, 1997).

3 The third member of the tripartite structure is the Home Secretary, who has a duty to promote the efficiency of the Police Service as a whole. The Police Department in the Home Office formulates national policy, while Her Majesty's Inspector of Constabulary (HMIC) carries out inspections of individual police forces. The role of HMIC was described in Home Office (1994) as 'the principal, but not the sole, source of professional advice to the Home Secretary and to the Home Office on all aspects of policing, both operational and management.'

While not part of the tripartite structure, it is important to note the role of the Treasury, which has consistently emphasised the need to reduce funding available for police services through a drive for greater efficiency and effectiveness. The Police and Magistrates' Courts Act of 1994 (subsequently amalgamated into the Police Act of 1996) introduced a formula-driven and cash-limited grant for the funding of police services, which is described later in this chapter. The Department of the Environment, Transport and the Regions has a growing influence on indicators through its role in local government.

The Treasury's impact on policing, beyond the funding allocation for the police service, is through the work of HMIC and the Audit Commission. The Audit Commission was established in 1983 with a twofold purpose: to ensure that local government provided 'wise and prudent administration'; and to devise and refine local government performance measures (Local Government Finance Act, 1982). HMIC, together with the Audit Commission, play an important role in police performance management through an extensive range of performance indicators which are described later in this chapter.

These various actors –

- Police authorities and their national body, the APA;
- The Home Office and its inspectorate, HMIC;
- Treasury and the Audit Commission;

are all stakeholders in policing. They all have a concern with the measurement of police performance and the results achieved by police forces.

However, the public are also stakeholders in policing, as the ultimate beneficiaries of those services. Whatever the public concerns about police purposes or performance, these are likely to be expressed through the political process (Smith, 1995b), both at national and local levels. This role is expressed in different ways.

- At a national level, Parliament is elected and the public's concerns with law and order issues will be reflected in the political process.
- These concerns may however, also be reflected at a local authority level, by those members who are appointed to Police Authorities.
- As part of the public consultation process, the public may also voice their concerns and expectations direct to police forces through Police and Community Consultative Groups (PCCGs).

This stakeholding public is the sole beneficiary of the results of police performance and police behaviour in relation to ethics and human rights.

This chapter describes the conflict in relation to performance management which results from the different purposes and expectations assumed by each of these stakeholders. We begin to consider this problem, first by utilising agency theory, and second by considering the various types of control systems.

Framework

Agency theory

Chapter 4 introduced the contractual theory of government. Agency theory is an outcome of economic theories of contract and builds from the assumption that one party, the agent (here the management of public sector organisations) carries out work on behalf of another, the principal. While agency involves trust, it is predominantly concerned with a system of contracts and incentives to ensure that agents (defined as self-interested) fulfil those contracts. The agency problem arises when the principal tries to ensure that the agent behaves in ways that are consistent with the principal's interests. The problem is exacerbated by the inability of either principal or agent to disentangle the separate effects of effort and chance on the results achieved. Consequently, there is an incentive for agents to minimise their effort and attribute failure to external factors.

Agency costs arise because of the need to ensure that agents act in the interests of their principals. Performance management (here defined as measuring, reporting and monitoring performance) is a method of ensuring such compliance. In the public sector, the agency problem is greater than the lack of common interests between principal and agent. The existence of multiple stakeholders – as in the case of policing – can result in inconsistent, imprecise or ambiguous purposes, performance expectations and performance management systems.

Given the complex structure of police governance described in this section, we can identify the various principals who have expectations of police performance and an interest in performance management:

- P1 is the public, which acts directly through PCCGs, indirectly through local authority representatives on Police Authorities; and also indirectly through their national parliamentary representatives.
- P2 is the Home Secretary, the (elected) secretary of state responsible for the police service.
- P3 is the Chancellor of the Exchequer, who exercises policy control through the Treasury.
- P4 is the (partly elected, partly appointed) Police Authority.

Although we are concerned primarily with the impact of performance management on police managers as the *ultimate* agents, we cannot avoid consideration of the role played by the *intermediate* agents – HMIC and the Audit Commission. Therefore we can identify three agents:

- A1 is the management of each force, headed by the Chief Constable.
- A2 is HMIC, the agent of the Home Secretary.
- A3 is the Audit Commission, the agent of Treasury.

Other 'tertiary' agents who influence policing include:

- Health and Safety Executive;
- Commission for Racial Equality/Equal Opportunities Commission;
- Police Complaints Authority.

Each of these principals – and their intermediate agents – exerts influence over the Chief Constable of each police force, who has responsibility for the performance of his/her force. The complexity of this relationship is shown diagrammatically in Figure 6.2.

In Figure 6.2, we can see the influence on police management (A1) by four principals – the public through PCCGs (P1), the Home Secretary (P2), the Treasury (P3) and the Police Authority (P4). We can also see the influence of two intermediate agents – HMIC (A2) and the Audit Commission (A3). This portrayal is complex because of the indirect role of the public in electing government and ministers and local authority members to police authorities.

There are two alternative models to agency theory:

- *Organisational field theory* comprises the 'totality of relevant actors' (DiMaggio and Powell, 1983: 148) who constitute a recognised area of institutional life: key suppliers, resource consumers, regulatory agencies, and other organisations producing similar products or services. Organisational fields are defined by relational linkages, shared cultural rules and common meaning systems (Scott, 1998). Scott and Meyer (1991) propose the societal sector as moving beyond organi-

Figure 6.2   Principal/agent relationships in policing

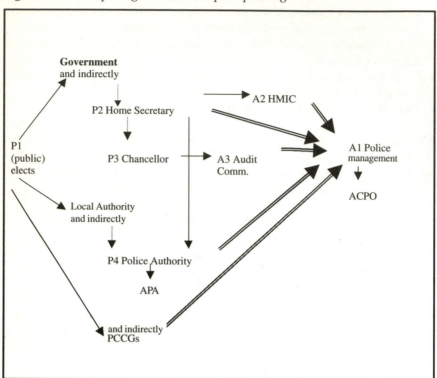

sational field. They define societal sector as a collection of organisations operating in the same domain together with other organisations that critically influence their performance.

- *Policy networks theory* recognises the plurality within the environment and the need to develop consensus between stakeholders. Policy networks are a development within organisational theory and emphasise the lack of clear decision procedures, goals or hierarchy. Management in networks is about 'creating strategic consensus for joint action within a given setting' (Kickert, Klijn and Koppenjan, 1997: 167). Government often occupies a unique position in networks, although it is not always the all-powerful actor it may appear to be.

The role of government is central in the management of police performance, albeit such performance is managed by various government 'agencies'. The adoption of organisation field or policy networks rather than agency theory adds little to an understanding of the problem of purpose and expectation, although it may add to a possible solution. We return to this later in the chapter.

We are primarily concerned here with the inconsistency, imprecision and ambiguity of purpose and goal expectations between different principals and intermediate agents, and with the effect of such ambiguity on ethical decision making by police officers and managers. These differences lead to a preference for different types of control systems that are reflected in how performance is measured, reported and monitored. We now turn to a consideration of these different types of control systems.

Control systems

Hofstede (1981) provided a useful typology for management control, recognising the particular difficulties faced by public sector and not-for-profit organisations. He identified six types of management control that he classified into two groups that we shall call, for simplicity, rational and values-based.

Most organisations display a rhetoric of rational, instrumental control systems based on goal-setting and performance management to achieve those goals, focusing on corrective action in the face of below-target performance (feedback). We return to values-based control later, but the rational rhetoric is well evidenced. Five types of control can be identified from the management control literature, particularly as they can be applied in the public sector: input, output, behaviour, outcome, and ritual. Each requires some measurement, or at least judgement about performance, usually in comparison with a target.

- *Input controls* relate to the provision of scarce resources that constrain activity. In the public sector concerns for economy may dominate decisions. Input controls are mainly financial, although they may also include non-financial limits (e.g. on staff levels). Inputs are dependent on the wider political process and budgetary allocations made as a result of that process.

- *Output controls* are concerned with measuring specific elements of organisational performance, principally the volume of activities carried out. These controls are a function of the demand for services and input constraints and result from the efficiency of resource allocation and utilisation. Measurement of outputs is typically in non-financial terms.

- *Behaviour controls* are imposed through policies and procedures, socialization processes, supervision, and rewards and sanctions that aim to reinforce desired behaviour and constrain dysfunctional behaviour. These controls have significant influence over resource allocation and utilisation. Measurement of behaviour is most commonly qualitative.

- *Outcome controls* are concerned with the effectiveness or societal impact of organisational activity. Outcome controls depend on policy appropriateness, demand for services, the adequacy of resources, and the effectiveness of their allocation and utilisation. Outcome controls will usually be qualitative because of the complexity of measurement.

- Ritual controls exist where there is imperfect knowledge of the means–end transformation process, a low availability of output measures or where the 'correct' behaviours cannot be identified. Ritual control provides the appearance of rationality in order to legitimate organisational activity as a result of the politically motivated desire to demonstrate rational behaviour. Ritual controls incorporate other forms of control, and may therefore be a combination of financial, quantitative and qualitative measures.

While not technically a control, a sixth measure can be introduced – that of *public demand for services*. As public sector organisations aim to satisfy public demand, that demand provides the principle motivation for organisational performance. The level of public demand for services is dependent on social, political, economic and environmental factors. The interaction between these six elements can be shown diagrammatically in Figure 6.3.

Figure 6.3 suggests that there ought, logically, to be a relationship between the demand for services, the resources provided, resource allocation and utilisation, and behaviours, in order to achieve outcomes. This chapter argues that there is no relationship between these controls in the police service, and as a result, ritual controls dominate. Consequently, these control systems provide little guidance to the ethical behaviour of police officers, given the ambiguities and inconsistencies between the different types of control.

Chapter 3 introduced the notion of stewardship, while the role of public sector performance indicators is concerned with accountability to principals (Smith, 1995a). To Figure 6.3 we must therefore add the role of external stakeholders. Figure 6.4 shows how different stakeholders may prefer different types of control.

In Figure 6.4, the Treasury view dominates input controls, its sole concern being the overall quantum of resources allocated to policing. Behaviour controls are the province of police managers. Output controls, being relatively easily measurable, are dominated by those agencies that have an interest in published performance and league tables. The general public and elected representatives are most likely concerned with the outcomes for society of police performance. Different stakeholders have become associated with different methods of performance management and hence different types of control mechanisms. The result is that attempts to

Figure 6.3 Control systems in the police

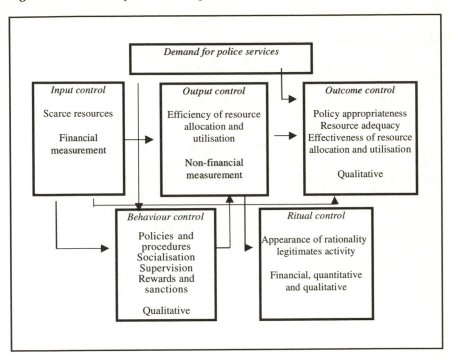

Figure 6.4 Stakeholder preference for control mechanisms

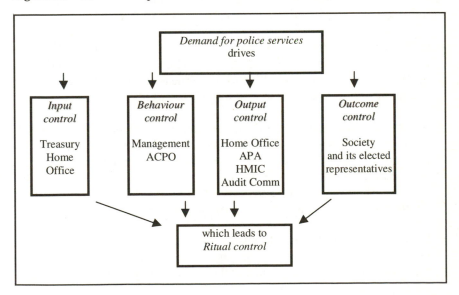

manage the performance of the police are ineffective, and recourse is only available to ritual controls.

Rational control v. non-rational control

The effect of ritual controls on individual ethical behaviour is to provide a view of the world that is pluralist yet lacking in internal congruity, although it is based on firmly held values.

Earlier in this chapter, we introduced the typology of Hofstede (1981) and his categorisation of rational and values-based controls. Values-based control systems are political, dependent on external power and influence, or use a 'garbage-can' model (following the early work of March and Olsen). The garbage-can model portrays decision making when 'fortuitous confluences' of problems, solutions, participants and choice opportunities occur via resolution, avoidance or oversight. These are non-rational (*not* irrational) processes that are dependent on external or internal structures of power and influence, negotiation processes and resource dependencies.

Hofstede (1981) argued that the key elements of non-rational controls were the values of actors, their models of the world and the rituals and symbolism that enable cognitive consistency. These values and rituals are culturally dependent (whether at an organisational, occupational, or national level). Hofstede argued that control reforms need to be sensitive to culture.

The contrast between a rational control-based and values-based response can be seen in the four case studies introduced in Chapter 5 (based on the four types of judgement developed by Kleinig, 1996a). If we follow the rational control-based model to these cases we see the following:

- In the case of the domestic dispute, police officers are more likely to see this as outside the scope of their role. The utilisation of their most limited resource (time) would lead to no measurable performance outcome, once they had attended within the target response time.

- In the same situation, if circumstances identify the incident as criminal, interpretative discretion may lead to criminal charges if the officers consider that recording the crime and the detection satisfies performance management. The most appropriate solution (negotiation) may be less important than the opportunity cost of officers' time in attempting to either resolve the incident or arrest and process the suspect.

- In the case of quality of life issues, discretion about priority is more likely to favour those issues that are subject to national or force performance indicators, particularly where rewards (promotion, favoured postings) may follow from such prioritisation.

- In the case of competing rights in a public demonstration, concern over cost may lead to decisions that reduce resources at the expense of putting officers or the public at risk of injury.

We would suggest that control systems that emphasise limited resources and achievement of PIs *may* influence the decision making of police officers and their managers towards outcomes that are not wholly consistent with ethics and human rights. On the other hand, the professional values of many police officers *may* lead them to neglect performance management issues in favour of the most appropriate operational (and ethical) outcome.

This chapter argues that police performance management displays the rhetoric of instrumentality and rationality, but that such rationality is a myth. In order to substantiate this, we need to look more closely at the development of police performance management, and the interest taken by different stakeholders in the management of that performance. We will demonstrate that ritual controls are necessary because of different expectations about policing performance and problems with the use of PIs and crime statistics; and because of the lack of any relationship between demand, resources, behaviour, outputs and intended outcomes. In the next section, we review each of these issues in turn.

Police performance management

The lack of agreement as to the purposes of the police, and the contrast between formal mission and practice was described fully in Chapter 2. This lack of agreement extends to the manner in which police performance is managed. Of the Overarching Aims and Objectives for the police service (Home Office, 1998b), only one (of three) aims and three (of eleven) objectives relate directly to crime. Yet despite the acknowledgement given by the Home Office in these new aims and objectives to the broader purposes of policing, crime still retains its dominant position as the main influence in the public perception of police performance.

Crime

Crime figures, though a dominant social fact, are not easy to interpret for a number of reasons:

- Official statistics are based on 'notifiable offences' and show only those offences recorded by the police and reported to the Home Office (Cm. 4162, 1998).

- The *British Crime Survey* (BCS) provides an alternative method of measuring crime, by surveying people in private households. Figures from the BCS suggest that less than half of all offences are reported to the police and only a quarter are recorded – 'the remaining 76% make up the "dark figure" of crime' (Mirrlees-Black *et. al.* 1998: 18). Explanations for this 'dark figure' include police not accepting a victim's account, considering the matter as too trivial to record, or recording the incident as a less serious offence.

- The difficulties in recording crime are evident in *Counting Rules*, the guidance provided by the Home Office to police forces to assist them in recording crime (Home Office, 1998d). These are complex and open to variations in interpretation.

- Increased crime figures between 1998 and 1999 were largely the result of changes in counting rules that took place after April 1998.

- Similar complications exist in relation to detection rates, in particular the use of secondary detections, i.e. those that result primarily from confessions gained during prison visits (which do not result in any additional penalty to convicted persons). Although they significantly influence crime detection rates, with effect from 1999/2000 the Audit Commission and the Home Office no longer accept secondary detections (Audit Commission, 1998a; Mayhew, 1999).

Finally, crime is, with the exception of the annual publications of crime statistics, not a dominant feature of police performance management. We need to consider police performance indicators to better understand the expectations of diverse stakeholders.

Police performance indicators

Carter, Klein and Day (1992) provide a comprehensive description of the introduction and development of PIs in the UK, using the introduction of the Financial Management Initiative (FMI) in 1982 as a starting point. Circular 114 of 1983 (Home Office, 1983) introduced the requirement for forces to set objectives and priorities and to allocate resources and deploy manpower in a way that would most effectively and efficiently secure those objectives and priorities.

The requirement to set performance indicators (PIs) had been heralded by the Citizen's Charter (HMSO, 1991), which introduced the expectation for police forces to set targets for answering calls from the public and responding to calls for assistance.

PIs are required primarily by the following agencies:

- Home Office
- Audit Commission
- HMIC, and
- ACPO.

We will discuss each of these in turn.

National key objectives
Home Office PIs have been introduced through the mechanism of Home Office key objectives, which the PMCA foreshadowed as national priorities for policing. The national objectives for policing are shown in Figure 6.5 below. Each of these objectives are supported by PIs.

As can be seen from Figure 6.5, national objectives (and their associated PIs) have frequently changed since 1998. Of particular significance is the elimination of objectives for detecting crime, high visibility policing and response to the public.[3] New priorities have been introduced for dealing with young offenders, working in partnership with other local agencies[4] and increasing the confidence of ethnic communities.[5] A separate emphasis has been given to drugs.

Despite these national priorities, other targets continue to appear. The five-year crime reduction targets introduced in 2000 (Home Office, 2000b) are aimed at reducing domestic burglary and vehicle crime in all forces and robbery in the large metropolitan areas. These have not formed part of the national priorities.

At the individual force level, the PMCA requires each police authority to 'determine objectives for the policing of the authority's area' (s. 7) which are consistent with the Secretary of State's key objectives (s. 37), after consulting the chief constable and the local community. The Association of Police Authorities (1998) believe that the primary significance of performance indicators is to 'give police authorities a structure for monitoring the performance of their individual police forces' (p. 16). However, the APA argues that the manner of inclusion of Home Office Key Objectives in policing plans has lead to a lack of differentiation between Home Office and local priorities.

Audit Commission PIs
The Audit Commission PIs result from its responsibility (under the Local Government Act, 1992 and the Audit Commission Act, 1998) to produce PIs that, by reference to cost, efficiency and effectiveness enable comparisons to be made of the standards of performance achieved. The first national publication of PIs by the Audit Commission took place in April 1995 (Home Office, 1996). These performance comparisons have been widely regarded within the police service as 'league tables'. The PIs required by the Audit Commission are shown in Figure 6.6.

Figure 6.5 National key objectives for policing

1994	1998	1999	2000
Maintain and, if possible, increase the number of detections for violent crimes	Maintain and, if possible, increase the number of detections for violent crime		
Increase the number of detections for burglaries of people's homes	Increase the number of detections for burglaries of people's homes		
Target and prevent crimes which are a particular local problem, including drug-related criminality, in partnership with the public and local agencies	Target *and reduce* local problems of crime *and disorder* in partnership with *local authorities*, other local agencies and the public	*Identify* and reduce local problems of crime and disorder in partnership with local authorities, other local agencies and the public	*Reduce* local problems of crime and disorder in partnership with local authorities, other local agencies and the public
Provide high visibility policing so as to reassure the public			
Respond promptly to emergency calls from the public	Respond promptly to emergency calls from the public		
	Deal speedily and effectively with young offenders and work with other agencies to reduce re-offending	Deal speedily and effectively with young offenders and work with other agencies to reduce *offending* and re-offending *by young people*	
	Target drug-related crime in partnership with other local agencies … (etc.)	Target *and reduce* drug-related crime in partnership with other local agencies … (etc.)	
		Increase trust and confidence in policing amongst minority ethnic communities	Increase trust and confidence in policing amongst minority ethnic communities

Note: Changes to wording of individual objectives are shown italic.

Figure 6.6   Audit Commission performance indicators[1]

Service	PIs[2]
Answering 999 calls	Number of calls; target time for answering calls; percentage of calls answered within target.
Incidents requiring immediate response	Definition of immediate response incidents; number of incidents; target time for response; percentage of responses within target times.
Crime	Total number of recorded crimes per 1000 population; number of violent crimes per 1000 population; household burglaries per 1000 households.
Crime detections	Percentage of all crimes detected; percentage of violent crimes detected; percentage of household burglaries detected (all detections are by primary means only); number of crimes detected by primary means per officer.
Repeat victimisation	Percentage of domestic burglaries where the property had been burgled in the previous twelve months.
Road traffic accidents	Number of road traffic accidents involving death or personal injury; percentage of accidents in which at least one driver tested positive for alcohol.
Handling	Number of complaints from the public; number of complaints resolved informally.
Availability of police officers	Number of police officers available for ordinary duty per 1000 population; percentage of uniformed operational constables' working time spent outside the police station and in public.
Public satisfaction[3]	Percentage of the public that is satisfied with the police services described in the other PIs.
Cost	Net expenditure per head of population on the police service.

[1] Adapted from Audit Commission (1998b).
[2] PIs for answering 999 calls, percentage of responses to incidents, working time spent in public and public satisfaction are estimated by sampling, in which case the method of sampling and sample size is reported.
[3] ACPO 'quality of service' PIs are now reflected in the Audit Comission's own PIs, and incorporate the need for systematic surveys to determine if the needs and expectations of the public are being met (Home Office, 1993b). They have been adopted by the Audit Commission to ensure that police performance is not seen solely in quantiative terms.

Other PIs

In addition to the Audit Commission PIs, certain other PIs must also be published. HMIC PIs provide 'contextual data' (Home Office, 1993a) about other aspects of performance. ACPO's 'quality of service' PIs are aimed at ensuring that police performance is not seen solely in terms of quantitative assessment and their PIs incorporate the need for systematic surveys to determine if the needs and expectations of the public are being met (Home Office, 1993a). Joint Performance Management PIs are an attempt to have common performance standards between the police and the Crown Prosecution Service in relation to the conduct of prosecutions. These non-Audit Commission PIs are summarised in Figure 6.7.

The dilemma facing police officers as to whether to prioritise performance management or ethics is in part assuaged by the ACPO quality of service indicators which attempt to measure public satisfaction with the quality of police services. In conjunction with HMIC measures such as the treatment of white versus non-white groups and the number of complaints by the public against police officers, the effects of the performance culture may be dampened a little.

Figure 6.7 Other performance indicators

Agency	PI
HMIC	A variety of measures of stop/searches of white and other ethnic groups; racial incidents; traffic offences; sickness absence; and the gender and ethnic mix of police officers.
ACPO	Percentage of people satisfied: with police action in response to 999 calls; with service received at police station enquiry counters; with initial police response to a report of violent crime, household burglary, or at the scene of a road traffic accident; with perceived level of foot and mobile patrol.
Required for Joint Performance Management (Police and Crown Prosecution Service)	Number of persons arrested for notifiable offences per 100 police officers; percentage of persons arrested for notifiable offences who were prosecuted/cautioned/dealt with by other means/subject of no further action.
Required by Publication of Information (Standards of performance) Direction, 1996	Target and actual performance for telephone answering and answering letters. Number of buildings open to the public and number suitable for access by disabled people. Information relating to equal opportunities policy, practices and monitoring.

Source: Police Service Performance Indicators (1997/98)

Best Value Performance Indicators

The performance culture found is, however, reinforced by the introduction of Best Value as a statutory duty from April 2000 (under section 4 of the Local Government Act, 1999). Best value impacts police authorities as designated best value authorities. The publication of best value performance indicators (BVPIs) for the police (DETR, 1999; Home Office, 2000a) reflect five dimensions of performance, shown below in Figure 6.8.

Most of these performance measures have consolidated existing PIs. Of interest however, are the targets to be set for BVPIs. Over five years, police forces are expected to achieve the performance levels of the top 25 per cent of police forces at the time the targets are set. The aim is to put most pressure on under-performing police forces and to narrow the range of performance between forces. Those forces already in the top 25 per cent are expected to seek continuous improvement (DETR, 1999: 21).

No sooner had BVPIs been published than the Public Services Productivity Panel (2000) reported on improving police performance, defining efficiency as the measure of police performance in meeting the Overarching Aims and Objectives for the money spent. The PSPP report goes beyond best value in recommending the construction of an 'efficiency index' based on a weighting of selected (primarily recorded crime) BVPIs related to the cost of providing police services for each force. The aim of the efficiency index is 'to actually discover what the true relationship is between inputs and outcomes' (p. 11).

Figure 6.8   Best Value performance indicators

Performance dimension	Number of BVPIs	Number of individual measures	Types of measures
Strategic objectives	4	4	British Crime Survey figures
Service delivery outcomes	8	17	Predominantly crime and detection
Quality	4	4	Response to incidents
Corporate health	14	14	Complaints, public satisfaction, female and ethnic strength, sickness, staff turnover and medical retirements, expenditure per 1000 population

Source: DETR (1999); Home Office (2000a).

Criticism of police performance management

Despite the Overarching Aims and Objectives constituting the latest statement of purpose for policing, there remains a considerable lack of consistency in police performance management. This inconsistency can be seen between the latest version of Home Office objectives, crime reduction targets (Home Office, 2000b), the proposed efficiency index, BVPIs and the PIs still demanded by the HMIC, ACPO and under Joint Performance Management. Concerns about PIs and measuring crime have been evident in the reports of the Audit Commission and HMIC, as well as the Home Office itself. There are substantial ethical dimensions to many of these concerns:

- The Home Office (1993a) warned that PIs *'do not all measure performance'* (emphasis added). This explicit warning appears to have been over-looked in the subsequent development of police performance management.

- The Audit Commission (1986) report *Improving Performance in Local Government* noted the problem of outcome measures by asking 'How much is vandalism and crime reduced by attendance at leisure centres, how much by crime prevention and detection activities of the police, and how much by the teaching of social responsibility in schools?' (quoted in Jowett and Rothwell, 1988: 30).

- The Audit Commission (1990) argued that 'definitions of "good" policing were still not adequately supported by objective indicators of performance' (p. 4). A later report, Audit Commission (1993), argued that the volume of crime is a measure of demand for police services, not a measure of police performance. This report noted the difficulties of aggregation despite differences in seriousness and ease of detection. This report also recognised that performance indicators skew activities, reinforcing the research by Likierman (1993) into the effects of PIs on middle managers in the public sector. The Audit Commission (1996) noted that conventional statistics could undermine a problem-solving approach to policing.

- In its review of police integrity, HMIC (1999a) found that the performance culture affected integrity, as a result of the tendency 'for some forces to "trawl the margins" for detections and generally use every means to portray their performance in a good light' (p. 19).

- The Citizen's Charter itself noted that a 'helpful, sympathetic, and effective' service (p. 25) was just as important as response time. This early recognition of the need for both measurable and qualitative performance has been largely forgotten in the historical development of police PIs.

PIs lead to a rationing of operational activity toward what league tables consider to be better performance, which is reinforced by the BVPI targets for top quartile performance. Rationing, or ruthless demand management as it was called in Chapter 2, results in decisions about scope, interpretative discretion and discretion about priorities that may have adverse consequences. Examples driven by rationing include response guidelines that eliminate police attendance for particular types of calls. It may also lead to ethical dilemmas such as redesignating an area as rural when PIs for response in an urban area are not being met, achieving a lower response time target rather than improved performance.

This description of the measurement of police performance through PIs and crime recording demonstrates the myriad of (changing) objectives, priorities and performance measures introduced by various agencies. We now consider the method of funding police services, to see if this helps to inform our understanding of different stakeholder expectations.

Police funding

Police funding has been cash-limited since the introduction of the PMCA in 1995. Funding is based on a complex formula and the assumption that 'the various kinds of policing need in an area can be related to the characteristics of the area and its population' (Home Office, 1998b: para. 1.3). Budget allocations are based on forces' relative need in six key areas:

- call management;
- crime management;
- traffic management;
- public order;
- community policing; and
- patrol.

In addition, police pensions and security needs are also taken into consideration, a proportion of the allocation being based on the (pre-PMCA) 1994 allocation, and a separate element recognising the costs associated with sparsely populated rural areas.

The Home Secretary determines the weightings to be given to each of these ten elements in the formula. Finally, over and above the formula, the ten forces in the south-east of England receive an area cost adjustment to reflect higher costs in those areas, and the Metropolitan Police receive an additional amount in respect of their capital city functions (Home Office, 1998b). The weightings allocated by the Home Secretary for 1998/99 are shown in Figure 6.9. No published changes have been made to these weightings, although it appears that minor changes are the result of a reduction in the pre-1994 factor from 20 per cent to 10 per cent.

The funding allocation shown in Figure 6.9 bears little relationship to the priorities allocated to policing by the overarching aims and objectives, by Home Office key objectives, or by any of the sets of PIs described in this chapter. Crime management receives only a quarter of the total allocation, despite the high profile given by *Criminal Statistics* and the *British Crime Survey* to levels of crime and detection rates. This is particularly surprising given the recent emphasis on crime reduction targets (Home Office, 2000b) and the inclusion of crime levels as the principal component within the proposed efficiency index (Public Services Productivity Panel, 2000)

By contrast, 15 per cent of the budget allocation is given to patrol, presumably to support high profile policing, despite the concerns expressed by the Audit Commission over patrol effectiveness (Audit Commission, 1996) and the removal of high visibility policing from national objectives in 1998. By contrast, 13 per cent of the allocation is paying for retired police officers as a result of an unfunded pension scheme, and 10 per cent is a result of past historical allocations that may be unrepresentative of present need. Despite the professed importance of the Crime and Disorder Act in prioritising youth justice and working in partnership with other local agencies, only 2.3 per cent of the allocation is for community policing.

Individual force allocations are based on a multiple regression analysis of a range of determinants such as resident population, daytime population, police establishment and pensions. These reflect the socio-economic characteristics of each area (Home Office, 1999d; Home Office, 2000c) although they are based on predicted rather than actual workloads and assumptions about cause–effect relationships.

Figure 6.9 Weighting for funding allocation to police forces

Element	Weighting
Call management	7.6%
Crime management	26.3%
Traffic management	6.2%
Public order	6.6%
Community policing	2.3%
Patrol	15.5%
Pensions	13.2%
Security	1.8%
Sparsity	0.5%
Pre-1994 factor	20%, subsequently reduced to 10%

Source: Home Office (1998b)

The introduction of cash-limited budgets and greater emphasis on performance indicators since 1995 parallels the increased demand on budgets from an unfunded police pensions scheme and the need for large-scale capital expenditure for national radio and information systems.

We have so far demonstrated the lack of consensus as to what elements of police performance are to be managed, how performance management should take place, the lack of compatibility between resource inputs and the diverse expectations of stakeholders, and problems with the use of performance indicators and crime statistics. This has been shown to impact on decisions made by individual police officers and their managers. How then are stakeholders to make judgements about police performance?

Judging police performance

Despite the broad spread of national and local PIs, there are three issues that have tended to dominate the national debate about police performance:

- crime;
- police numbers;
- police expenditure.

We address each of these in turn.

Crime

Taylor (1998) analysed forty years' criminal statistics. His analysis demonstrates the sharp rise in crime, despite a fall in the period between 1993 and 1997. Figure 6.10 provides a summary of key figures from Taylor's research.

Figure 6.10 Analysis of criminal statistics

	1958	1992	1997
Recorded crimes	669,000	5,383,000	4,467,000
Recorded crimes per 100,000 people	1,500	10,500	8,600
Average annual rate of increase in number of recorded crimes over 40 years (%)			5.4%

Source: Taylor (1998).
Note: In the 1990s, the number of recorded offences fell in each year from 1993 to 1997, the longest sustained fall during the 40-year period (Taylor, 1998).

Police numbers

In judging police performance, levels of crime need to be related to police strength and HMIC have produced data on the productivity of police officers. Extracts from this data are shown in Figure 6.11.

These figures show that crime has increased disproportionately to the increase in numbers of police officers, which have remained relatively static since 1985. While detection rates per officer have remained constant, the percentage of crime detected has fallen because of the increase in the volume of crime.

Police expenditure

By contrast, there has been an increasing concern by the Treasury with the level of public expenditure going to policing, which rose from £1.6 billion to £3.3 billion between 1979 and 1984. As can be seen from Figure 6.10, this was not to fund new police officers, but was a consequence of the Edmund-Davies Committee recommendations on police pay (Police Foundation and Policy Studies Institute, 1996). Increases in funding also went to finance equipment, primarily information technology (HMIC, 1998a).

An Audit Commission (1997) report on police performance showed that increased resources do not automatically improve levels of service. The Commission and the Home Office both argue that improvements in funding should lead to improvements in performance (Audit Commission, 1997: 20; Audit Commission, 1998b: 2; Home Office, 1999a: 21).

The variation in spending on police services throughout the country is also a matter of concern for the Audit Commission. In 1999/2000, expenditure on policing per head of population varied from about £256 in the City of London to £103 in West Mercia. Changes in inflation-adjusted spending ranged from a 20 per cent increase in Durham to a 7.5 per cent decrease in Warwickshire (Audit Commission, 1999).

The number of police officers has itself become a proxy measure of police performance. Routine press reports about falling numbers and calls for increased funding ignore the HMIC and Audit Commission efforts to

Figure 6.11 Trends in crime and detections per 100 police officers

Year	Police Strength	Recorded crime '000s	Recorded crimes per 100 officers	% detected	Detections per 100 officers
1980	114,543	2,520	2,200	39.5	870
1985	120,116	3,416	2,844	35.5	1,009
1990	126,777	4,364	3,442	31.6	1,088
1993	128,290	5,317	4,144	25	1,035
1996	126,901	5,034	3,967	27	1,022

Source: HMIC (1998a), Appendix 9, p. 185.

replace police officers with civilian staff wherever possible (HMIC, 1998a). The number of police officers is an inadequate measure given the large number of civilians carrying out work previously carried out by police officers. What is important, though not reported, is the change in the number of operational (i.e. those in face-to-face contact with the public) police officers over time.

Concerns about crime, investment in policing and police establishment are undoubtedly the context in which managerial reform continues in the police service.

This has a powerful impact on the individual police officer trying to make sense of his/her ethical responsibility. Consequently, if unchanged, the performance culture is likely to continue to dominate police practice. The next section suggests how we might move beyond the rational control system imposed by a contractual perspective to a new values-based and learning-oriented paradigm that may be more supportive of human rights and ethical considerations.

Towards a new paradigm

There has been substantial criticism in the management control literature about financially dominated performance measures in business firms (for example Meyer, 1994; Kaplan and Norton, 1996). Equally it would be possible to criticise public sector organisations that are dominated by too many non-financial performance measures. A critical feature of the balanced scorecard is that there needs to be balance *among* measures of different facets of performance. Kaplan and Norton suggest financial, customer, internal process, and innovation measures in their 'balanced scorecard'. Fitzgerald *et. al* (1991) suggest a balance among results (competitiveness and financial performance) and determinants (quality, flexibility, resource utilisation and innovation) for service firms.

However, in applying these concepts to policing, we would argue that there ought also to be internal congruence *between* the different measures themselves. To independently measure demand, inputs, processes and outputs and to ignore any inter-relationship between them is to produce merely a wide range of dissociated measures, rather than any holistic interpretation of organisational performance.

At present, police performance management is *unbalanced*. Maintaining spending within budgets that are historical, but which do not reflect rising demand, and in which (the Home Office formula) budgetary allocations do not reflect priorities may be necessary but is insufficient to achieve performance expectations. Productivity measures may also be necessary, but are equally insufficient to achieve the desired quality of service and meet the expectations of the public. Maintaining behaviours may be a method of management control for police managers, and this may ensure a more qualitative response, provided behaviour is not solely governed by quantitative performance measures.

Despite these conflicts, police officers typically adopt a 'coping' behaviour to meet the demands placed on them despite resource limitations and performance expectations. This is consistent with the finding by Laughlin (1996) of 'higher principles' in the caring professions in which professional behaviour may be inconsistent with available resources, productivity measures and desired (productivity) outputs. These 'higher principles' are consistent with the value-based controls described by Hofstede (1981).

However, the differential rewards for complying with ethical versus performance expectations can be expected to influence the behaviour of police officers and managers. While sanctions may result from transgression of ethical infringements, quantitative performance expectations may have a higher profile, particularly where these are reflected in individual officers' Performance and Development Reviews (PDR). The PDR can be expected to have a greater connection with promotions and transfers to favoured postings for officers deemed 'successful' as measured by the performance culture. And what support is there for police officers subscribing to their values – the 'higher principles' – rather than to the performance culture?

Three further case studies can be used to exemplify this conflict:

Case Study 1
A youth, well known to police, continues to carry out thefts of motor vehicles. Despite prosecution, he continues to repeat the offence. The resulting effect is clearly seen in section level crime figures and in the drain on police resources to deal with the youth.

Case Study 2
A gang, well known to police, carry out multiple domestic burglaries to support a drug habit. Methadone treatment programmes have been suspended by the local hospital due to financial constraints. The resulting effect is clearly seen in section level crime figures and in the drain on police resources to deal with the offences.

Case Study 3
A high profile murder investigation has consumed a substantial amount of police resources for more than 12 months, with little prospect of an early arrest. The impact on resources is being felt by other investigations.

These cases raise the problems faced by police officers and their managers, whose performance at both section level (through PIs) and individually (through the PDR) is based on rates of crime and detection. In the first two cases however, police performance is constrained by:

- the decisions made by other criminal justice agencies;
- the actions of other agencies, especially education, social services and health.

If recorded crime and costs are the principal measures of police performance, police officers may be tempted to give less regard to ethical and human rights issues, either to the suspects or to the victims of crime. There *may* be a tendency to obtain prosecutions that result in long-term imprisonment in order to avoid repeat offences by the same individual (case studies 1 and 2 above exemplify this).

On the other hand, the significant ongoing costs, where little short term result is likely (case study 3), may lead to the suspension of an investigation earlier than would otherwise be the case. This might be carried out in order to reallocate resources to those (perhaps lesser) crimes that may be easier to detect and so improve measured performance.

In relation to case study 2, one chief constable publicly commented that, had he the power, it would be more effective to reduce the rate of domestic burglary by using the police budget to fund a methadone treatment programme in his area.

What the police service needs is a way forward, and this is unlikely to be found in either performance management by multiple measures or in the creation of a single efficiency index. The problem in all police performance measures is the aggregation of dissimilar crimes with dissimilar importance, dissimilar causes, and dissimilar difficulties of detection.

If policing is to be genuinely committed to a problem-solving approach, then we need to make sense of what is happening at the incident level in each police section. We need to understand how those incidents are resolved, and develop patterns to aid in understanding. This understanding cannot come from a rational control-systems approach, in which objectives or goals remain unchallengeable. By contrast, an organisational learning perspective permits questions about purposes and expectations as much as about the resource-behaviour-outcome relationships. Through processes of organisational learning, the police might increase their knowledge and understanding about how to solve the causes of crime and disorder. Only after this understanding should aggregation take place.

Organisational learning processes already exist in the police. The debriefing of firearms and public order incidents leads to improved procedures and training. Sharing of information within and between forces takes place through training events and in regional ACPOsponsored committees. Sharing knowledge is also a major role of the National Crime and Operations Faculties.

While preventive work with other agencies and proactive, intelligence-led policing is high on the government agenda, the control paradigm has not changed. It controls the more easily measurable – like fast response and detections – and this is what gets done because of PIs and league tables. Consequently, little learning takes place because it gets squeezed out by the volume of controls and the lack of recognition of the interaction between different PIs. Learning may lead to discarding the 'myth of the magic formulae' and to a fundamental change in the whole framework of purposes, activities and targets for the police, and to more reliable judgements about police performance.

Hofstede (1981) argued that rational control systems do not learn as they aim to keep activities on target. By contrast, value-based systems are learning systems. We argue that to begin such an organisation learning process, the police service needs to move beyond the contractual state with its agency relationships to a 'policy networks' approach.

Earlier in this chapter, we briefly contrasted organisation field and policy networks with agency theory and suggested that a policy networks perspective may yield a possible solution to the problem of ambiguity. In particular, policy networks might provide the opportunity for multiple actors to reach consensus about goals, priorities and performance management systems. Such consensus would then need to be reflected in legislation that defines the role of different government agencies. There is some evidence in the more recent developments of overarching aims and objectives and best value performance indicators that these different agencies are already beginning to work together more effectively. We will return to this in Chapter 8, where we discuss operational accountabilities and oversight.

Adopting a policy network perspective in which the aim is to reach consensus about goals, priorities and performance management systems implies learning. Moving from a control-oriented paradigm to a learning paradigm that encourages risk-taking, experimentation and accepts failure as a cost of learning may lead to better knowledge and under-standing about cause-effect relationships and the best means of achieving desired results, however they may be defined.

Conclusions

Many years ago, Jones and Silverman (1984) argued that 'the inherent dominance of efficiency over effectiveness will encourage monetary value rather than social value in policing' (p. 31). A focus on the effectiveness of policing, i.e. on the outcomes for society, is missing from police performance management. The dominance of measures of public demand for services and measures of activity (behaviour) and output have overshadowed any concern with outcome measures. This is unlikely to be rectified by an efficiency index.

Effective performance management requires not only agreement between stakeholders as to purpose, but compatible expectations about police performance. Such expectations ought to be reflected in the methods of control adopted and the performance management system that is inherent in those different methods of control.

No consistency of purpose, expectation or performance management presently exists in policing. Therefore, in the control paradigm, ritual control dominates. The appearance of rationality is satisfied by the publication of statistics on expenditure, objectives, performance and crime. The public may believe that these are all inter-related. However, despite the value in any individual measures, there is an absence of rationality because of the absence of understanding about the relationship between input, behaviour, output and outcome, i.e. the lack of understanding of cause and effect relationships. The figures suggest a 'magic formula' by which resources can be converted to actions and actions into outcomes for society. Managers adopt this ritual form of control, as it provides the rationality for managerial behaviour, while legitimating the organisation with its principals.

Consequently, tensions exist between principals and police managers-as-agents and agency costs in police forces are high because of the need to satisfy multiple principals and intermediate agents, and because of the lack of attention by either HMIC or the Audit Commission to compliance costs.

Calls for the costing of police services, 2 per cent per annum efficiency savings, the introduction of best value legislation and a proposed efficiency index may serve only to further confuse the measurement of police performance by adding further variables or complexity.

The inconsistency, imprecision and ambiguity of performance management makes judgements as to performance by any of the principals, intermediate agents or police managers-as-agents virtually impossible. This also leads to ethical and human rights challenges for police officers faced with the requirements (and the rewards) that follow from subscription to the performance culture.

This chapter has proposed that the police service:

- move from the notion of contract and agency to that of a policy network in which purposes and performance management might be developed more by consensus and cooperation;

- recognise that police performance management displays the rhetoric of instrumentality and rationality, but that such rationality is a myth. Crime and PI data in their present form are inadequate to manage police performance;

- move from a rational, control-oriented paradigm to a learning-oriented paradigm, based on values or 'higher principals';

- adopt processes of organisational learning that permit questions about purposes and expectations as much as about the resource-behaviour-outcome relationships that may occur, and which can be used to understand the causes of incidents.

Left unchanged, the performance culture imposed by tight control systems will not be supportive of efforts towards human rights. The framework of values in the organisational learning paradigm is consistent with the professional clinician model. Professional autonomy that reflects discretion, diagnosis and problem solving will enable greater attention to ethics and human rights issues, and may ultimately lead to a safer, more secure society.

Further reading

The impact of performance on police ethics has not been well covered in the literature. It has tended to be treated as a separate area, hence most of the major references in this chapter are from organisation theory and accounting. A number of the chapters in Leishman, Loveday and Savage (*Core Issues in Policing*, 1995) provide a good overview of the issues of performance and policing. HMIC's report *What Price Policing?* (1998a) and the report of the Public Services Productivity Panel (*Improving Public Performance*, 2000) offer a vision of the future approaches to public service efficiency indices. As a counterbalance to this the work of Kaplan and Norton ('Using the balanced scorecard as a strategic management system', 1996) and Fitzgerald *et al.* (*Performance Measurement in Service Businesses*, 1991) provide more balanced approaches to performance measurement.

Notes

1 In this chapter, we use the term performance management to encompass how performance is measured, reported and monitored by external stakeholders.
2 Police and Magistrates' Courts Act, 1994 – see later in this chapter.
3 Although the Home Secretary's explanation (Home Office, 1999d) was that these had not reduced in importance.

4 Consistent with the government's approach, through the Crime and Disorder Act of 1998, to develop Community Safety strategies that addressed the causes of crime.
5 In response to the Macpherson Inquiry into the murder of Stephen Lawrence.

Chapter 7

Operational ethics

Introduction

In this chapter we have chosen three areas of operational policing to illustrate the complexities of 'operational ethics'. We will start by considering covert policing. Even the title of this type of policing, suggesting as it does the use of deception and less than transparent means, seems to be in conflict with 'ethical policing'. This is certainly the stance taken by a number of authors who have examined the area. We will suggest that covert policing is an essential part of policing – 'necessary in a democratic society' – and one that can be carried out ethically and in compliance with human rights.

Our second area – the policing of 'dangerousness' – is strongly connected to covert policing. This area of policing, involving the management of the risk posed by a small group of people to their fellow citizens, is an increasingly important part of policing (Neyroud, 1999). It is also one that poses serious dilemmas for police officers trying to balance the safety of the community against the rights of individuals.

Some authors have seen the third area, the use of force, as the core of policing (Bittner, 1975). Using force clearly contradicts the values of dignity and respect that the ethics of duty promote. Yet, we will argue, the effective and fair deployment of force is a cornerstone of good policing. Indeed, throughout the chapter, we will be seeking to develop the idea of compliance frameworks, which can support proper professional standards in these and other key operational areas.

Covert policing

The 1990s saw an increase in intelligence-based, 'proactive' and covert forms of policing in the UK and Europe. There was a corresponding focus on and concern about the issues raised by such activity, particularly the use of informants; intrusive surveillance; 'proactive' policing; continuing development in the nature and internationalisation of crime and the technology available to combat it.

There has been relatively little primary research on covert policing, partly because of the difficulty of research in such an area. The research that there has been has often tried to separate it into neat boxes such as 'informants' and 'electronic surveillance'. In practice, the elements of 'covert' policing are inextricably connected. Firstly, since the aim is to gather intelligence and evidence with a view to detecting or disrupting crime, very few operations can afford to rely exclusively on one approach. Indeed, good practice would strongly support the deployment of as many means as possible in order to triangulate the findings of the one. Secondly, the various methods share common features. They are covert, 'offender centred', involve deception, interference with individual rights, particularly intrusion into privacy and raise issues about the accountability and ethics of policing.

The debate on covert policing has too often separated into a dialectic between those who start from a pessimistic view of the state surveillance as advancing 'big brother' and those eager to utilize almost any technology in the aid of the 'fight against crime'. This simplistic analysis needs revising in the light of work such as that of Ericson and Haggerty (1998), who, in applying Beck's ideas to policing, have identified that the issues of privacy, trust, surveillance and risk management are intimately connected and are part of a new and complex 'contract' between the citizen and the state. The original contract has, in their view changed as society has changed. The problem, therefore, is not, as Marx (1988) has stated it, the use of undercover or the development of technology, but the 'question of *how to control the use* to which these crucial issues are put' (Garland, 1995: 4).

There are two broad areas which need to be controlled: deception and intrusion into privacy.

Deception

Marx (1988) identified that the approaches to deception divided into two broad schools: 'ethical deception' and 'deceptive ethics'. The first was supportive of deceptive means and relied either on social contract theory (citizens have granted the police the right to use such exceptional means) or utilitarianism (it is ethical as long as it is used for good and important ends). In the second approach – 'deceptive ethics' – the main arguments were drawn from the ethics of duty and, therefore, rejected any means that involved lying and rule-breaking by the state, such as may be involved in undercover and participant informant operations (Zander, 1994). Additionally, proponents of this approach raised serious concerns about the broader, symbolic implications of state deception for society (Durkheim, 1959 and Levinson, 1983). A further objection can also be raised from the ethics of virtue, in that the deployment of deception sits uneasily with qualities such as honesty.

On the other hand, those supporting 'ethical deception' have argued that deception may not only be acceptable in policing, but, as in handling a kidnap (see the case study in Chapter 3 for an example of this) essential in preserving life. There are, therefore, acceptable lies. So where are the boundaries? Skolnick (1975) has drawn a distinction between investigation, where deception can be acceptable, and interview and trial, where it cannot. A similar distinction can be seen as implicit in the way that ECHR allows interference with private life in certain circumstances, but provides no similar exceptions to the right to fair trial. Delattre (1989) suggested that whilst the morality was complex there were a number of limits – such as entrapment and exposing police and citizens to physical harm. These limits can be set out through legislative principles and internal guidelines supported by effective ethical standards.

Intrusion into privacy
A similar balancing act between conflicting rights – those of the society, the victim and the suspect – is provided by the issue of intrusion (Moore, 1983). Electronic and physical surveillance, databases and informants can all be argued to be 'intrusive' (Justice, 1998). The boundaries of ethical practice require careful consideration of the human rights principles we identified in Chapter 4 (Justice, 1998).

Marx (1988: 206), having weighed the arguments on deception and intrusion carefully, concluded that *'covert means were sometimes the best means'*. This raises the question of how a police officer can judge the 'right circumstances' in which to deploy covert means and the right means to deploy. This can best be understood by considering the means alongside the potential consequences of each approach. A useful way of setting this out is the four-way model of the consequences adopted by Marx (1988):

1 Desirable/intended
The most obvious desirable and intended consequence must be that the proposed approach is effective in detecting or preventing crime. Klockars (1985) and Brodeur (1995) have suggested that there is little evidence that covert policing is effective. In a British context Dorn, Murji

and South (1992) have questioned the use of buy and bust operations, whilst Dunnighan and Norris (1995a) have challenged the effectiveness of police use of informers, arguing, in particular, that the Audit Commission's (1993) equation of reward money with detections was fundamentally flawed.

There is certainly good reason to support Dunnighan and Norris's arguments. The Audit Commission did not properly calculate the very considerable costs of recruiting, handling and controlling informants (Hanvey 1995). However, Dunnighan and Norris, and Brodeur, in their turn, have failed to consider the very extensive evidence about the importance and effectiveness of informants:

- They are vital in detecting 'invisible' or 'consensual' offences such as drugs, corruption and vice.
- They are important in allowing investigation of secret, organised or terrorist groups.
- They are essential in the detection of robbery and volume crimes such as burglary.

Equally, there is good evidence to suggest that surveillance – both physical and electronic – is effective in investigating serious and volume crime (Eck, 1983 and Matthews, 1996), provided that its use is clearly focused (Knight, 1995). It cannot simply be a matter of effectiveness of covert policing methods – they must be more effective than the alternatives – deception and intrusion must be a last resort not the first (Marx 1988). However, certain categories of crime and criminals are clearly beyond investigation without the use of covert methods (Vahlenkamp and Hauer, 1996). This raises a balancing ethical question about any law enforcement system which can only investigate simple cases or offenders lacking the sophistication and wealth to cloak their crime in privacy (Wilson, 1978 and Clutterbuck, 1997).

The case study in Figure 7.1 illustrates a complex burglary investigation, involving an organised conspiracy. It is just such offenders who have become increasingly difficult to detect by 'conventional' means. Moreover, the variety of different methods, all covered by an authorisation trail, would provide the sort of strong corroboration that is important to secure safe and effective convictions in such cases.

2 Desirable/unintended

Brodeur (1995) suggests that there is little evidence of a deterrent effect resulting from covert policing. However, it seems likely that the ample evidence of criminal tactics being changed to avoid detection (Mativat and Tremblay, 1997) would be replicated in a proper study of the response to

Case Study 1: 'Desirable and intended' and 'Desirable and unintended'
A police crime analyst, applying geographic and crime pattern analysis techniques to the Force's crime victim database, identifies a pattern of high value burglaries in which the victims have all been on holiday at the time of the crime. Further inquiries and analysis reveal that the victims all booked their holidays direct with the company and flew out of the same airport.

The analysis of internal telephone records at the company reveal that all the victims had spoken to a single booking clerk. The Detective Chief Inspector leading the investigation decides to place the clerk under surveillance and requests research on his private telephone calls. Both the surveillance and the telephone metering data reveal that the clerk makes regular contact with a member of a known criminal gang, who have been identified through informant information as being responsible for high value burglaries.

A number of options are considered to further the investigation. Research on the forensic evidence from the previous burglaries reveals very little other than confirmation of the similar method. It is clear that only a proactive operation will lead to the detection of the burglaries. The DCI decides that the seriousness of the crime justifies a covert operation. He therefore deploys two undercover officers, posing as travellers, to book a holiday and then appear to depart from the airport. The address that the officers provide to the booking clerk is on a well known high value estate. The surveillance team then monitors the clerk's subsequent meeting with the gang member in a public house.

When the burglars turn up at the premises later that night they are detained and subsequently charged with burglary. Each stage of the operation has been documented, entered in the policy log and subject of an authorisation process separate from the investigation team.

covert methods. This, in turn, would suggest both disruption and an indication of deterrence. A more obvious desirable consequence of covert policing – particularly of electronic and physical surveillance – is the reduced reliance on confession evidence (Maguire and Norris, 1992). Furthermore, there is potentially greater managerial control over both target choice and methods, because of the internal authorisation and planning process required in covert operations. Both these advantages are well illustrated in the case study 1.

3 Undesirable/intended
There are six main areas of potentially 'undesirable' but, arguably, intended consequences:

- 'Licensing criminals': either through the use of participating informants or 'deals' to encourage cooperation.
- Police instigation of crime, in particular in 'sting' operations where the boundaries of entrapment are often unclear.
- Violations of privacy.
- Violations of trust, through the use of 'sources' who compromise their client or professional confidentiality.
- Subversions of due process, such as using electronic surveillance to gain evidence outside the interview and, therefore, the protections of the codes of practice.
- Coercion of the vulnerable and juveniles to become informants by applying pressure or inducements.

Central to these areas is the issue of accountability, since both informant handling and the 'proactive' operations concerned have been judged to sit outside an adequate formal framework of authorisation, review and inspection (Justice, 1998). Case study 2 illustrates just such a 'proactive' or 'anticipatory' operation, which, in the eyes of the European Court, stepped across the boundaries of desirable, because the police appeared to have created a crime that they had no reason to believe would have taken place without their intervention. But such breaches of rights are not inevitable risks nor necessarily unacceptable. For, given a balancing set of public interests, such as the prevention, disruption or detection of serious crime, and a proper framework of accountability, it may be acceptable for an informant to participate in crime or for a private dwelling to be entered to place a listening device.

> *Case study 2: 'Undesirable/intended*
> This case study is based on the European Court of Human Rights case of *Teixeira del Castro v. Portugal* (1998). In that case two under-cover police officers on a drugs operation approach V.S., a known drugs user, who is suspected of minor dealing in order to pay for his own habit. They hope to identify his dealer and, to this end, offer to buy heroin from him. Unaware that they are police officers, V.S. agrees to find them a supplier. V.S. mentions the name of Francisco Teixeira del Castro as being someone that might be able to find them some. V.S. does not know Teixeira del Castro's address and has to call round to F.O.'s house to get it. F.O., V.S. and the two undercover officers then drive together to Teixeira del Castro's address. The

latter comes out and the two officers offer to buy 20 grams of heroin and produce a quantity of banknotes. They are very persistent in encouraging him to get the drugs for them. Finally he agrees and, accompanied by F.O., he goes to the home of another person, J.P.O. and obtains three sachets of drugs, totalling 20 grams. Teixeira del Castro then returns with the drugs to V.S.'s house and hands them to the undercover officers, who promptly identify themselves and arrest Teixeira del Castro for dealing drugs.

At no point in the operation did the undercover officers seek any judicial or independent authorisation for their targeting of Teixeira del Castro, nor did the latter have any previous convictions or any prior intelligence against him indicating that he was dealing drugs.

The European Court held that 'the two police officers actions went beyond those of undercover agents because they instigated the offence and there is nothing to suggest that without their intervention it would have been committed. That intervention and its use in the impugned criminal proceedings meant that, right from the outset, the applicant was definitively deprived of a fair trial.'

(Case available at www.echr.coe.int)

4 Undesirable/unintended

It is more difficult to argue that this last set of consequences could ever be acceptable, including as they do:

- Harm to third parties.
- An escalation of crime through non-enforcement or covert facilitation.
- Physical or psychological harm to undercover officers or informants.
- Disorganised and conflicting law enforcement, a process magnified by internationalisation.
- Corruption, either 'outcome misconduct', 'noble cause' or venal.
- Erosion of 'trust' in society generally and confidence in the police and criminal justice system, in particular.

Covert operations that produce these consequences cannot easily be justified as 'ethical' and these are risks that managers must seek to manage out. Recognising the potential for any operation to result in harm, serious breaches of rights or corruption are a vital part of the risk assessment process that must precede any authorisation of covert operations (ACPO, 1999c).

> *Case study 3: 'Undesirable and unintended'*
> A criminal intelligence division in North Holland, a specialist CID
> unit with its own separate line control, embarked on a 'proactive'
> operation to tackle major drugs importation, using participant
> informants and controlled delivery of drugs. The operation led to an
> escalation of drugs importation, informants controlling police, police
> corruption or, at least, complicity and a considerable shock to public
> confidence in the police.
>
> The conclusion of the government-led inquiry into the scandal was
> that poor and distant management, police operations which went
> outside the legal framework and a lack of democratic oversight, had,
> together, contributed to the problems.
> (Van Traa, 1996)

However, even the Dutch parliament, confronted with the example in
case study 3, did not conclude that covert operations were, therefore, unacceptable (Van Traa, 1996). Like Marx (1988: 89–107), they recognised the
'complexity of virtue' involved in such operations, a complexity which
must necessarily encompass not only a careful consideration of the means,
but also a balancing of the potential risks against the competing public
interests. Marx emphasised the need for such a balance 'because, at their
worst, undercover tactics are so troubling and, at their best, so filled with
ethical and operational dilemmas, they must be used with extreme
caution, and only after consideration of alternative means and the cost of
taking no action' (p.206).

Ethical and human rights compliant covert policing?

The sensitivity of covert policing and the dilemmas, which Marx set out,
mean that there are strong arguments for the 'balancing of interests' to
occur within an oversight process which is independent from the decision
maker. This principle of independent, often judicial, oversight is well
established in European[1] and US law (Kleinig, 1996a). But it is not simply
external systems that are important. There were two elements to the Van
Traa committee's recommendations: better internal management and control systems and a better external framework of accountability. The Van
Traa recommendations, the Justice report *Under Surveillance* (1998)[2], the
ACPO Code on Covert Policing and the Regulation of Investigatory
Powers Act 2000[3] together provide a framework which begins to meet
these internal and external requirements.

Figure 7.1 Model of compliance with ethical and human rights principles

	Compliance requirement	*Source of compliance*
Tactical/Operational The day-to-day implementation and management of covert policing operations	• Manual of standards on covert policing • Trained staff (such as informant handlers and controllers) • Record-keeping and audit trails • Leadership, supervision and support.	• ACPO manuals of guidance on covert policing. • National Intelligence Model (ACPO, 2000b). • ACPO manuals and RIPA codes of practice.
Strategic Chief Officer management and control of covert policing	• Intelligence/covert policing strategy • Nationally agreed standards • National training standards • Controls and audit systems • Leadership	• National Intelligence and Covert Policing Standards (ACPO, 2000b and 1999c).
Legal and societal The legal and societal control systems	• Clear and comprehensive legislative provision with supporting guidance • Independent oversight/audit of applications and operations • An independent complaints system • Public consultation about the nature and extent of of covert policing • Democratic oversight of covert policing	• RIPA 2000, the Police Act 1997 and the accompanying Codes of Practice under both Acts. • The Commissioner system (RIPA) and Police Complaints system. • PCCGs set up under Section 106 Police and Criminal Evidence Act. • Parliamentary scrutiny of the Commissioner (RIPA) and the Police Authority.
Ethical principles The ethical principles which must underpin covert policing	• Respect for personal autonomy • Beneficence and non-maleficence • Justice • Responsibility • Care • Honesty • Stewardship	• As set out above in Chapter 3.

Figure 7.1 draws these issues together and sets them out in the form of a 'model of compliance' with ethical and human rights principles. At first sight the model indicates that the UK has, with the implementation of RIPA, a strong framework. However, it is important to look behind the formal framework. If we divide it into internal and external controls, the following are important qualifications.

Internal

There are six main areas of internal controls: frontline supervision; internal guidelines (ACPO, 1999c); authorisation procedures; budget; performance management; review.

Frontline supervision in the CID has been widely criticised for being tied down with its own caseload and not prepared to monitor integrity (Baldwin and Moloney, 1992; Stockdale, 1993; Dunnighan and Norris, 1995b). However, this pessimistic view does not hold good for intelligence-led work, where the nature of the work and the processes such as tasking and coordination, provide greater opportunities for managerial intervention and budgetary control. Furthermore, the ACPO intelligence model requires greater involvement from senior uniform managers in the tasking process (ACPO, 1999c). Their lack of involvement was a crucial factor in the Dutch problems.

Behind many of the criticisms of the CID, its management and its involvement in intelligence-led policing are concerns raised by studies of the culture of policing and, particularly of the detective. Detectives have been portrayed as 'entrepreneurs', granted a high degree of autonomy and showing a very proprietorial attitude to informants and their information (Ericson, 1993 and Hobbs, 1988). At the same time, it has been suggested that informal rules are more important to police officers than formal rules and that there is a gulf between management and frontline officers' cultures (Reuss-Ianni and Ianni, 1983). We have suggested in Chapter 5 that this is an unduly pessismistic view and that considerable changes in operating culture are possible and have been achieved (Brown, 1997 and Chan, 1997).

Guidelines and authorisation procedures are not always obeyed or enforced in practice (Dunnighan and Norris 1995b). But they have been shown to be an important and effective element in limiting officers' discretion (Wilson 1978, Maguire and Norris 1992). Furthermore, the change to a statutory framework is likely to be far more effective than purely internal procedures (Justice, 1998) and have a similarly professionalising effect to the changes brought about by PACE (Brown, 1997).

Performance management has been demonstrated to be both difficult and, especially where applied as a crude drive for quantity, dangerous (Dunnighan and Norris 1995b). A particular problem has been that of specifying meaningful objectives (Wright, Waymont and Gregory, 1993).

Here, a move away from a managerialist approach to a more professional, standards-based and qualititative methodology seems very overdue (see Chapter 6).

External

There are several dimensions to the external framework: legislation; democratic control; inspection and audit; judicial and Commissioner oversight; complaints procedures.

The covert surveillance legislation has been criticised for being confusing and providing a series of overlapping and conflicting regimes (Justice, 2000) and for being over-intrusive in providing powers to gather electronic data (FIPR, 2000). Furthermore, there has been no serious attempt to provide a more international framework, which, given the shift to global policing we identified in Chapter 1, is a major flaw (ICJ, 1999). However, with RIPA and its Codes and Police Act 1997, there is a reasonably comprehensive basis for 'legality' to underpin covert policing and this is a vital step towards ethical and human rights compliance.

Democratic oversight is limited by both the tripartite structure which restricts police authority intervention in 'operations', and the secrecy of those operations, with a consequent lack of information about their conduct and outputs (Jones, Newburn and Smith 1994: 27). There is scope for forces to develop the way that they share information about the nature and control of covert operations through local consultation processes.

Inspection and audit have been important in promoting good practice (Audit Commission 1993 and ACPO, 1996)

In relation to judicial and commissioner oversight: despite criticism about the potential for non-disclosure of evidence (Sharpe, 1994 and Dunnighan and Norris 1995b), the exclusion of evidence under Section 78 of the Police and Criminal Evidence Act 1984 plays a critical role in controlling police methods, as Marx (1988) has documented in a US context. The requirement for prior approval by a Commissioner in cases of serious intrusion was a major change and provided a substantial discipline in the system, alongside the very detailed application process required by the Commissioners. Last but not least, the Crown Prosecution Service has an important role in advising, reviewing and discontinuing cases, which has been underestimated (Justice 1998).

There is an additional element to the complaints procedures, which we have already suggested are not entirely satisfactory, in the form of a tribunal. The latter has been criticised for a lack of transparency and teeth (Justice, 2000).

If we take the challenges of covert policing and our analysis of the framework for compliance together, there are some grounds for optimism. The cultural change towards increasingly evidenced, audited and independently scrutinised operations is a major one for police forces seeking to move to a more intelligence-led approach. Firstly, progress has been made (Maguire and John, 1995). Secondly, energetic leadership – and ACPO has taken an energetic lead in this area – can change the whole tenor of policing (Foster 1989). Finally, as Chan (1997) has shown, police culture is not impervious to changes in the external environment. Putting these three together, it is clear that internal guidelines and policy statements are an important first step, particularly where there is clear support from the top. 'Covert Policing Standards', which the Association of Chief Police Officers developed, provided a vital step towards professional standards in covert policing. To make them work they need underpinning with effective training, a better appreciation of the skills of risk management and a more proactive, interventionist style of management, including the deployment of covert methods against their own staff. All of these, in turn, need reinforcement from legislation, external and internal monitoring systems, quality reviews, altered reward systems and better remedies for the citizen. Most, if not all, of these are in place.

Policing dangerousness

There are many issues, such as risk assessment, intelligence and intrusion into privacy which are common to both covert policing and 'policing dangerousness'. The latter is part of the increasing shift in policing from incident-driven reaction to policing 'whose objective and intent is the promotion of security and the minimisation of risk' (Johnston, 1997). Typical of this new style of policing is:

- The use of databases of previous convictions and previous reports of crime and the application of analytical techniques such as offender profiling, geographic and crime pattern analysis to identify potentially dangerous offenders and, more controversially, suspected Potentially Dangerous Offenders (PDOs) (Ericson and Haggerty, 1998).

- The use of risk-assessment tools based on actuarial calculations of the likelihood of suspects offending or reoffending and the harm they might cause (Grubin, 1998).

- Multi-agency approaches involving police, probation, social services and housing providers bound by 'protocols' on sharing information and joint management of offenders (Neyroud, 1999 and Nash, 1999).

The impetus for these developments has been partly a professional search for ways of deploying new technology and knowledge to achieve better prevention and detection of serious offences, partly a response to previous failures such as the criticisms of police handling of the Yorkshire Ripper case and partly, but probably most strongly, the need to meet the enormous public demand for security from the perceived and well-publicised threats posed by serious sex offenders and those with serious mental illness (Boateng, 1999). The legislative framework in the UK created by the Sex Offenders Act 1997 and the national debate in the USA around 'Megan's Law' (Hebenton and Morris, 1995) and in the UK about 'Sarah's Law' have added to these pressures, creating an expectation that the police and other public authorities can and will prevent serious offending.

The Human Rights Act adds to the debate in the UK by simultaneously tightening the restrictions on the police interfering with their targets' rights and imposing positive duties on the police and other public authorities to protect life and 'physical integrity' (Starmer, 1999). The European Court has, in the Osman judgement clearly laid out the boundaries of the police obligation to protect life:

> As to the scope of that obligation … it must be established to [the courts'] satisfaction that the authorities knew or ought to have known at the time of a real and immediate risk to the life of an identified individual or individuals from the criminal acts of a third party and that they failed to take measures within the scope of their powers which, judged reasonably, might have been expected to avoid that risk.
>
> (*Osman v. UK*, 1999)

The impact of *Osman* and a number of other cases involving child protection[4] is to open up police operational decision making to scrutiny and encourage the same greater emphasis on professional standards as we have already argued are essential in covert policing. The cases also identify a number of moral and operational dilemmas for the police:

- Intrusion *v.* protection: the police and other agencies are faced with having to balance the degree of intrusive activity – covert policing, probation supervision and controls on housing and employment – with the need to protect the public, including, often, the offenders themselves. This balance, which to the public and the media is seen in simple terms of minimising any risks, may necessarily involve weighing the risks of offending with the benefits that could be expected from effective treatment, which may require the offender to be trusted and treated in the community.

- Openness and honesty *v.* private and family life: the demand from the public for information about dangerous offenders, particularly sex offenders, living in the community is frequently in tension with the offender's rights to private life and the requirement for the police and other agencies to be open and honest. The debate about 'community notification' about offenders has placed police in the invidious position of guardians of the public interest and often seeming to be protecting the offender not the community.

- Cash-limited managerialism *v.* protecting rights: the first two dilemmas have to be seen against the background of a dominant managerialist approach to public service, which provides a cash limited budget and constraining performance indicators. The latter make no mention of or allowance for the preventive activities involved in policing dangerousness or for the costs of balancing and protecting rights. This tension between managerialism and human rights is one we have dealt within Chapter 6.

As with the dilemmas posed by covert policing, policing dangerousness requires a balancing exercise. The framework within which this takes place in the UK is much less formal than that for covert policing. Aside from the Sex Offenders Act, most of the tools such as multi-agency protocols and risk assessment methodologies are not covered by legislation and are frequently not standard (Grubin, 1999). The compliance framework appears substantially less robust. The police are accountable for their judgements through judicial review, civil cases and human rights challenges and will need to continue to develop defensible standards of decision making, risk assessment, training and partnership working. Yet again, increased professional standards appear to be the best route to 'ethical' policing.

Police and the use of force

With the police use of force we turn, for the last of our three operational areas, to an area of policing which, like covert policing, starts with a difficult moral dilemma. For, although the use of force has been described as the core of policing (Bittner, 1975), it has also been argued, like deception, to be intrinsically wrong, because it conflicts with the ethics of duty, and specifically with the dignity and personal autonomy of its subject (Kleinig, 1996a). However, from a different standpoint, it is 'morally obligatory' (Miller, Blackeler and Alexandra, 1997) for police officers to protect life – another aspect of respect for personal autonomy – and preserve order, which often require the potential for force or its actual deployment. This dilemma of duties leads to a utilitarian balance requiring that the 'exercise of force needs to be ethically justified by the ends that it realises' (Miller, Blackeler and Alexandra, 1997: 83) or to be, as the text of Article 2 of ECHR states, 'absolutely necessary'.

Another argument about the use of force in policing has concentrated not on the intrinsic wrong but on the inevitability of police misconduct. Waddington (1999: 158) has argued that police officers operate 'beyond the limits of respectability' and 'repeatedly at the invitational edges of corruption'. In the case of force, the problems of defining that 'edge' mean that police are often in danger of crossing it. At one extreme this frequently exposes police officers to the accusation of assault, at the other police officers abuse their authority and misuse force against vulnerable, power-less or minority communities. Whether we accept Waddington's argument about the inevitability of abuse or not, we must accept the 'enormous responsibility – and corresponding opportunity for abuse – on individual members of the police force' (Miller, Blackeler and Alexandra, 1997: 83).

The key both to Kleinig's dilemma and Waddington's criminological perspective is justification. There are four issues which we want to explore in this section: the grounds for use of force; the use of excessive force or force as misconduct; the use of inappropriate force; making the use of force ethically and human rights compliant.

Kleinig's approach to justification places the use of force into the 'contractual' relationship between police and citizen. In return for the authority to use force, police must justify its use. Kleinig suggested some of the key dimensions of justification were as follows:

- Intention: must always be 'honest' and not improper, such as 'for punishment' or 'contempt of cop' (Waddington, 1999).
- Seemliness: must not be 'inhuman or degrading'. This links well with the case law under Article 3 of ECHR.[5]
- Proportionality: must be made strictly necessary by the subject's conduct or circumstances.
- Minimisation: must be the least force necessary and, therefore, officers must be trained in a range of options and capable of deploying them appropriately.
- Practicability: must be relevant to the legitimate aims the officer is seeking to accomplish, not a substitute for something else.

Kleinig's approach, which matches many of the principles underlying ECHR, begins to define the boundaries of 'acceptable' force. These principles are only one part of the justification for force. Three other elements are also important: the methods of force deployed; the competence of the officer; the strategic and legal/societal framework (Miller, Blackeler and Alexandra, 1997).

Firstly, we must deal with the methods deployed and the concept of the 'continuum of force' or a range of options available to the officer, ranging

Figure 7.2 The continuum of force

Non violent options	Tactical communication
Use of physical force only	Physical force: ranging from restraint techniques up to defensive strikes
Non-lethal options	Handcuffs CS spray Batons Use of dogs
Less-lethal options	Plastic baton rounds
Lethal options	Firearms

Note: This table has been derived from the main options available to UK officers.

from 'tactical communication' through to lethal options. This has become a key doctrine in the training and equipping of both US and UK police officers. The approach starts from the presumptions of 'minimisation' and 'practicability'. Following these, the use of force, to meet the test of absolute necessity, must first of all be actively avoided, through the use of 'tactical communication' or 'conflict management' techniques (Geller and Toch, 1996). Only once these have failed or are clearly inappropriate, can the officer justify the use of physical force or defensive or offensive weapons (see Figure 7.2).

The continuum approach in Figure 7.2 is hierachical or linear. It has been supplemented in the UK by a 'conflict resolution' model because of the implicit presumptions to escalation that the hierarchy of options can create. Hence, the linear model might suggest that a lower option, such as tactical communication is necessarily followed, when unsuccessful, by a more forceful one, such as the deployment of CS spray. The UK model (ACPO, 2000a) places use of force decisions in the context of the offender's behaviour, information about the offender and the response to the officer's tactics. This approach, in turn, recognises the importance of research that has challenged the 'split-second-syndrome' (Fyfe, 1989), in which it was argued that officers do not have the opportunity for deliberative actions because assaults happen suddenly and without warning. Scharf and Binder (1983) demonstrated that this was rarely the case, particularly in the more serious cases, and that there were five distinct phases to an encounter: anticipation; entry and initial confrontation; dialogue and in-formation exchange; final frame decision; and aftermath. To this Geller and Scott (1992) have added a sixth phase after dialogue in which there was an opportunity for the deployment of non-lethal options. This analysis of violent situations is vital. The phased development, which is illustrated in Figure 7.3, reinforces the importance of the careful and considered conflict resolution model. It emphasises the necessity of officer training in both tactics and decision making and it offers the chance for supervisors to intervene, particularly in the early stages (Reiss, 1980).

Given that force must be justified and that a 'complex' continuum approach seems to fit the requirements of 'absolute necessity', we need next to consider whether force that is not 'absolutely necessary' should be

Case study 4: Justification in use of force
A 25-year-old man has broken up with his girlfriend. He is depressed and suicidal. Having taken a mixture of drugs and alcohol, he decides to commit suicide and to do so by getting shot by the police. He steals a car in the early hours of the morning and drives it to a remote location, where he knocks on a farmhouse door and tells them to call the police because he has got a gun and is ready to shoot anyone who comes by. The police control room dispatches units [*anticipation*].

An unarmed police unit arrives first at the scene and is directed by the senior officer in the control room to keep a safe distance and report [*entry and initial confrontation*]. They tell the control room that the man is standing in the road holding a pistol. He appears drunk or drugged and is shouting to them to come and see whether he is serious. The unarmed unit is joined by two armed units, who are authorised to arm up by the senior officer, because of the clear and confirmed threats from the man. The armed units are instructed to contain the scene and negotiate, whilst the senior officer sought to get further units, including a dog unit, to the scene.

One of the armed officers begins to talk to the man [*dialogue and information exchange*], who makes it clear that he is prepared to shoot someone and starts levelling his weapon in the direction of the officers and then lifting it to his shoulder again. The dog unit arrives and the lead armed officer, who has assumed command of the scene, decides to try and disarm the man using the dog. The dog is sent in [*deployment of the non-lethal option*] and approaches the man, who turns and shoots at the dog, injuring it, and then turns his weapon towards the handler. One of the armed officers, who believes that the man is preparing to shoot at the dog officer, fires once [*final frame decision*] and the man begins to fall. The two armed officers move forward rapidly and disarm the man and then begin to administer first aid [*aftermath*]. The man is quickly removed to hospital with serious, but not fatal, injuries.

treated as misconduct. This has been the traditional, discipline approach to the use of force. However, there are strong arguments for suggesting that this is neither practical nor productive. Whilst the boundaries of justification can be drawn, they are still not precise, but are contingent on the circumstances confronting the officer, the officer's own skills and equipment and the organisational context (Waddington, 1999). Geller and Toch (1996) argued that the 'training, supervision and other support systems in police departments currently are oriented in too many jurisdictions toward avoiding scandalous, liability-generating, or grossly substandard uses of force by officers' (p.295). Instead, they suggested, professional standards in the use of force will only be obtained if there is more concentration on the coaching and development of officers whose use of force is 'reasonable' rather than 'highly skilled'.

The conflict resolution model requires considerable skill from the officer in assessing situations, communication and, ultimately, if required, in deploying force minimally. It seems likely, given this complexity, that a great many cases of use of force may still be 'appropriate', but are not 'highly skilled', nor misconduct. This argues for a shift in the traditional control systems towards a more professional model, encouraging high skills through accreditation, mentoring, peer coaching and supervisor monitoring (Geller and Toch, 1996). This has the additional advantage of shifting the benchmark of 'use of force' away from the narrow 'edge' of justification towards the 'highly skilled' (Klockars, 1996) or 'commendable' use of force (Geller and Toch, 1996).

Developing a more professional model to deal with use of force leads on naturally to the development of a compliance model. There have been a number of approaches to this in the USA and in the UK. We have chosen to use three of these: a key judgment from the US Supreme Court, to which the Police Foundation presented expert testimony (Kleinig, 1996a); Geller and Toch's (1996) seminal collection of papers presented following the Rodney King beating; the work of the Association of Chief Police Officers in the UK to audit policing and 'Keeping the Peace' policies in advance of the implementation of the Human Rights Act 1998 (ACPO, 1999a and 2000a). It is important to distinguish, as we have done in describing the model for covert policing, between the tactical/operational level, strategic and legal/societal. The last two provide, respectively, the management framework and the context of use of force.

There are clear, common themes between the three approaches set out in Figure 7.3:

- **Tactical/operational:** accredited training, standards in tactics and equipment which minimise the use of force and the injury to officers and record-keeping.
- **Strategic:** Clear policy framework and standards emphasising

Figure 7.3 Approaches to the use of force

	United States Supreme Court[1]	Geller and Toch (1996)	Association of Chief Police Officers[2]
Tactical and Operational	• Kind of weapons available to the officer • Operational tactics on deployment, engagement and warnings • Training and recertification	• Conflict management training • Intervention training of officers to reduce 'bystanderism' • Coaching and mentoring of officers to make them 'highly skilled'	• Training which is accredited and maintained in conflict management and each specific weapon tactic deployed • A manual of operational tactics • Individual record-making
Strategic	• Reporting and review systems for the use of force • A clear framework of policy designed to minimise the use of force	• An 'officer safety' initiative • A departmental style that emphasises 'community policing' and 'peace-keeping' rather than 'crime-fighting' • A clear policy emphasising minimal use of force • A national reporting system on the use of force	• An 'officer safety' strategy[3] • Monitoring of use of force locally and nationally • Review of tactics and equipment in the light of monitoring • A clear command and control structure, with a cadre of trained commanders
Societal/legal	• A legal framework that emphasises 'reasonableness' in balancing the 'intrusion' of force with the necessity of action	• Public consultation about the use of force, including sharing • Effective complaints system with an independent element	• 'Legality'; a clear framework of accessible and available law governing the use of force • 'Remedy' for the citizen, including an independent remedy in serious cases

Notes
[1] The United States Supreme Court judgement in the case of *Tennessee v. Garner* (1985) set out the main parameters for US Police use of force (Kleinig, 1996a).
[2] This is based on the ACPO Human Rights Toolkit (ACPO, 1999a), which is discussed at greater length in Chapter 11 and the ACPO 'Keeping the Peace' Manual (ACPO, 2000a).
[3] This point is also emphasised by the report of the HMIC into Officer Safety (HMIC, 1997).

minimum use of force and officer safety, effective monitoring and review processes.

- **Societal/legal:** Effective consultation, complaints systems and a clear legal framework.

The additional element that Geller and Toch (1996) emphasise is the personal responsibility on each officer and manager to ensure professional standards are maintained, both personally and by their colleagues. 'Bystanderism' or the passive observance of unjustified or inappropriate force being exercised is not only unacceptable, but a clear breach of the moral obligation to protect life (Article 2 of ECHR) and preserve physical integrity of others (Article 8). Culturally, this is challenging, because, as we have seen in Chapter 5, loyalty to colleagues is a strong value in policing.

Conclusions: towards ethics in operational policing

The three areas of covert policing, policing dangerousness and use of force each present complex moral balances for policing between the ethics of duty, utility and virtue. The first and last areas have been fertile areas for scandal and misconduct in the last quarter of the twentieth century. Policing dangerousness has the potential to provide equally fertile ground in the twenty-first century.

What we have sought to describe in this chapter is not merely the difficulties and dilemmas facing policing – there is a rich academic literature devoted to this – but also the shape of 'compliance'. In this argument 'compliance' is standard, individual, organisational and societal, achieved by a professional model of policing operating in an effective legal and democratic framework. In chapter 11 we shall return to this theme of compliance to look at how this sort of model can be applied effectively and dynamically across the police service and policing generally.

Further reading

On covert policing the outstanding book is Gary Marx's study of surveillance in America (*Undercover: Police Surveillance in America*, 1988). The Justice report *Under Surveillance* (1998) is the best treatment of covert policing and human rights compliance. Policing dangerousness has not yet been well studied. Nash (*Probation, Police and Protecting the Public*, 1999) provides a good treatment of the mechanics of police and probation officers managing offenders. Ericson and Haggerty (*Policing the Risk Society*, 1998) provide the best theoretical study of the police and risk management. There are a number of detailed research studies of risk assessment and the related processes published by the Home Office (such as Grubin, *Sex*

Offending against Children: understanding the risk, 1998). Geller and Toch (*Police Violence: understanding and controlling police abuse of force*, 1996) is a comprehensive treatment of the police use of force. The report of HMIC on *Officer Safety* (1997) is an important study of the potential compliance framework. From a different perspective, the Police Complaints Authority report on batons (*Striking a Balance: the police use of new batons*, 1998) provides critical treatment of police responses to officer safety and use of force.

Notes

1 Cases such as *Amann v Switzerland* (1999), *Huvig v France, Kruslin v France* and *Kopp v Switzerland* for instance.
2 One of the authors was a member of the Justice Working Group that advised on the report.
3 We shall refer to this Act as RIPA.
4 Cases of *Z. and others v UK* and *T.P. and K.M. v UK* (1999).
5 Cases such as *Ribitsch v Austria* (1995).

Chapter 8

Organisational ethics

Introduction

In this second part of the book we have gradually developed our ideas about the police officer as a 'professional' and the type of performance and operational frameworks that are needed for policing to be ethically and human rights compliant. In Chapter 5 we were primarily concerned with the individual officer as a professional operating within the organisational culture. In the following chapter we then examined the implications of the managerialist performance model. We concluded that this model was not wholly congruent with the much broader balancing act that the new world of ethical, human rights policing was likely to demand. We then moved to examine three areas of operational policing and ask whether it was possible to see a professional, compliant approach emerging. We concluded that such an approach was emergent, to different degrees, in each of the areas.

The debate in Part 2 has, therefore, thus far, provided a picture of emerging change. However, just as we suggested above that policing faced choices between different futures, it is very evident that there are important choices for the police organisation in its relationship with its environment and stakeholders. As we have started to suggest, in discussing performance and operations, these choices have a vital part to play in developing ethical policing and establishing the authority and legitimacy of policing.

In this chapter therefore we move on to consider the organisation in its context and the issue of operational accountability. We will continue the argument begun in Chapter 6 and develop it further by considering the implications of the Patten report – the most authoritative examination of police accountability in the UK since the Royal Commission in 1962 –

together with the developments post-Macpherson. Patten (1999) suggested a new framework of governance that acknowledged the pluralism of policing and society. The soul searching after Macpherson has encouraged police forces to look for more effective and more transparent mechanisms for consultation and oversight and has been accompanied by a radical review of the approach to complaints against police (KPMG, 2000 and Liberty, 2000). We will seek to draw these together with the principles of human rights and suggest the outlines of a new accountability framework.

The second part of the chapter will move from accountability in general to consider the complaints systems and corruption and misconduct. Here, after setting out some of the main aspects of corruption, we examine the challenges to the organisation presented by the need to tackle corruption. We will suggest that human rights compliance requires a high degree of independence in the investigation of the most serious complaints, whilst the continuing development of ethical policing needs an 'intelligent watchdog' which is a key part of the learning cycle rather than one driven by managerialist conceptions.

The third part of the chapter deals with the increasingly important issue of policing diversity. It has been argued that 'diversity' is a natural consequence of a postmodern world (Johnston, 2000). Simple, homogeneous, geographic communities have given way to the complex and plural. The aftershocks of Macpherson (1999) have forced UK police forces to confront the impact of their policies on minority communities and have encouraged some to seek new ways to engage with communities and new approaches to the oversight and transparency of controversial operational areas. We will explore the implications of these new approaches by examining the issue of stop and search powers.

'Operational accountability'

The accountability of operational policing has been a source of major debate, particularly in the UK, as we noted above in our review of the literature on police ethics in Chapter 1. We will look at a number of aspects of that debate, including the different types and dimensions of accountability. Given the powers that the police are entrusted with and the key societal functions they perform, accountability is a crucial aspect of the ethics of policing. It is fundamental to the achievement of 'consent' and 'legitimacy' and the maintenance of 'authority' (Morgan, 1989 and MacLaughlin, 1991). Margaret Simey described its importance thus:

> Accountability is not about control but about responsibility for the way in which control is exercised. The distinction is a fine one but of

fundamental importance. In other words, accountability is not an administrative tool but a moral principle ... of those to whom responsibility is given an account of their stewardship shall be required.

(Simey, 1985)

Stewardship we have already defined as one of the key principles for policing. Patten subdivided Simey's 'account' into the 'subordinate and obedient sense' and the 'explanatory and cooperative sense', bringing together two distinct ethical tracks. The first, 'obedience' – to the community's needs and the law – is clearly linked to the ethics of duty. The second, 'explanation and cooperation', which emphasise the partnership between police and the community, seem more closely aligned with the ethics of care. These two elements of accountability can be seen as complementary, because explanation and cooperation might be argued to be a vital part of meeting the needs of the community.

They can, equally, be seen as in collision. For, we have suggested, in discussing the professional clinician model of policing, 'empowerment' and autonomy in decision making are vital. There is a significant tension between empowerment, in the form of decentralised decision-making and top-down models of accountability, particularly in the form of an increasingly detailed managerialist performance model, which seem to fit better with 'obedience'.

Accountability is, therefore, not a simple concept or one that has attracted easy consensus. Johnston (2000) highlighted three dominant perspectives on accountability: managerialist; radical; interactionist. Taking these in turn:

The managerialist view on accountability

This view, which we have covered in detail in Chapter 6, sees the police as a business with stakeholders and 'customers' to whom account is given through performance against indicators. Preferred methods of accountability include a simple index of efficiency, league tables which can be easily compared and the budget. Accountability is, therefore, input and output based.

The radical view on accountability

The radical view, of which Simey and Jefferson and Grimshaw (1984) were key proponents, stressed democratic control over police policy, priorities and decision-making, including the exercise of discretion. This approach, in which process rather than inputs and outputs is dominant, suffers from a limited conception of 'democracy'. For it assumes an elected body that is truly representative and enjoys wide participation. It therefore

Figure 8.1 The dimensions of police accountability in the UK

Type of accountability	Main elements	Subordinate or obedient?	Explanation or cooperation?
Democratic	Police Authority and Home Secretary	Strongest relationship of obedience to central gov't (Patten, 1999 and Johnston, 2000), despite Police Authority role growing with policing plans and best value (Jones and Newburn, 1997)	Police Authority role in consultation on policing plans and in linking with crime and disorder partnerships.
Legal	Primary legislation, particularly PACE, RIPA, judicial review and civil claims (see Chapter 10)	Legal accountability growing with the increase in quantity and range of legislation. Removal of legal immunity (*Osman v UK*) to increase exposure of police to challenge in operational areas	Duties to cooperate with local partners under the Crime and Disorder Act (Section 17) are untested for their impact on police policy making.
Performance	Performance indicators (see Chapter 6)	Main elements of the framework are centrally imposed.	As we set out in Chapter 6, the PIs rarely provide an effective explanation of performance and some discourage partnership.
Financial	Cash-limited budget	Major element of central control (see Chapter 6)	The complexity and lack of transparency in the funding formlae make understanding the links between national funding and local delivery opaque (see Chapter 6)
Audit/ Inspection	HMIC force and thematic inspections and Audit Commission national studies and local audits.	Major element of central control, providing standards and link to the appointment of chief officers	Published HMIC reports provide some important qualitative data on performance and professional standards.

Contract	The Policing Plan, Crime and Disorder Plan and Best Value and and Performance Plan.	The chief constable has a key involvement in the drafting of the plans and must have 'regard' to them. Plans have to include national priorities. The overlapping of plans adds a layer of confusion.	Important part of a 'contract' with the community over priorities (Savage and Charman, 1995).
Consultation and participation	Police Consultative Committee and local beat and parish meetings	No formal mandate to influence policy.	An important element in local dialogue, but with variable impact (Morgan and Newburn, 1997 and Brown, 1997).
Partnership	Crime and Disorder Partnerships, Drug Action Teams, Area Child Protection Committees, amongst many	Police control of the information and coercive powers frequently means that police are the dominant partners (Neyroud, 1992).	Much of the partnership working happens outside public scrutiny and there are few formal mechanisms for enforcement of obligations between partners.
Independent oversight	• Police complaints system • Lay visitors	• Lack of public confidence in the independence of the investigation (Macpherson, 1999 and Liberty, 2000).	• Lack of transparency and disclosure of investigating officers reports (Macpherson, 1999). • Lay visitors adding some transparency to custody (Morgan and Newburn, 1997).
Internal	• Force values • Force policies and procedures • Internal audit and controls • Performance and development reviews of individual officers	These systems and the leadership which supports them are a vital part of the link between operational policing and the Policing Plan.	Lack of lay involvement and transparency restricts the ability of internal controls to impact public confidence, particularly amongst disaffected groups.

conveniently ignores the history of 'majority tyranny' and political corruption that blighted many US police forces before Vollmer and Wilson's new professionalism. Furthermore, the important PSI studies of democracy in policing have shown that 'democracy' is better defined through a broad set of parameters, including equity, service delivery, responsiveness, transparent information and participation (Jones, Newburn and Smith, 1994 and Jones and Newburn, 1997).

The interactionists' view on accountability

On the other hand, interactionists like Manning (1977), have been sceptical of any attempts to hold operational policing to account, whether by internal rules or external mechanisms. Such scepticism has been confounded by changes such as those brought about by the introduction of the Police and Criminal Evidence Act (Brown, 1998). The key lesson from the interactionist studies is the importance of change working with the grain of police values and professional practice.

The three approaches cannot easily be compared directly, because not only do they share very different conceptions of accountability, but also they each rely on very different methods to secure that accountability. Yet, in truth, police are accountable through a wide variety of mechanisms, which reflect elements of all three approaches. We summarise the scope, plurality and effectiveness of these systems in Figure 8.1.

The number of different strands of accountability has sometimes been held up by police officers – particularly senior police officers – as evidence that the service is 'very accountable'. However, the quantity of accountability should not be confused with the quality. What becomes clear from the analysis in Figure 8.1 is that the quality of accountability is significantly skewed. The majority of the most powerful, subordinating processes are between central government and the local police force. Progressively, as we move to local and then very local levels, the processes become more and more explanatory. This begins to question whether the police are able to be 'responsive' to local needs or are left merely seeking to explain national priorities and the limits of their resources to tackle local problems.

The added complication is that not only have the police limited resources and limited scope for manoeuvre within the centralised framework, but also the development of a 'diverse, loosely coupled network of public, commercial, voluntary policing agencies' (Loader, 1999: 9) means that the police are no longer the only or in some areas the main policing agency. Furthermore, the growth of national, transnational and international policing through national agencies, bilateral agreements and multi-national agencies has added several distinct and not altogether well integrated elements (Johnston, 2000). The new complexity of accountability is represented in Figure 8.2.

Figure 8.2 Levels of policing and their relationship to government[1]

Type of policing	Relationship to national government	Level
International	Above government	Super-macro
Transnational and cross border	Between governments	Macro
National policing	By government	Macro
Local police force	By government	Meso
Council run community safety, patrols and wardens	Through government	Meso
Private policing	Beyond government	Micro
Citizen	Below government	Micro

[1]This table has been developed and expanded from Loader (1999).

It is evident from Figure 8.2 that there are growing areas at the macro and micro levels of policing where the existing tripartite structure, which we described in Chapter 6, does not assist. MacLaughlin (1991) has argued that to maintain 'consent' and 'legitimacy' and, therefore, authority, the police must able to explain and justify their actions. With so much policing outside the direct responsibility of police and with relatively weak mechanisms at the local level, where the service is actually delivered, there appears to be a serious problem for police in explaining and justifying their performance in crucial areas such as crime and disorder, where so many other agencies and individuals play a role. To the problems already identified we must also add the fact that none of the existing mechanisms at local level have proved particularly effective in involving groups, such as the minority ethnic communities, who are disaffected with their policing (Bowling, 1999).

Patten (1999), who was seeking to find a solution to the policing of a divided community, one part of which had largely lost confidence in its police force, outlined proposals which go some way to addressing the local accountability deficit. In the place of the largely explanatory police – community consultative groups, which Scarman (1982) and the Police and Criminal Evidence Act bequeathed to the mainland, Patten suggested a new local body, the District Policing Partnership Board. Their relationship with the Police Authority is represented in Figure 8.3.

Patten's model provides a much more powerful local body, with elected and independent members 'representative of the district in terms of religion, gender, age and cultural background' (Patten, 1999: 34). The ability to call for reports and hold local commanders to account recognises the shift to devolved operational policing that we discussed in Chapter 6. Moreover, Patten encouraged both the Police Board and the District Board

Figure 8.3   The Patten model of accountability (Patten, 1999)

Long-term (societal)	Government/Devolved Assembly	• Broad principles • Broad objectives
Medium-term (strategic)	Police Board	• 3–5 year strategy • Monitoring performance, including operations • Appointment of Chief Officers • Coordination of its work with other policing agencies • Link to the Ombudsman
Medium-term (strategic)	Chief Constable	• Annual Plan • Operational responsibility
Short-term (operational)	District Policing Partnership Board	• Receiving reports and reviewing local performance • Contributing to the strategy • Annual report • Power to raise additional rate which can be used for public or private sector resources

to promote partnership and, by providing a power to levy at the district level, gave the local body some muscle to lever such relationships.

It must be said, however, that Patten's model is still heavily focused on the public police. The DPPB (District Policing Partnership Board) has only limited scope to leverage other partners and agencies by encouragement and the local levy. Patten's model falls short of the 'active regulation' approach that Loader (1999) and Blair (1999) argued is essential to cope with the plural policing economy. Loader would have a much more dramatic shift to a body that was capable of regulating each aspect of that economy and of contracting with both public and private bodies for policing services. This model has the attraction of introducing competition within the 'market', but presents a very significant challenge in preserving the integrity and independence of action that human rights demand of police authorities. Equally Blair's model, which would give the police the central role in 'active regulation' of other public and private providers, has been criticised by Loader for putting a service provider into the role of regulator. However, given Patten's framework of more active Police Board and DPPB control, Blair's model might move the police towards the more genuinely 'enabling' role, which we outlined in Chapter 2. Such a move would be timely given that government under the banner of 'neighbourhood renewal', has accelerated the development of citizen, estate and parish patrols (Travis, 2000).

If Patten, possibly supplemented by an element of Blair and Loader's active regulation, offers better accountability at local level, he does not solve the transnational and international relationships. These are no longer simply a matter of bilateral exchanges as Patten seems to suggest, but are increasingly key operational partnerships. Inevitably, this is drawing the supranational bodies such as the EC into the law and order arena. The debate on accountability at this level has only just started, but is becoming increasingly urgent.

Patten, Blair, Loader and new mechanisms at transnational and international level offer the potential for a new distributed policy network and system of accountability. Given less emphasis on a forest of performance indicators and more emphasis on the quality of outcomes and clarity of explanation, they may begin to move police accountability towards a better balance of duty, care and virtue and away from what we have described as 'ritualism'. However, these changes on their own will not be enough to meet the challenge of human rights. In handling critical incidents, developing policy to meet disaffected groups and in investigations of police misconduct and complaints new approaches and greater independence are required. Explanation needs to move from ritual to transparency and understanding.

Two important changes to meet these challenges have emerged from the shadow of Macpherson. The first, 'Independent Advisory Groups' have been developed largely to meet the urgent need to restore confidence in police amongst the minority ethnic communities. The second, independent investigation and management of police complaints, was a recommendation of Macpherson, but had already become essential after the European Court of Human Rights raised serious doubts about the independence of the Police Complaints Authority. Furthermore, alongside Patten, an independent Ombudsman had already been created in N. Ireland.

Independent Advisory Groups (IAGs) have the potential to open up police policy making and operational decision making. Developing models involve the creation of a group of 'lay advisors', including the most trenchant critics of current police performance, and their participation in policy making, performance monitoring, critical incident management and review.[2] It may be too early to assess the outcomes, but the immediate implications in the area of race relations is a shift away from the decide-and-defend approach which the previous models of accountability encouraged.

This new world of transparency and openness is not without its own hurdles. If the aim, as Bowling suggests, is to be 'appropriate, relevant and accessible' (Bowling, 1999: xxi), this begs the question of 'to whom?' Being open and developing lay oversight does not solve the problem of conflicting advice, restricted resources, plural communities and, therefore,

153

plural priorities. For example a large rural force with a small minority ethnic community will face the need to balance the numerically small needs of those minority communities alongside the very different needs of the rural areas. This local balancing act is likely to be complicated in the UK by the perceived minority status of rural issues in central government policy making and in the funding formula (see above Chapter 6).

Nevertheless, greater lay participation does offer the police a better avenue to articulate and test their judgements. By bringing lay involvement in close to the decision makers it enhances the personal responsibility for decisions that the complex framework we have described above tends to disperse and dissipate (Kleinig, 1996a). However, as Goldstein (1977) has argued, being responsive (in this case to lay advice) should not be confused with being accountable. Lay advice can suggest and encourage a course of action and demand an explanation, but a police manager has to balance the needs of various interests, decide, evidence that decision and then be held accountable. It is in this latter stage that the better local mechanisms suggested by Patten link with the development of lay involvement by providing a forum for the balancing of interests to be tested and debated.

Complaints, misconduct and corruption

Bowling's support for lay involvement also extended to the investigation and management of complaints against the police. The lack of confidence in the independence and transparency of the UK system was a major criticism in the Macpherson report (1999). We will, therefore, examine the case for independent investigation of complaints, assess two of the proposed models and then look at the implications for tackling misconduct and corruption in the service.

The Macpherson report recommended independent investigation of serious complaints and concluded that 'investigation of police officers by their own or another police service is widely regarded as unjust and does not inspire public confidence' (Recommendation 58). This has been supported by a number of studies (Liberty, 2000), which suggest that:

- Complainants and the public do not trust a system in which the police investigate their own complaints, even where there is an independent oversight body such as the Police Complaints Authority.

- The unique position of the police as the possessors of coercive power and as gatekeepers to the criminal justice system meant that there was a strong presumption towards an independent system, which was reinforced by the 'comradeship' value of police culture.

- Although there were problems with cost and staffing, with securing police co-operation with independent investigators and with the problems of dual investigation,[3] these were outweighed by the benefits of independence for public confidence in the police.

However, although independent models of investigation may be desirable and an essential requirement of human rights,[4] they are not without their problems. Perhaps the most important one for our proposed professional model is that the police do not have control or early access to the learning from complaints. We have already identified in Chapter 7, in considering use of force, that such learning is vital to assist police to develop really skilled practice. This link between complaint and learning has been a significant problem with the Police Complaints Authority's approach. Whilst there has been an attempt to achieve this by publishing studies of more general problems such as the use of batons or CS (Police Complaints Authority, 1998 and 1999), the secrecy and culture of non-disclosure encouraged by a focus on maximising discipline findings has inhibited fast-time learning. The very strength of an independent model – its real and perceived separation from the police – may, therefore also be one of its Achilles' heels, unless in building the new organisation some form of partnership can be forged between it and those within the service committed to ethical approaches.

The importance of such a learning partnership has been emphasised by Newburn's research on the nature and origins of police misconduct and corruption (Newburn, 1999). He concluded by arguing 'the central facet of any anti-corruption strategy should be an emphasis on "ethical policing" ' (p.47). That emphasis needed to include a commitment to the sort of principles we outlined in Chapter 3, a clear code of ethics, to which we return in Chapter 10, and visible and open leadership. Newburn's analysis suggested that this was more important than the contribution that an independent process of investigating corruption could make. The latter might increase public confidence in the complaints system, but only the former was more likely to impact on the cause of those complaints in the first place. To understand this argument we need to review the main lessons of the research on corruption.

One of the reasons why ethical policing is so central to the control of corruption is because, as Kleinig (1996a) has stated, corruption is at heart an ethical problem. Precise definitions are difficult, but they all revolve around the means, ends and motivation for acts which may not necessarily involve misconduct, but which are intended to further personal, professional or organisational advantage rather than the public good (Newburn, 1999). Hence, corrupt behaviour ranges from the out and out avaricious to the type of 'noble cause' corruption that Rose argued was a major feature of the 'old regime' (Rose, 1996). The key to the damage that corruption causes lies in this perversion of the integrity and equity of the service delivered and the consequent diminution in the moral authority and legitimacy of the police and criminal justice system.

Corruption is not a new problem. Indeed, Newburn's review showed that it was pervasive (in all societies), continuing and present at all levels of the service. A series of major corruption enquiries has challenged the standard police defence to corruption (and racism) in which it is argued that the problem is confined to a 'few bad apples'.[5] Instead, the lessons of these enquiries are that it is systemic not individual. In support of this approach Sherman (1974) outlined what he felt were the causal factors, dividing them into 'constant' and 'variable':

Constant factors included:
- Discretion
- Low managerial visibility
- Low public visibility
- Peer group secrecy
- Managerial secrecy or a sharing of the peer group values
- Status problems of the police role
- Association with law breakers and organised criminals

Variable factors included:
- Community structure
- Organisational characteristics, such as the level of bureaucracy, quality of leadership, sub-cultures and ethical framework
- Legal opportunities for corruption such as the policing of vice
- Corruption controls, both internal and external
- Social organisation of the corruption itself
- 'Moral cynicism'

Sherman's analysis suggests that modelling corruption requires the same disciplines as modelling crime. Ekblom's model of crime reduction (Ekblom, 1999) may, therefore, be just as validly applied to corruption as to community safety. Ekblom's model divides crime into three distinct, but interconnected parts: the distil factors; the proximal factors or the event; the reinforcing factors. Thus we can take Sherman's analysis and overlay Ekblom's model (Figure 8.4). If we then follow Ekblom's approach to preventing crime, we must seek to 'to *intervene* to *disrupt* the conjunction of criminal opportunity, either by changing the situational or offender-related precursors in advance of the criminal event, or by preventing them coming together' (Ekblom, 1999: 10). Combining this with Newburn's analysis of the main controls on corruption we can see the outlines of a broad anti-corruption strategy.

Figure 8.4   Ekblom's model of community safety and crime reduction applied to Sherman's analysis of the causal factors in police corruption

Distil	Proximal	Reinforcing
• Discretion • Peer group and managerial secrecy • Status of the police role • Community structure • Organisational characteristics	• Low managerial visibility • Low pulic visibility • Association with law breakers • Legal opportunities for corruption through vice policing	• [Lack of] effective corruption controls • Social organisation of the corruption • 'Moral cynicism'

Ekblom (1999) divided the main approaches to prevention into the offender-oriented and the situational. We have slightly adapted his terminology, but taking the first group, we can discern five types of intervention that might be relevant.

Early or remedial intervention

This includes recruiting standards, screening and training and developing the recruit's understanding and confidence in handling ethics. The open discussion of ethics and corruption was seen as vital by Goldstein (1975).

Supplying officers with resources to avoid corruption

This is principally through *cognitive* or *social skills enhancement*: firstly, by placing a strong emphasis on ethics and professional standards in long-term personal development and by encouraging mentoring; secondly, by creating an open organisation in which the reporting of concerns about professional standards is regarded as part of an individual's vocation, not an exceptional act of 'whistleblowing' (HMIC, 1999a). Punch (1994) suggested that this might be enhanced by access to an 'ethical commission', which might include lay involvement, when officers are faced with difficult dilemmas. Thirdly, a key aspect is 'positive symbolic leadership' (Punch, 1994 and HMIC, 1999a) which sends a clear message about the standards and values of the chief officers.

Changing current life circumstances

Changing life circumstances of officers by raising their professional self image (a morally ambivalent self image was seen by Sherman (1974) as a major factor in the slippery slope to corruption), by reducing conflict or compromising positions by officer safety programmes and 'community policing' approaches.

Restricting resources for corruption

Restricting resources for corruption by clear standards and active management on areas such as information security and informant management, which are major areas of compromise.

Deterrence and discouragement

This comes about by increasing the risk or effort and reducing the perceived benefits of corruption. It is clearly important to deploy the same intelligence-led approach to detecting and disrupting corruption as is applied to all major crime. Certain types of policing and certain situations are substantially more corruption-prone than others and, as such, may warrant the use of proactive methods, including focused integrity testing. This might involve targeted covert operations, checks on bank balances and drug testing. However, the enthusiasm for such methods (HMIC, 1999a) needs to be firmly tempered by the requirements of human rights[6] and a concern for the adverse impact such approaches can have on the trust in the organisation (Marx, 1988). It is important that the whole organisation knows the overall strategy, that it is properly resourced and works to clear guidelines, so that enthusiasm for tackling corruption does not spill over itself into corrupt practice against internal suspects (Punch, 1994).

Situational intervention

On the *situational* side, the focus of preventive methods is variously on:

- *Improving internal security* through better, clearer and properly monitored policies.
- *Design of the wider environment* – placing enhanced controls and checking systems in high risk areas such as covert policing as we have suggested in Chapter 7 and providing clear rules through an ethical code and guidance on ethical decision making (see Chapter 10).
- Facilitating the presence, motivation and capability of *corruption preventers* in their exercise:
  - of *'self-defence'* by encouraging public complaints. This is one area where the independent investigation agency would be advantageous. However, the impetus for such a campaign would be better as a joint initiative by police forces and the agency.
  - and in the wider environment of formal or informal *surveillance* or *social control* by encouraging all staff to report concerns and encouraging supervisors and managers to adopt 'active' and interventionist styles (HMIC, 1999a).

Using Ekblom and Newburn in this way emphasises that corruption needs a strategic approach, based on careful analysis, rather than a piecemeal response to individual problems. It confirms that independent investigations are only a small part of such a strategy, which must, in fact, be driven by the leaders of the service and actively owned by their staff (HMIC, 1999a). Less optimistically, the parallel with crime reduction also supports Newburn's rather gloomy conclusion that 'rarely is it the case that such problems are "solved". Rather, the more realistic aim is usually to attempt to minimise the impact of the problem' (Newburn, 1999: 47). Waddington (1999), equally pessimistic, regarded corruption as an inevitable accompaniment to policing, but also emphasised the wider societal factors that contribute. He stressed, in particular, the need for police to have adequate powers to do their job so as to avoid the temptation for 'institutionalised rule breaking and rule bending' (Waddington, 1999). He might also have added the need for a political climate that does not overemphasise a bean counting culture that can add performance corruption to the long list of potential misdemeanours. For corruption is a product of the community, the culture and the organisation and can only be prevented by all three working in partnership.

Policing diversity

One aspect of that 'partnership' which has come under critical scrutiny has been the relationship between police and minority communities. This is, as Newburn has said of corruption, a universal, pervasive and continuing problem. We will concentrate here on this aspect of policing diversity, on the ethical implications of Macpherson and how they might be applied to one area of operational policing – stop and search. We will seek to draw some conclusions for the wider policing of diversity at the end of this section.

The policing of racial diversity has been brought into stark focus in the UK by Macpherson (1999). The latter concluded his inquiry report by saying that:

> The need to re-establish trust between minority ethnic communities and the police is paramount ... seeking to achieve trust and confidence through a demonstration of fairness will not in itself be sufficient. It must be accompanied by a vigorous pursuit of openness and accountability.
>
> (Paras 46.31–32)

Macpherson's comments came nearly 20 years after the Scarman report (1982) in which the police had been absolved from 'deliberate bias or prejudice' in policy and senior management direction. For Scarman this absence of witting racism was enough to rebut the charge of 'institutional racism'. In the intervening years, as Bowling (1999) has documented, the evidence of wilful acts and omissions was mounting, from both official and unofficial sources. Examples include the failure to prevent or investigate racial attacks properly, hostile or unsupportive treatment of victims, a failure to involve the community effectively in tackling racial attacks and policing against ethnic minority communities through the disproportionate use of stop-search and arrest powers.

To Bowling's list of 'service delivery' criticisms could be added an equally long list of internal issues. Broadly, these divide into four areas: the failure to recruit ethnic minority staff; the poor record on retention and promotion of those who have been recruited; the 'white' working culture of the organisation; direct and indirect discrimination (Holdaway, 1996). Many of these issues were raised by Scarman (1982) and yet were still major areas of comment in the HMIC thematics on diversity and race in the late 1990s (HMIC, 1997b and 1998b).

It is against this background that Macpherson's verdict of 'institutional racism' by the police needs to be seen. In an important section of the inquiry report he linked this to four factors:

- The actual investigation into Stephen Lawrence's death, including the treatment of Stephen's family, the victim and witness support, family liaison, the failure of many officers involved in the case to recognise the racial motivation of the crime and the general lack of urgency.
- The national disparity in the 'stop and search' figures.
- The national 'under-reporting' of 'racial incidents', which Macpherson linked to the inadequate police response and consequent lack of confidence in victims to report.
- The failures in police training in racism awareness and race relations identified in *Winning the Race* (HMIC, 1997b and 1998b).

(Macpherson, 1999: Para. 6.45).

None of these issues was unique to the case of Stephen Lawrence, nor indeed to a UK context (Chan, 1997). What was different was the way that Macpherson and his team interpreted these issues and the template of 'institutional racism' against which they judged them:

The collective failure of an organisation to provide an appropriate and professional service to people because of their colour, culture, or ethnic origin. It can be seen or detected in processes, attitudes, and behaviour which amount to discrimination through unwitting prejudice, ignorance, thoughtlessness and racist stereotyping which disadvantage minority ethnic people.

(Para. 6.34).

Thus, the police organisation was 'collectively failing", despite the acknowledged commitment of many individual officers to anti-racism. This is an important shift from Scarman's position, which accepted that the absence of deliberate bias by the majority of officers was sufficient to justify their actions. In this sense they had discharged their negative obligation not to discriminate. The key change between this and Macpherson's approach was that the basis of the judgement had moved from the avowed intent of officers and managers to the outcomes of their policies and operational practice. This shift is doubly significant in the light of human rights. For, as we have seen in Chapter 4, ECHR places not only negative but also positive obligations on public authorities to avoid discrimination. The impact of these twin obligations are neatly summed up in Article 2 of the International Convention on the Elimination of all forms of Racial Discrimination, which requires positive steps to be taken to 'amend, recind or nullify' such discriminatory practices. As Bowling (1999) has argued, in this new world post-Macpherson, to be anti-racist means 'organisations must *actively* work towards eliminating racism' (p. *xxi*).

The 'ethical policing' of diversity requires, therefore, active leadership, intent that is turned into practice, analysis of results and a preparedness to change rather than defend discriminatory outcomes, all of which needs to be done, as Macpherson suggested, in the 'open'. This is, however, not a straightforward challenge as the issue of stop and search can illustrate. The disproportionate use of stop and search powers against visible ethnic minority citizens was a major issue in Scarman's inquiry (Scarman, 1982), was identified by Home Office research as a problem (Willis, 1983) and was flagged up in Macpherson (1999) as a major source of concern. It also figures as a major debate in the US (Kleinig, 1996b), where the history of race relations and the problem of race-based discrimination has been even more chequered.

A number of initiatives had already started before Macpherson. In the 'Tottenham' experiment (NACRO, 1997) a local project sought to improve the way in which stop and search powers were used and enhance community confidence. The experiment deployed four principal strategies: a leaflet for those stopped which explained police powers and citizen rights; the removal of stop and search from individual and team 'league tables'; improved targeting of suspects; senior management commitment. The experiment produced a very limited impact on the outcomes of stop and search but did identify shortfalls in knowledge, skills and training amongst officers. Post-Macpherson a series of pilots were started to improve on Tottenham and these were evaluated by the Police and Reducing Crime Unit (Quinton and Bland, 1999). At the same time the Metropolitan Police undertook a major research project (Fitzgerald, 1999). We have summarised the main lessons of these pilots and projects and the legislative changes brought about by the Human Rights Act and the amendments to the Race Relations Act (which have brought operational policing within its scope) in Figure 8.5.

The arguments under strengths, weaknesses and opportunities are broadly consistent with, respectively, utility, duty and care. The balance between them points, as Fitzgerald and Quinton and Bland begin to set out, towards an emerging model of ethical practice:

- *Tactical and operational*: just as we saw in our discussion of the use of force in Chapter 7, the evidence suggests that raising professional standards of those whose performance is in the middle – between misconduct and excellence – is critical. Training, mentoring and monitoring

Figure 8.5   SWOT analysis of the use of Stop and Search powers

Strengths	*Weakness*
• Up to 12% of all arrests result from stop and search powers, particularly those for going equipped and offensive weapons (Fitzgerald, 1999). • Many more result in important intelligence which contributes to detection (Fitzgerald, 1999). • Targeted policing, using stop and search, has been identified as an effective policing strategy (Home Office, 1998a).	• Disproportionate use against black and Asian young men (Brown, 1997). • Impact on police-community relations (Holdaway, 1996). • Poor professional skills (NACRO, 1997 and Fitzgerald, 1999). • Evidence of unlawful use of the powers to gather intelligence or for 'social control' (Fitzgerald, 1999). • Searches in public have a wider impact on those who observe police actions (Fitzgerald, 1999).
Opportunities	*Threats*
• To achieve more effective use of police resources by better targeting and professional skills (Quinton and Bland, 1999). • Better training and situational skills (NACRO, 1997, Quinton and Bland, 1999 and Fitzgerald, 1999). • Better supervision of discretion (Quinton and Bland, 1999). • To deal with some minor street crimes, such as personal possession of cannabis by informal action and no arrest (Fitzgerald, 1999). • Lay and community involvement in the strategy, target setting and evaluation of stop and search (Quinton and Bland, 1999 and Fitzgerald, 1999).	• Article 14 challenges under the Human Rights Act. • Breach of the provisions of the Race Relations Act. • Insecurity and low morale of officers concerned about complaints, civil claims and HRA actions reducing the effectiveness of stop and search (Fitzgerald, 1999). • Criminalising young black and Asian men (Fitzgerald, 1999).

of performance are vital. Improved recording of the stops and the evidenced decisions that supported the exercise of the powers, more involved supervision and clear interventions where there are problems are also important.

- *Strategic*: A strategy for the use of stop and search which is based on the evidence from the research such as Fitzgerald's and which emphasises effective practice. Clear and visible leadership, which makes active use of the monitoring data.

- *Societal and legal*: It is vital that the strategy, its deployment and its effects are shared, debated and disseminated to the community through lay advisory groups and Community Safety partnerships. If, as Fitzgerald argued, stop and search is an important part of reducing street crimes that cause substantial fear in the community, then the tactic should be a major part of the 'contract' in the Community Safety plans. If the more active model of accountability proposed by Patten were to be implemented then, it should figure high on the local board's agenda.

A final, vital, part of continuing to develop ethical stop and search is the performance framework which is used to evaluate it, how that framework is used and by whom. Fitzgerald has demonstrated just how corrosive quantitative approaches have been in encouraging numbers of stops without any proper control over their legality, the way in which discretion was being exercised, the discriminatory outcome or the community's concerns. We have, therefore, to find a better-balanced framework, which reflects all of these and which can be used in partnership with the community. In Chapter 6 we touched on the balanced scorecard model developed by Kaplan and Norton (1996) and Fitzgerald *et al.* (1991) and stressed the advantages of such models because they were capable of linking and balancing a wide range of measures, quantitative and qualitative, internal and external. A similar model needs to be fashioned for stop and search and used as the 'tin-opener' with which to drive the professional and ethical use of the powers. Such an approach, which acknowledges the situational, organisational and community aspects of this and many other aspects of policing would meet Norris and Norris' test for developing 'good policing':

Because police practice cannot be fully determined in advance by prescriptive policies or training manuals we would argue that there can be no ideal practice. Good practice cannot be simply taught or replicated but it can be developed. This development is a personal achievement that in part depends on the repeated application of

skills and situated judgement. But it also depends on a morally informed professional self-awareness, which is most likely to be
fostered by a critical community of practitioners

(Norris and Norris, 1993: 219).

In talking of a 'morally informed professionalism' we need in concluding
this section to recognise that at the heart of the debate about stop and
search and the wider debate about policing diversity is an important
change to one of policing's long held assumptions, that good policing is
about delivering the same service to everyone. This version of the
principle of equity has been held up to defend colour-blind and gender
non-specific policies, which to a large degree the Scarman approach
supported. Development of race and equal opportunities in policing have
been slow and, at times, uncertain (Brown, 1997). Implicit in the
Macpherson report (in such areas as family liaison) and increasingly
explicit in the debate about race and equal opportunities after it is a shift
from the 'golden rule' – treat others as you would be treated yourself – to
what has been described as the 'platinum rule' – treat others as they want
to be treated. This shift has far-reaching implications for the future
policing of diversity and, indeed, equal opportunities and runs in parallel
to the debate about the rights of victims in the criminal justice system. For,
against this background, how do the police faced with a victim's demand
for further investigation balance that need against the next victim or
potential victim without continuously failing? To some extent this is an
inevitable dilemma of human rights, where a cacophony of demand has
somehow to be turned into harmony. We have suggested above that the
police will only be able to do this if they secure wider community
involvement in that process.

Conclusions

This chapter brings us to the end of Part 2 of the book. We have sought
here to show the dilemmas of ethical policing through the use of examples
and by focusing on four areas: the personal ethics of the professional
officer; the ethics of performance; the ethical problems presented by three
critical operational areas; the ethics of the organisation, its accountability
and the ways it addresses two of its most pressing problems, corruption
and the policing of diversity.

What has emerged from these chapters is:

* A professional model that stresses evidence-based practice.
* A performance framework that must move towards values and away
from managerialism.

- A compliance framework that links individual practice to leadership and community oversight.
- New approaches to accountability that open up the organisation to lay and outside scrutiny.

In the final part of the book we will explore how these four areas can be developed and ethical policing progressed through managing people, managing the organisation's values and judgements and managing compliance effectively.

Further reading

On accountability the Patten report (1999) is, as we have suggested in the text, an important contribution. The series of books produced by the Policy Studies Institute as a result of a long-running research project on accountability in policing provide a comprehensive treatment of 'democracy in policing' (Jones, Newburn and Smith, 1994) and the impact of the Police and Magistrates Court Act (*Policing After the Act*, Jones and Newburn, 1997). Johnston (*Policing Britain*, 2000) devotes much of his central chapters to the subject and provides a strong treatment of the local–national, public–private dimensions.

On corruption, Newburn's succinct Home Office research paper (*Understanding and Preventing Police Corruption*, 1999) gives an excellent summary of the existing literature. Barker and Carter (*Police Deviance*, 1986) give a more detailed treatment to individual aspects of the problem. The various international reports on the corruption scandals, which are well summarised in Newburn, are important not least for the first-hand accounts of the problems. Rose (*In the Name of the Law*, 1996) provides good coverage of corruption and the criminal justice process.

On diversity, Macpherson (*Report of the Stephen Lawrence Inquiry*, 1999) is essential reading, particularly Chapter 6 and the conclusions. Bowling's (1999) book *Violent Racism* is an outstanding account of the development of policy, the police response and the impact on police legitimacy. The second edition has a preface that contextualises the issue to Macpherson and the developments since Macpherson. Holdaway (*The Racialisation of British Policing*, 1996) offers broader treatments of race and policing. Kleinig (*Handled with Discretion*, 1996b) has three essays debating race and discretion in a US context. Fitzgerald (*Final Report into Stop and Search*, 1999) and the shorter Home Office report (Quinton and Bland, 1999) bring stop and search up to date: Fitzgerald's paper is a particularly strong treatment of the complexity of the issue and the solutions. Brown's article in Francis, Davies and Jupp (*Policing Futures*, 1997) puts race into the wider context of equal opportunities.

Notes

1 The comments in this section are derived from experience in West Mercia.

2 This refers to criminal investigations being conducted at the same time as the complaints investigation.

3 There have been a number of cases such as *Govell v UK* (1999) and *Aksoy v Turkey* (1996) where the European Court has been very firm about the need for an independent remedy where there are concerns about the exercise of powers which interfere with rights.

4 For instance, Wood (1997).

5 Cases such as *Teixeira del Castro v. Portugal* (1998) suggest that 'random integrity testing', which has been suggested in some anti-corruption strategies may well offend the principles of Article 6 of ECHR. As Marx (1988) has argued, it is vital for investigators to distinguish between the questions 'is this person corruptible?' and 'is he corrupt?' Only the second suggests that there is some prior justification for interference with rights.

PART 3

In Part 2 we developed our discussion of police ethics and human rights by examining four areas of ethics in some detail – personal, performance, operational and organizational. In this final part of the book we turn to some of the ways in which the approach we have defined in Part 2 – the new professionalism of ethically and human rights compliant policing within a new, open contract with the community – might be achieved.

This part of the book is divided into three parts:

- Human resource solutions: in particular, recruitment, training and the development of the 'learning organization' in policing.
- Decision making, codes and control systems: we examine the case for an ethical code and the links with decision making.
- Auditing compliance: we look at how police might use policy audit to develop ethical compliance and build a virtuous cycle of learning and good practice.

In the conclusion, in Chapter 12, we then seek to draw the threads of the book together, look back at the themes that have emerged from our discussion and present our final vision of the future of policing, ethics and human rights

Chapter 9

Human resource solutions

Introduction

We discussed in Chapter 8 the subjects of early or remedial intervention, supplying officers with resources to avoid corruption, and recruitment of ethnic minority officers. A professional model that stresses evidence-based practice was recommended with performance and development reviews, appraisals and a performance framework moving towards values and away from 'managerialism'. We are going to build on all these subjects in this chapter and share with the reader the consequences of neglecting these processes in law enforcement organisations. It is of paramount importance, in establishing ethical behaviour in police officers, to commence that process from the very start of the recruitment system. The elementary step is to identify which competencies, skills, abilities and values we require in a police officer.

We shall be using a case study from a police department in the USA[1] to help illustrate our discussion:

> *The Rampart study*
> In late 1997 and early 1998, three incidents occurred in which Los Angeles police officers were identified as suspects in serious criminal activity:
>
> * The incidents began when three suspects robbed a Los Angeles Bank of America. The investigation into that robbery led to the arrest of a police officer and his girlfriend, an employee of the bank.
> * The second incident involved the false imprisonment and beating of a handcuffed arrestee at the Rampart substation by a serving

police officer. Two other officers were present and acquiesced to the beating.

- The third incident involved the theft of three kilograms of cocaine from the Department's Property Division that led to the arrest of another officer.

A thorough investigation into all the incidents, through a Board of Inquiry, demonstrated that many of these officers allowed their personal integrity to erode and their activities certainly had a contagious effect on other staff. The scandal devastated the police department's relationship with the public and threatened the integrity of the entire criminal justice system.

The Board of Inquiry reported: 'Distrust, cynicism, fear of the police, and an erosion of community law and order are the inevitable result of a law enforcement agency whose ethics and integrity have become suspect.'

The Board in the Rampart Inquiry categorised its recommendations into several areas:

- Testing and screening of police officer candidates
- Personnel practices
- Personnel investigations and management of risk
- Corruption investigations
- Operational controls
- Anti-corruption inspections and audits
- Ethics and integrity training
- Job-specific training

We also will use the headings from the inquiry in this chapter. Of course, the police in the USA have not been the only law enforcement organisation to suffer corruption. There have been many examples in the UK and Australia. Chan (1997) reports in detail on the findings of the Rusher report which relate to changes in police recruitment, selection and training.

Recruitment of police officers

The type of person law enforcement agencies do not want is fairly clear. More difficult is to define those traits police recruiters are searching for.

However, we could do worse than utilise the extensive research carried out by management expert Stephen Covey. Covey (1989) studied all of the 'success literature' in the USA going back to 1776 and discovered an interesting fact. It was only in the last fifty years that a phenomenon he described as the 'personality ethic' had become established as the criterion for success. Prior to that period, success had been achieved through the 'character ethic'. The personality ethic focused on attributes such as superficiality, image consciousness, skills, techniques and quick fixes through human and public relations techniques and positive mental attitude. The character ethic however, featured integrity, humility, fidelity, temperance, courage, justice, patience, industry, simplicity and modesty. Is there any question about which of these models we would like to see in police recruits?

Another aspect apparently lacking in current police recruitment and selection campaigns is the recognition of emotional intelligence (or EQ – emotional quotient) in potential recruits as opposed to the more usual search for IQ (intelligence quotient). The dimension of EQ takes account of reason and intuition; two traits most people would welcome in police officers. Goleman (1996) describes emotional intelligence as the abilities of self-control, zeal, persistence, and the ability to motivate oneself. Goleman tells us that there are widespread exceptions to the rule that IQ predicts success; at best IQ contributes about 20 per cent to the factors that determine life success, which leaves about 80 per cent to other forces. In view of these heavily weighted factors, we cannot neglect emotional intelligence in our search for ideal recruits. Continuing with this theme, Cooper and Sawaf (1996) attribute as little as 4 per cent of real world success to IQ and therefore the remainder may be related to other forms of intelligence. In their book entitled *Executive EQ*, they recommend the value of the four cornerstones of emotional intelligence: emotional alchemy, emotional literacy, emotional depth and emotional fitness.

Testing and screening of police officer candidates

In our case study, pre-employment information on four of the profiled officers raised serious issues regarding their employment with the Police Department. The serious issues were that the recruits had criminal records, problems in managing their personal finances, drug addiction and histories of violent behaviour. The Police Department recommended that they should be disqualified but despite this the officers were employed by the Personnel Department. As a result, the Board of Inquiry recommended recruit screening and visits to home addresses to establish suitability. The lesson here is that there must be clear criteria in the recruitment and selection of police officers; but first the criteria must be established. We shall discuss several approaches on recruitment and selection: the 'competency' approach, the 'values' based approach, and various selection criteria and issues. We shall also discuss how the police recruit is 'socialised' into the police organisation and whether this changes his or her values and attitudes. We will then examine the 'reflective practitioner' approach, and finally police training.

During the last decade it has been established that the profession of policing is competency based – that is, it is a practical activity and therefore should be judged against performance criteria rather than academic standards. Competency is defined by Klemp (1980) as 'an underlying characteristic of a person which results in effective and/or superior performance in a job'. Exley (2000) says that personal competencies are all about the individual: self-awareness, self-regulation and motivation; ability to understand emotions and how they affect others; knowing self-strength and limitations; having the self-confidence to commit and achieve; ability to take the initiative and be optimistic about the outcome; ability to cope with new things. Also, social skills determine how the individual relates to others: ability to sense other people's feelings and read the mood of a group; to inspire and build relationships; to work in teams; to listen and communicate. The competencies Exley lists are attributes the police service should be seeking in recruits, but she says that competencies needed by recruits may differ from job to job. The list also looks similar to that proposed by Goleman (1996) on emotional intelligence which we set out above.

Competencies used at recruitment cannot predict the applicant's success in the job or how long they intend to stay with the organisation. It was also suggested that strict adherence to the competencies might result in an organisation filled with 'clones' who did not have the ability to innovate or create. Keenan (2000), who has completed 20 years of research into this area, tells us that 43 per cent of organisations in the UK say they are using competencies in their recruiting. He favours the competency approach to recruitment 'with its focus on observable behaviours and its use of systematic methods to identify these, [which] would appear to be the most appropriate way at present, to specify the abilities needed to do the job. Competency-based interviewing techniques are also used to elicit competencies reliably and accurately'. Doerner and Nowell (1999) describe a new approach called 'B-PAD'. This is a behavioural-personnel assessment selection process whereby the candidate submits to several videotaped scenarios which are then assessed by trained assessors. In the study, B-PAD was found to be free from bias in the selection process. The system appears to be similar to selection assessment centres.

The police service in the UK has adopted a competency-based approach towards recruitment, selection and promotion. All ranks in the service have a list of competencies against which they are assessed for their 'performance and development review' (PDR) and annual appraisal. Then there are competency-based assessment centres for recruitment, selection for specialist posts and promotion.

PDR – essential competencies
- Professional and ethical standards
- Communication
- Self-motivation
- Decision making
- Creativity and innovation

PDR – other competencies (apply to some role/ranks, and not others)
- Leadership
- Managing and developing staff
- Operational planning
- Strategic thinking

Within the competency framework, detailed behaviour statements or performance criteria are also published and we will return to the subject of the PDR later in this chapter. In adopting the competency-based approach several principles should be observed:[2]

- Competencies need to be relevant to the job
- The recruitment process must relate to these competencies (i.e. advertisement, short-listing and interview process)
- Careful consideration needs to be given to the planning of questions and the scoring process to ensure that all candidates are given the same opportunity to demonstrate their competencies and that the evidence is recorded in the event of a challenge
- Interviewing should require the candidate to evidence their possession of the competence by giving an example of how they used their experience to deal with an issue. Hypothetical questions should be avoided.

The competency-based approach towards recruiting and selection has many advantages. According to Wood and Payne (1998) these are:

- Experience with a range of organisations show they improve accuracy in assessing people's suitability or potential for different jobs.
- They facilitate a closer match between a person's skills and interests and the demands of the job.
- They help prevent interviewers and assessors from making 'snap' judgements about people or from judging them on characteristics that are irrelevant to the job in question.

- They can be used to underpin and structure the full range of assessment techniques – application forms, interviews, tests, assessment centres and appraisal ratings.
- By disaggregating an individual's profile into specific skills and characteristics, development plans can more accurately be targeted to areas of true development need.

An alternative method of recruiting to that of the competency route is that of values-based recruitment. Core values of an organisation are the 'essential and enduring tenets of an organisation. A small set of timeless guiding principles … core values have intrinsic value to those inside the organisation' (Collins and Porras, 1996). Most police forces in the UK have compiled statements of their organisation's values, and the ACPO Statement of Common Purpose and Values is discussed in Chapter 10. The two techniques, competency-based and values-based, are not mutually exclusive – many of the competencies reflect organisational values. The key for ethical policing is their emphasis on consistent standards and an ability to define the acceptable and the excellent.

Various selection criteria and issues

Psychological testing
Most law enforcement agencies currently use psychological tests to inform the selection process and to add dimension to assessment and development centres. Whilst psychological testing is an appropriate tool, it is sometimes used in an inappropriate manner. Such tests can be used to assess a potential recruit's overall mental fitness but it is doubtful whether they can be used to judge if the person will make a 'good police officer'. As the earlier case study evidenced, it is also important to decide if the tests are going to 'weed in' or 'weed out' candidates and the requisite criteria.

Educational standards of police officers
Society in general is changing and police officers must reflect their society. Police officers must be able to understand information they receive and operate complex machinery such as computers, radios and drive automobiles in an exemplary fashion. In setting exacting personal and professional standards for recruits into the police service, there is a question as to the educational standards required. The USA has demanded high educational standards for law enforcement officers. A study carried out in the USA (Kakar, 1998) indicated that police officers with higher levels of education report themselves performing better than others with lower levels of education. This trend continued throughout the officers' careers. An earlier study conducted in the USA by the Police Executive Research Forum (PERF) in 1989 found that overall the results suggested

that police executives found more advantages of college education for police officers than disadvantages. The research was able to identify a substantial number of indicators where the recruits with 'college education' (or graduates) performed better than those without higher education qualifications

The situation in the UK on educational standards of police officers will be rectified by the introduction of common minimum standards, a new competency framework and standards protected by a national training strategy; the Police National Training Organisation (NTO). (See HMIC, 1999c) The implications of these developments will be discussed later in this chapter.

Gender issues

There is also a changing structure in society that has resulted in an increase in dual income families and growing proportions of women and ethnic minority workers. According to research in the USA (Peters, 1997), women managers are better at relationships, planning, goal setting and follow through; all attributes we would welcome in police officers. Contemporary research (Scott, 1999 and Westmarland, 1999) revealed that women, who are a minority of the workforce in the UK police service, are breaking through the 'glass ceiling' and reaching the highest levels of management. This appears to be a general trend as in 1987 only 5 per cent of managers in England and Wales were women; today 52 per cent of management is female, 18 per cent being in senior management (Tucker, 2000). The police service has some way to go to catch up with these ratios, but there is slow and steady progress.

Diversity issues

The police service has learned some hard lessons from the omission of recruitment and selection of ethnic minority police officers. Following the report by Sir William Macpherson into the racist murder of Stephen Lawrence (Macpherson, 1999), the Home Secretary set up a task force to progress an action plan aimed at stamping out 'institutional racism' in the UK police service. This included setting targets for individual police forces to achieve in the recruitment of ethnic minority recruits. In practice, the recruitment of police officers often does not reflect the ethnic diversity which exists in the population of the country. 'Reflecting the diversity' is not merely a simple matter of statistics, but a strong message about the inclusiveness of the police service.

Training

According to Norris (1992), the 'reflective practitioner' is:

> Someone who makes conscious and systematic attempts to act in the light of the values of the service and to judge, and improve, the quality of professional action in the light of those values.

Such a person would therefore appear to be the type of recruit the police service should be seeking. In addition, Berkley and Giles (1999) state that a reflective practitioner is one who:

- Requires a deeper understanding of the knowledge involved.
- Sees and responds to everyday practices through a reflective lens.
- Wants to live out 'caring' as everyday practice.
- Needs to create time to enable reflectivity to take place and for new ideas to emerge.
- Values the concept of empowerment.
- Is acutely aware of the characteristics of interpersonal encounters.
- Is ready to apply experience into manageable reality.
- Has an awareness of their own values and the need to live them out.
- Has the ability to critically analyse practice.
- Encourages team discussion and team decisions.
- Is willing to discuss experiences and account for action.
- Is not afraid to say 'I do not know'.

In the early 1990s the training of police recruits in England and Wales was fundamentally changed. According to Beckley (1990) the police service in England and Wales were looking for supermen and superwomen to be law enforcement officers. They were seeking applicants who could use discretion and who had skills and abilities under the following headings:

Desired character traits:

- Able to monitor personal performance.
- Good communication and relationship with others.
- Investigative skills.
- Job and general knowledge.
- Decision making, problem solving and planning skills.
- Practical effectiveness.
- Clear and succinct written reports.

Poole (1985) and Norris (1992) recognised the importance of experiential learning and that most police officers only learn by actually doing the job. However, there was not general agreement on how to support continuous professional development through reflection on experience. Reflective practice has not taken a very firm hold in police training. However, good reflective practice is not entirely extinct. Research on developing reflective practice in training relating to the use of police firearms concluded:

The principles ... include a positive motivational context, learner activity, interaction with others and a well-structured knowledge base. For the tutors on the National Firearms Instructors Course this list provides a workable and succinct rationale for what the course is trying to achieve with students in the promotion of experiential learning through reflective practice.

(Clarke and Francis-Smythe, 2000)

The training of police recruits in the UK underwent significant change again in 1998 to its present centralised Probationer Training Programme (PTP) with an improved structure and direction and emphasis on aims, objectives and measurable learning outcomes. The aim of the new programme was to provide probationers with the necessary skills, knowledge, attitudes and understanding to enable them to fulfil their future roles as police officers. However, in the learning objectives, there is no mention of police ethics or professional behaviour. Those aspects would be left to the training modules of the programme delivered within the probationers' police force under the guidance of a tutor constable. The tutor constable is a fundamentally important member of the training process as he or she will provide the all-important 'on the job' training and should be a good role model. In assessing the effectiveness of this arrangement, it is only necessary to say that there is not a national standard for the training of tutor constables nor are they given any training in police ethics or educationally sound guidance on vocational assessments. It is therefore difficult to see how standards of ethical and professional behaviour can be inculcated into the recruit through training.

Discretion

The use of discretion has clear links to police ethics when one considers the decision making of a police officer to exercise or fail to exercise a statutory police power when dealing with a citizen. Use of police powers to stop, search, arrest, detain, interrogate and seize property clearly indicate the possible infringements of civil liberties and human rights. It would therefore seem vital to train officers in the use of their considerable powers – a training that we have suggested above needs to be part formal input, part personal development, but the key grounding has to be in the early months of induction.

Socialisation of police recruits into the police service

A longitudinal study was conducted in Australia (Christie, Petrie and Timmins, 1996) to investigate the effects of education and training and early role socialisation upon police recruit attitudes. The research found that the university education programme, which the induction included, had little effect on attitudes but the subsequent exposure to the police academy and the job of policing had a more substantial and deliberalising effect. In another study (Hvingtoft-Foster, 1993), occupation socialisation of police probationers was examined in the UK. It was found that formal and informal training had a profound effect as a socialising force. This fact was re-iterated in a similar study (Lawrie, 1995), carried out in Kent and London, which also revealed that gender and the ethos of the particular police force are important issues in the socialisation of probationers.

In an American study (Little, 1990), it was proposed that there were five ways in which police recruits receive occupational socialisation:

- Formal educational curriculum
- Practical training
- Anecdotal information from instructors
- Anecdotes told amongst themselves
- Anecdotes transmitted to instructors for verification

Studies carried out in Australia, by Bryett and Harrison (1993) pose a three-stage transition process in the socialisation of police recruits into the organisation:

- Events preceding the actual joining
- Joining or becoming part of the organisation
- 'Full member status'

There are many factors to consider in all of the stages, many of which relate to the recruit's prior knowledge or relationship with the police service through family or local connections – the 'generational progression' into the police service. This phenomenon is very strong in police forces in the UK and USA. Baron and Greenberg (1990) state that 'these individuals provide a wealth of information (not all of it accurate) which strongly colours the perceptions and expectations of all recruits'.

As we have seen (Rampart case study), there is a necessity for complex joining procedures for police officers. Kenney and Watson (1990) state that most law enforcement agencies have come to accept the need to screen police candidates. Authors in this subject area always return to the theme that police officers are 'civilians in uniform' and nowhere is this more true than in the UK where policing is generally regarded as being delivered with consent of the community. The difficulties that this complex role imparts upon the police officer are that, although he or she is required to interact with society and accept societal values, the officer will also be expected to stand back from society, make decisions impartially, with discretion and in the public interest – in other words, adopt high ethical standards. According to Bennett (1984) there is a 'unique set of attitudinal and behavioural expectations or working norms that differentiate police officers from the public.' Therefore, we can only conclude that the training of probationer police officers is of immense importance in the socialisation process as recruits have little or no criteria by which to judge their experiences. They need to contextualise their previous and subsequent experiences, knowledge and understanding into police service scenarios before they can hope to live up to the high standards their public expect of them. Research and experience has revealed that this situation is not assisted by the approach of experienced police officers and the so-called 'canteen culture' which recruits must go through to reach 'full member status'. Research by Graef (1989) produced the following quote from a trainer:

> Of course we train them to do it properly at training school, but in their first two years probationers are faced with a set of values in the canteen and in the station generally they must at least pretend to go along with in order to be accepted.

Personnel practices

Returning to our 'Rampart' case study, it was discovered by the inquiry that several supervisors in the case had not received personnel evaluations in years. Tightening up the system of performance management and staff appraisals rectified this omission. In the UK, as a result of guidance from the Home Office (HOC 43/96), the police service adopted a new performance management and staff appraisal system in the late 1990s that was intended to apply to all staff. The aim of the PDR system was to improve the Forces' quality of service by developing individuals and provide:

1 A clear understanding of requirements and links
2 Feedback and coaching to improve performance
3 Identification of individual strengths and weaknesses
4 Personal Development Plans[3]

Although the system was designed to be consistent with, and complement, internal procedures for job selection and promotion, that aspect was very much ancillary to its main function. The feedback and action planning functions of the PDR operated as shown in Figures 9.1 and 9.2.

The performance management aspect of the PDR was based on individual objectives that linked to divisional or departmental objectives and upwards to organisational and eventually national objectives.

Individual police officers and particularly supervisors and managers, have a personal obligation to pay attention to their own self-development. Supervisors and managers have further responsibilities in relation to their

Figure 9.1 PDR de-brief model of giving feedback

Giving feedback

Figure 9.2 PDR action planning

Action planning

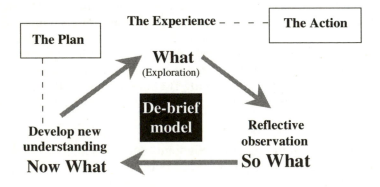

team members to ensure that effective and honest appraisals are carried out and that career development opportunities are available for all. To complete worthwhile career planning it is first necessary for the individual to know himself or herself. Open-minded and receptive people should feel able to ask for support and feedback from relevant people in their organisation such as line managers and colleagues. The ability to give and receive feedback effectively is an essential management skill that is underrated in the police service. Also, managers in the police service should not forget that one of the core competencies required for their post is that of 'developing people'.[4]

Figure 9.3 Model of performance management

Objectives

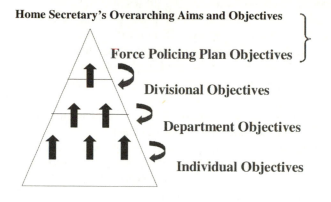

**Personnel investigations, operational controls
and anti-corruption inspections and audits**

These aspects have been covered in other chapters in this book and will
not be reiterated here. However, to assist the understanding of the reader,
we will continue with information about the Rampart case study. The
Board of Inquiry investigation found that clear patterns of misconduct had
gone undetected and investigators had not taken complaints against
police action seriously. The complaints were mainly investigated internally rather than passed on to the internal affairs group. The Board of
Inquiry found the most discouraging aspect of this was the failure of
supervisors and managers to oversee work. Because of the lack of
supervision, errors were not detected and this was further exacerbated by
the lack of an effective auditing system. We have discussed the aspect of
integrity checks and professional standards in chapter 8 and will not
therefore add more here.

Ethics and integrity training programs

The conclusions from the Rampart enquiry are important in our search for
high professional standards and ethical behaviour in police officers all
round the world, especially in the UK, as we shall explain. The Board of
Inquiry found:

> We must revitalize and reinforce our core values in the minds and
> hearts of all our personnel so that each and every employee
> understands their responsibility to uphold the integrity of the
> Department ...

The Board recommended that the two key elements of such approach must be:

- A thorough review of the existing ethics and integrity courses for topic continuity, proper delivery based on the needs and job duties of participants, and trainer preparation and credibility.
- A comprehensive training program on ethics, integrity, mentoring, and leadership, involving critical thinking, problem solving, and decision-making strategies for addressing ethical dilemmas in policing.

Clearly, it makes logical sense to discuss ethical issues widely and train police officers so that they understand ethical dilemmas. It is incumbent on the organisation to support and guide police officers when they perform their complex and difficult role in society. There are many reasons for this, not least that of personal and vicarious liability, but also the health, safety and welfare of staff. Despite the emphasis laid on professional and ethical standards, there is not a specific session or lesson on the subject of police ethics contained in the national curriculum for the training of recruits, supervisors or first level managers in the UK police service. There are specific training courses available[5] to senior managers in police ethics, but trainers would argue, and certainly the Rampart enquiry would indicate, that training on police ethics is essential for all levels of staff in the organisation.

On the subject of putting integrity to work, Cooper and Sawaf (1996) say:

> It is one thing to discuss and commend integrity – which is something most business people are wont to do. Yet putting it into action requires a keen perception, intuition, and conscience, backed by ongoing reflection.

We discuss in Chapter 10 the need for exemplary ethical and professional standards to emanate from the senior managers to act as role models for the rest of the organisation. To use a sharp contrast from which to learn we should examine not only the lessons from the Rampart enquiry but an example from a law enforcement agency with self-confessed problems of corruption, the Indian police service. Corruption within the Indian police organisation is not a new phenomenon and folklore has always associated police with extortion and brutality. A recently published research paper (Verma, 1999) on the subject called for a major transformation of organizational structure, management practices, supervision procedures, decentralization of power, creation of a local accountability system, even a change in role and functions of the police in society.

So far as the International Association of Chiefs of Police (IACP)[6] was concerned in 1999, 'Ethics is our greatest training and leadership need today and into the next century'. IACP recommend that training in ethics commences from the police recruit throughout the officer's career and includes decision-making models and the discussion of specific values or moral anchors. This theme is repeated in the Rampart enquiry which states that ethics training must be carried out in an adult learning environment and should be delivered in the form of discussion rather than lecture.

Personal development of staff

Instilling professional and ethical standards into the police organisation

We have discussed the difficulties of instilling professional and ethical standards into the police service through our examination of the Rampart case and our look at the Indian police organisation. One method the police service could adopt from commerce and industry is the 'learning organisation'. Chan (1997) contends that cultural change can occur through organisational learning, but that a fundamental change in police culture will be required. As she says, 'Many of the negative aspects of police culture seem to have been developed as anxiety-avoidance mechanisms rather than innovative problem-solving strategies'. According to Finger and Brand (1999) it is necessary to go through a four-stage process of structural changes to bring about the objective of becoming a learning organisation: unlearning cultural obstacles; conversion learning; continuous improvement; creating a learning culture. Finger and Brand (1999) and Beckley (1998) suggest that the learning organisation model can be adapted successfully to the public sector, although it is not in widespread use.

The learning organisation

Senge (1990) was one of the first proponents of the 'learning organisation'. In his book *The Fifth Discipline*, he outlined his theories of 'systems thinking' and 'personal mastery', which include the principle of self-development. Leadership was recommended to build a 'shared vision' through team learning and for managers to transform themselves into designers, teachers and stewards to support and guide the people in the organisation. Senge (1990: 22) notes that many organisations have a learning disability which he explains through the parable of the boiled frog. The disability operates through blinkered approaches and the unwillingness to learn from mistakes and experiences. A similar phenomenon is noted by Argyris (1986) in the form of 'non-learning' when carrying out the practices of:

- Protecting yourself unilaterally – by avoiding direct interpersonal confrontation and public discussion of sensitive issues that might expose you to blame.
- Protecting others unilaterally – by avoiding testing assumptions where the testing might evoke negative feelings and by keeping others from exposure to blame.
- Controlling the situation and task – by making up your own mind about the problem and acting on your view, by keeping your view private and by avoiding the public enquiry that might refute your view.

The essence of personal mastery, according to Senge, is learning how to generate and sustain creative tension in our lives. Learning in this context does not mean acquiring more information but expanding the ability to produce the results that individuals truly want from their life. Senge is not alone in announcing this philosophy as Covey (1989) articulated his 'habit 2' of 'begin with the end in mind' in his book *The Seven Habits of Highly Effective People*.

The creation of a learning organisation is not possible unless people at every level in the organisation practice the principles of lifelong learning. People with Senge's 'personal mastery' and self-awareness, openness and honesty are more committed to tasks, they take more initiative and they have a broader and deeper sense of responsibility in their work.

An important principle to understand is that of organisational learning. This concept has been studied in depth by Dr Cliff Bunning (1993)[7] who states that the primary emphasis is upon the need for senior executives to display vision, courage and integrity in leading the organisational transformation that is needed for organisations to become superb at learning and innovating. While accepting that the term 'organisational learning' is merely a metaphor as, having no brain, organisations cannot learn, Bunning emphasises that when individuals within the organisation learn, the organisation as a whole needs to be prepared to listen and respond to the learning.

Pedler, Burgoyne and Boydell (1991) offered a list of the conditions under which a 'learning organisation' can be achieved:

- Learning strategy
- Participative policy-making
- Informating (IT used to inform and empower people)
- Formative accounting
- Internal exchange
- Reward flexibility
- Enabling structures
- Front-line workers as environmental scanners

- Inter-company learning
- Learning climate
- Self-development for all.

The police service as a learning organisation

Becoming a 'learning organisation' is widely recognised in commerce and industry as best practice for organisations that go through considerable change in a constantly demanding environment. The police service is constantly going through change and has 'flattened' its management structure considerably over the past few years – it is therefore the ideal candidate to become a learning organisation. A learning organisation has managers who create an environment where the behaviours and practices involved in continuous development are actively encouraged. Of course, this means that managers will need the skills and ability to foster the learning organisation and bring it into life. They need to recognise the necessity and benefits of developing the careers of their staff and they then need to utilise the new effectiveness of staff once developed. This means that they have to release some control and allow staff to flourish. Less secure managers may find this aspect of the learning organisation threatening, but to achieve the innovative, open and secure ethos for the organisation to grow, it is absolutely necessary to foster such an atmosphere.

Critically, whichever version of the 'learning organisation' is adopted, the central features that are relevant for 'ethical policing' are clear: the encouragement of an open organisation; the sharing of information; the fostering of learning; the development of individual and organisational capability.

This subject brings us to the next development: the Police National Training Organisation (NTO). The Association of Chief Police Officers (ACPO) put forward an application to become a National Training Organisation for the police service. As this is written, the application is under consideration by the DfEE. NTOs have five strategic aims:

- Raising strategic capability
- Improving competitiveness
- Giving advice on education and training
- Qualifying the workforce
- Developing effective partnerships.

This is an important step which should lead to training and development of staff in police organisations in the UK being appropriately needs-analysed, planned, quality-controlled, evaluated and reviewed.

'Whistleblowing' in the police service

Beckley (1997b) wrote about the phenomenon of public interest disclosure or 'whistleblowing' in the police service and the detrimental effects it had on the careers of individual participants. It would not be accurate to report vast strides forward in the police organisation in this arena; however, some progress has been made. Firstly, the UK Government introduced the Public Interest Disclosure Act of 1998 which recognised the necessity to protect disclosures made within the organisation, to an industry regulator or, to a lesser extent to an external source. However, the Public Interest Disclosure Act does not apply[8] to police officers; therefore internal disclosure or alternatively corresponding with the Police Authority are the only routes. Secondly, most police forces in the UK have introduced proper grievance procedures that are being used by staff, thereby indicating confidence and satisfaction with outcomes of the procedures.

There are also 'dignity and respect' and 'equal opportunities' policies to properly recognise and support the wide diversity of today's organisations. The aims of the dignity and respect policy from West Mercia Constabulary are to provide all staff with the right to be treated with dignity and respect at work; provide an informal stage without redress to formal investigation or disciplinary action; and assure individuals that allegations will be treated seriously. Management responsibilities to the policy are: to promote a working environment free from harassment, discrimination, victimisation and bullying; setting standards, communicating and explaining policy and procedures; reflecting on their own management style; and being responsive, supportive and taking individuals who complain seriously. Dignity and respect policies will also complement and link to force policies on managing diversity and recruitment and selection.

Conclusions

We have examined many issues from the Rampart case study as we have progressed through the topics in this chapter. It is important that the police service learns from its mistakes and continuously improves itself through organisational and individual learning. In terms of recruitment and selection, it is clear that the organisation should be influenced by attributes such as the 'character ethic', emotional intelligence, competences and personal values of potential recruits. Research has indicated that applicants with higher educational qualifications are more suited to police work than those with lower educational qualifications, although recruitment policies should be flexible, open and transparent and identify competency criteria and minimum standards for recruits. Once recruits have been appointed to a law enforcement agency, they should be socialised into the organisation with care and trained using appropriate teaching and learning techniques. All law enforcement organisations should have clearly articulated values statements and all police officers should be trained in police ethics throughout their career. Organisational learning, particularly relating to ethical and professional standards issues, can be pursued through the learning organisation model. Operation of this model in police organisations would require leadership from chief officers in the police service and to ensure the organisation is on message executive officers must be role models for staff. We will further discuss the ethical codes of the police service in Chapter 10.

Further reading

There are a myriad of publications on the subject of competencies and the reader may make their own choice on this subject. There are few publications on the specific subject of police competencies, recruitment and selection, but books such as Goleman's *Emotional Intelligence* (1996) and Cooper and Sawaf's *Executive EQ* (1989) would offer a different perspective on personal attributes of recruits.

Information on police training is mainly covered by material published internally, but principles can be extended from many private and public sector sources.

Good publications on management principles in the police service are hard to find, therefore the authors would recommend general reading from Steven Covey's *Seven Habits of Highly Effective People* (1989) and Peter Senge's *The Fifth Discipline* (1990). The latter book also covers organisational learning and reading may be augmented by reference to the many works of Pedler and Burgoyne. In addition to the cited sources, information about personal learning can be obtained from the excellent books of Alan Mumford and Peter Honey.

Notes

1 Obtained from the Los Angeles Police Department website: wqww.lapdonline.org.
2 Information kindly supplied by Sue Harper, West Mercia Constabulary Human Resources Dept.
3 Source: a speech given by W.G. Nelson, Assistant Chief Constable, to the Autumn Conference of the Association of Chief Police Officers.
4 See 'The Core Competencies at each Rank' from The Police Staff College, Bramshill.
5 For example, the police management programme for inspectors at Bramshill Police Staff College, and the Certificate in Professional Policing (Ethics), a postgraduate course offered by Teesside University.
6 Material taken from the website of the International Association of Chiefs of Police: http://www.theiacp.org/

7 Dr Cliff Bunning is Professor of Human Resource Management at the International Management Centre, Pacific Region, Brisbane, Australia.
8 As per Section 200 of the Employment Rights Act 1996 as amended by the Public Interest Disclosure Act 1998, Part IV and Section 47B.

Chapter 10

Decision making, codes and control systems

Introduction

We will be concerned in this chapter primarily with the issue of ethical codes and decision making. As we have discussed earlier in this book, the image and reputation of the British police service have become tarnished during the 1990s, leaving its reputation in low regard. The question all police officers should be asking themselves is, what can be done to redress this situation and how can police officers achieve greater professionalism? We have mentioned professional codes above in discussing 'professionalism' in Chapter 5. In company with many other professional bodies and associations, the police service in this and other countries have proposed the introduction of statements of ethical standards.

Ethical codes

The first ethical standards in the police service probably date back to the instructions given to Metropolitan Police officers by Robert Peel in 1829.[1] This statement emphasised the preventive nature of policing envisaged at the outset of law enforcement in the UK. Internationally, the next recorded efforts appear to be in the USA in 1928 from the celebrated work of August Vollmer and his protégé, O.W. Wilson. In 1937 the Federal Bureau of Investigation introduced 'The Pledge', recommended for all law enforcement officers and in 1955, through the move to professionalise the police, a code of ethics was prepared. Finally, in 1991 the International Association of Chiefs of Police (IACP) published the most widely used code, the Police Code of Conduct (IACP, 1991). Meanwhile, the United Nations developed its Code of Conduct for Law Enforcement Officials and not to be outdone, the Council of Europe (Whitehouse, 1997) produced a Declaration on the Police.[2]

Returning to the UK, the Royal Commission on the police said in 1960 that the duties of the police are unique.

> The constable must be vigilant both to use his authority adequately and instantly as occasion demands, and at the same time never to exceed it. We are satisfied that this individual responsibility is more onerous than any delegated to, or assumed by, a member of any comparable profession or occupation. Responsibility of this kind, to be properly and reasonable exercised, demands high moral standards and a nice exercise of judgement.

In 1985 the Metropolitan Police (Metropolitan Police, 1985) produced a slim, well-written handbook that contained a code of professional duties for the information of all officers. Endorsed by the then Metropolitan Police Commissioner, Kenneth Newman, and written by Albert Laugharne, Deputy Commissioner, this was a far-sighted document that still warrants our attention to this day for its incisive and intuitive principles. Unfortunately, it was written in rather inaccessible language, which may have led to the response of apathy by its intended audience who largely ignored the enlightened messages it contained. The code of professional duties the book expounded looks good today, especially in its inclusion of specific human rights and freedoms.

Although the Statement did not produce much direct result, it did contribute to the introduction of the Police Service Statement of Common Purpose (ACPO, 1990) and there is some evidence that this was a key part of a very important drive for 'quality' in policing in the UK through the early 1990s (Waters, 1995). Alongside this, there have been several attempts in recent years to introduce or revive interest in a police code of ethics. According to *Police Review* in 1998 (Adams, 1998) the Association of Chief Police Officers (ACPO) recommended the introduction of a code of ethics that had been prepared in 1992.

This same code of ethics was mentioned in the Patten report (Patten, 1999) on policing in Northern Ireland and recommended as good practice. The commission set itself six policing benchmarks (Cramphorn, 1999) against which it tested its proposals; effectiveness, efficiency, impartiality, accountability, representativeness and respect for human rights. The report went on to say:

> Codes of practice on all aspects of policing, including covert law enforcement techniques, should be strictly in accordance with the European Convention on Human Rights.

Figure 10.1 ACPO draft Statement of ethical principles (1992)

As a member of the police service, I will aspire to:

1 Act with fairness, carrying out my responsibilities with integrity and impartiality.

2 Perform my duties with diligence and a proper use of discretion.

3 Display self-control, tolerance, understanding, and courtesy appropriate to the circumstances in my dealings with all individuals, both outside and inside the police service.

4 Uphold fundamental human rights, treating every person as an individual and display respect towards them.

5 Support my colleagues in the performance of their lawful duties and, in doing so, actively oppose and draw attention to any malpractice by any person.

6 Respect the fact that much of the information I receive is confidential and may only be divulged when my duty requires me to do so.

7 Exercise force only when justified and then only use the minimum amount of force necessary to effect my lawful purpose and restore the peace.

8 Act only within the law, in the understanding that I have no authority to depart from due legal process and that no-one may place a requirement on me to do so.

9 Use resources entrusted to me to the benefit of the public.

10 Accept responsibility for my own self-development, continually seeking to improve the way in which I serve the community.

11 Accept personal accountability for my own acts or omissions.

Although all the high quality and idealistic work we have listed above on ethical frameworks into policing was completed and circulated, none of it was widely accepted or introduced into policing in the UK, except for the ACPO Statement of Common Purpose and Values. Yet, since its development there has been a plethora of enquiries into how the police of this country operate (Audit Commission, 1993), on its role (Audit Commission, 1996) and responsibilities (Home Office, 1995), how the police are accountable and how they fit into the criminal justice system (Cm 2281). Despite all this debate, there is still no service-wide accepted comprehensive document that contains a statement on ethics in policing in England and Wales.

If we were to summarise the current statements of ethical principles, it would be as follows:

Figure 10.2 Existing ethical standards in the police service in England and Wales and Europe

Ethical standards in England and Wales
- Oath of Office
- Statement of Common Purpose and Values (reproduced above)
- Code of Conduct (Police personnel procedures)

Ethical codes in Europe
- The United Nations Declaration of Human Rights
- The Council of Europe Convention on Human Rights
- The United Nations Code of Conduct for Law Enforcement Officials
- The Council of Europe Declaration on the Police

Amongst this list, even the oath of office requires updating in the light of the recommendations of the Patten Report (Patten, 1999) on policing in Northern Ireland, to take into account the renewed emphasis on human rights and the positive duty on police officers to uphold and protect the rights and freedoms of members of the public they serve (Recommendation 2).

The Code of Conduct introduced under the Police Act 1996 (and Regulations) is in a completely different form to the Police Regulations it replaced. The headings of the code, which commenced operation on 1 April 1999, are as follows:

Figure 10.3 The headings of the Police Code of Conduct (1999)

- Criminal offence
- Sobriety
- Care of property
- Appearance
- General conduct
- Lawful orders
- Confidentiality
- Honesty and integrity
- Politeness and tolerance with fairness and impartiality
- Use of force and abuse of authority
- Performance of duties

Despite its aspirations, the Code's effectiveness rests on the foundations of the previous system – based around the Police Complaints Authority – which has been heavily criticised for a lack of genuine independence by staff associations and the European Court.[3] Above all, the Code of Conduct, which is primarily designed to outline the boundaries of punishment for poor performance, is not a substitute for a positive, aspirational code of ethics, which provides a guide to good professional standards.

Necessity for police ethical codes

Having reviewed both the plethora of statements and noted the lack of a single, authoritative code of ethics, we now need to ask why, after nearly

200 years of managing without one, the police service in the UK now requires such a document? We will examine the desirability of such a code shortly, but is it *necessary*? There are four major factors suggesting that it is:

1 Constitutional reform in the UK has moved towards written rather than abstract or notional constitutions. The Human Rights Act 1998, coupled with the proposed Freedom of Information Act,[4] will alter fundamentally the way policing is carried out in this country.[5] In particular, police officers will have the added requirement and duty of respecting and upholding the human rights of every citizen. The Human Rights Act will give citizens the right to compensation, and other appropriate remedies, through the courts if public authorities such as the police infringe their 'human rights and fundamental freedoms'. This will bring a new focus towards ethical behaviour by police officers who will be called upon to account for their actions.

2 Secondly, there are long-standing trends in the courts to establish culpability for personal liability and accountability (Ashworth, 1994) in the field of public safety, both to the individual and corporately (Beckley, 1997).

3 Lastly, there has been widespread public concern over police actions as outlined in the first part of this book. The concern appears to stem from the 'means and ends' argument that equates to the 'Dirty Harry' syndrome linked to 'noble cause corruption' (Kleinig, 1996).

4 Finally, there is the public disquiet and lack of confidence in the police complaints system (Beckley, 1997b).

Kingshott (1999) went on to argue that the police do need a code of ethics because, although the vast majority of police officers believe in the work they are doing as a vocation:

- Sometimes officers are over-enthusiastic.
- They lack leadership and direction.
- They succumb to the pressures of public expectation.
- They 'gild the lily'.
- They break or circumvent the law.
- Sometimes lack professionalism (e.g. Macpherson Enquiry).[6]
- There are a few corrupt officers.

Even if a code is necessary, it has been argued that it is unlikely to produce the expected benefits (Davis, 1991 and Donahue, 1993). However, a more optimistic view is that public trust in the police will be enhanced by a code of ethics (Vicchio, 1997 and O'Malley, 1997). Kingshott (1999) suggested that the benefits of the introduction of an ethical code for the police could include:

- An improvement of public perception of the police role.
- Improved confidence and trust in the organisation.
- A significant reduction in unethical behaviour in the organisation.
- An awareness of the ethical implications of decision-making.
- Education to achieve sound ethical decision-making skills and thereby improve the quality of service delivery to the society being policed.
- Development of officers' personal morality.

Kingshott concluded that officers would not actively oppose a code and he proposed that the introduction of a code would have benefits for (i) the individual, (ii) the organisation and (iii) society in general because a code of ethics is no more than a codification of good behaviour and enhanced professionalism.

This raises the important issue of what a code should try to cover. This requires us to revisit the reasons why ethics are important in policing. Research (Vicchio, 1997 and O'Malley, 1997) has established the issues relating to the importance of ethics in policing and the 'ideal ethical police service':

- To identify the ideal
  - the ideal is what we strive for.
  - no person or organisation can ever meet the ideal all the time.
  - the objective is to bring reality as close as possible to the ideal.
- To learn duties, rights, obligations.
- To acquire knowledge for rational decision-making.
- To demonstrate the relationship of honesty and ethics to public trust.

The ideal ethical police service

- Free of corruption
- Honest
- Restrained in the use of force
- Professionally competent
- No improper acceptance of gratuities
- Integrity (trust, competence, professionalism, confidence)
- Inclusive: no 'us' against 'them'
- Everything done in private would be done as if in public
- Policies formed with a consideration of justice
- Mistakes treated as opportunities for learning
- Free of bigotry and valuing diversity.

We should also take account of the societal controls of behaviour, ethics, religion and the law when we ask the question, what would a code of conduct contain? According to Haggard (1993), the code should contain the following cocktail: fairness, care and attention, control and courtesy, respect, collegiality, confidentiality, use of force, stewardship, education and self-development, and accountability. Indeed, we quickly find that the literature identifies a set of core principles matching closely to the ones we described in Chapter 3.

The last element, as Ashworth (1994) suggests, is that police ethics are closely linked to human rights; that is a conclusion also reached by an ACPO working group on policing and human rights (Beckley, 1999). The group examined the areas of police work that will be affected by the adoption of the Articles of the European Convention of Human Rights and produced a list of the 'top ten' impacts. Police ethics was listed as the number one impact upon policing as a result of this legislation. Coupled with the later introduction of the Freedom of Information Act, the significance and necessity of an invigorated examination of police ethics becomes clear.

On its own the code is not enough. As Alderson (1998) has argued, police officers – or any criminal justice professionals (Rutherford, 1993) – will find it impossible to act ethically without the right socio-economic and political conditions. The other key element that is missing is moral leadership. This subject has also engaged research (Adlam, 1997) to identify the ethical profile of police managers and the moral ethos of police organisations. The outcome of the research established that police managers 'are well placed to lead ethically' and found that:

> There are, plainly, some grounds for optimism concerning the moral ethos of police organisations. There are also grounds for optimism concerning the 'moral expertise' of police in the middle managerial ranks of the service.

Alderson, who also emphasised the importance of leadership, suggested the following declaration should also be adopted:

Police leadership: a declaration
I will seek to inculcate high ethical humanitarian standards into carrying out of duties by officers under my command, whilst at the same time accepting their need to use force, sometimes deadly force, in the lawful performance of duty, and the need to use powers granted to us by governments so that we may protect the people, their freedoms, and their property, in accordance with the spirit of the implied social contract.

I will not ask, demand of, or cause any officer under my command to carry out duties and actions which are contrary to the laws of my country, or to those laws of international covenants and treaties such as the Universal Declaration of Human Rights and its protocols, and the European Convention on Human Rights and Fundamental Freedoms which have been adopted by my government.

All this I promise in the cause of justice, freedom and the common good.

(Alderson, 1998)

Conclusion on ethical codes

On the question of introducing a code of ethics for the police service, Sir John Woodcock, Her Majesty's Chief Inspector of Constabulary, said (in 1991):

That change will be threefold, each inter-dependent with the other. First, the rights of the customer of police services will be raised to the pinnacle of all police activity. Secondly, human right issues rather than the control of crime will come to the forefront of police thinking, albeit that the human rights of the majority can be deeply threatened by growth in crime. Thirdly, there will be a recognition that fair and equal treatment of all police and civil staff is not an end in itself but additionally a mirror image by which the public discerns the nature of police treatment of minorities.

(Woodcock, 1991)

As we have seen the developments since have emphasised the need for such an approach: more covert policing, with all the ethical hazards (Chapter 7); a performance culture that adds ritual but not proper standards (Chapter 8); a lack of clear standards in difficult areas such as the exercise of discretion (Chapter 5); a collapse in public confidence in the integrity of the service and its competence (Chapter 1). On the other hand, there has been a marked shift in public service towards 'standards in public life' (Nolan, 1995) and a significant trend in commerce and industry towards 'values-driven' and management with integrity.[7]

'Integrity' now features strongly in documents published by Her Majesty's Inspector of Constabulary. In his 1989/99 annual report he said:

The underpinning guiding principles provide a constant reminder a constant reminder of the crucial mechanisms to achievement, with integrity, partnership and acceptable local priorities featuring strongly.

The HMIC thematic inspection on police integrity confirmed that the vast majority of police officers, support staff and special constables working within the 44 police forces in England, Wales and Northern Ireland are honest, industrious and dedicated (HMIC, 1999a). But it warned:

> Every time an officer abuses the trust placed in him or her by the public, the collective image of the Police Service is damaged.

It also said:

> As in so much of policing, integrity has been taken for granted in training and as a consequence has received far too little emphasis.

Key recommendations of the inspection report can be summarised as follows:

- Active supervision
- Review selection and training so as to enhance the integrity of staff
- Better vetting
- Rigorous audit of high risk information and activities
- Clearer standards and leadership on integrity from Chief officers.

The recommendations are a timely reminder. However, the police may be able to take some comfort from the fact that some research (Adlam, 1997) suggests that the police service has made significant progress in promoting good ethical behaviour. In addition, some of the key building blocks are in place:

- The Code of Conduct.
- the Personal Development Review (PDR) system (Home Office, 1997) should place greater emphasis on self-development and the responsibility of police managers to ensure the development and coaching of their team of staff.

Further challenges include the need for an increased emphasis on training on human rights, ethics and community and race relations. Clearly, innovative methods of training will be required to achieve a substantial shift of 'mind set' from the 'canteen culture' described in the Macpherson report and other papers (Kingshott, 1999). The first glimmers of innovation and hints of the direction to take are emerging through the use of ethical decision-making models and 'open and transparent' methods of managing (Beckley, 1999).

We would argue that all of this would be easier and more effective once a proper, comprehensive code of ethics has been agreed. Only then can the coupling of recruitment, selection, training and leadership in promulgating human rights and ethics begin to achieve the goal of professionalising the police service (Villiers, 1997).

Decision making

An effective code of ethics is also a prerequisite of developing a more effective approach to decision making. This has some urgency, because as we already emphasized, from the commencement of the Human Rights Act 1998 it will be necessary to review the use of all police powers and policing decisions in the light of the principles of that Act and ECHR. *Compatibility* against ECHR principles will involve a scrutiny against the principles we identified in Chapter 4: legality, proportionality, necessity and relevance, equality of arms, proper remedy. At first sight, this seems rather cumbersome and a burden upon efficient and effective policing activities, but operating in this way will soon become second nature, as similar thought processes already occur. Furthermore, during late 1999 and early 2000, in advance of the implementation of the Human Rights Act in the UK, all police policies and practices were tested for compliance against the compatibility criteria using an 'audit tool kit' devised by ACPO. The aspect of auditing polices will be further discussed in Chapter 11.

The introduction of a human rights framework into UK law requires police officers to uphold and protect positively the rights of citizens. This will mean a fundamental change in thinking and decision making, especially in the use of discretion. Every decision on whether to arrest, search, and report for an offence or merely caution, use as an informant or obtain intelligence will require evidenced and justified decisions.

The Association of Chief Police Officers (ACPO) quickly realised that there would be considerable impact on everyday operational policing as a result of the provisions of the Human Rights Act. This is not because police officers in the UK consistently abuse the human rights of individuals; it is simply that certain police powers, procedures and the outcome-oriented operating culture do not always comply with the above ECHR principles. ACPO formed a working group on policing and human rights that set out to examine the impacts of ECHR principles on operational policing. The resultant list of 'non-compliant' working practices, policies and procedures was considerable. The challenge was to overhaul them to identify best practice in the light of the revised ECHR paradigm and to ensure compliance. This revision of working practices and introduction of enhanced and improved procedures should be seen as an opportunity, not a threat, towards greater professionalism and integrity of the entire service.

Two particular areas of concern in UK and ECHR decided cases are those of the rules of natural justice and the quality of decision-making in operational policing. Indeed, law students need go no further in their study of administrative law than reference to cases involving police forces which highlight poor decision making, heavy-handed tactics in dealing with police staff and lack of appreciation in the meaning of quality of service. The remainder of this section will examine the two themes of decision making and the rules of natural justice to highlight their importance and give some practical pointers towards good practice.

Decisions

The management teams in the police service, like all publicly accountable organisations, make decisions that are not always to the taste of all the public they serve, nor to that of all their individual employees. At present, the police service does not have to justify itself at shareholders meetings or public meetings where aggrieved individuals have a right of audience. In view of this, the legal system has built in a process of checks and balances to address this issue by way of judicial review and this system will remain after the commencement of the Human Rights Act. Judges expect a high standard of decision making in public authorities and have set that standard in decided cases. They also expect that decisions will comply with the principles of the rules of natural justice. Upon commencement of the Freedom of Information Act, decisions made by public authorities will be open to scrutiny by interested parties. Additionally, the Human Rights Act (section 7) will allow individuals whose rights have been infringed by public authorities to be awarded damages by the courts. Historically, the amount of damages awarded by the European courts has been low, the theory being that it is more important to establish individuals' rights than punish public authorities. Courts may grant such relief or remedy, or make such an order (within its powers) as it considers 'just and appropriate', in order to afford 'just satisfaction'.

A person claiming to be a victim of unlawful acts committed by a public authority may either bring proceedings against it in the appropriate court or tribunal or rely on the Convention right concerned in any legal proceedings. For these reasons, it has been argued[8] that the scope of judicial review will be widened after the commencement of HRA. In short, human rights have increased the scrutiny of police decision making.

Judicial review[9]

There are four major grounds where the UK courts will consider judicial review and intervene to supervise and control decisions of public authorities:

- 'Illegality' or 'ultra vires' – decisions made beyond the power of the authority
- 'Irrationality' or 'unreasonable' – unreasonable decisions
- 'Procedural impropriety' or breach of the rules of natural justice
- 'Proportionality'.

As can be seen, there are strong connections between these 'tests' and the principles of human rights. This connection is strengthened when we turn to the authoritative and most instructive case in this area – 'Wednesbury'.[10] This case, contemporary with the drafting of ECHR, provides the following guidelines for a 'reasonable decision':

- It must be a real exercise of discretion – human rights extend this 'active' discretionary principle to tactical operational decisions.
- It must have regard to relevant matters.
- It must disregard non-germane matters.
- It must not be vitiated by bad faith of dishonesty – a clear link with the ethics of virtue.

Legal opinion is divided about the impact of the Human Rights Act on this case. Some have argued that the courts will also consider the *merits* of decisions (Puddephatt, 1999). Others[11] suggested that judges would be cautious. In the case of Smith,[12] the court said that where ECHR is involved, the courts will scrutinise decisions and reasoning very closely and *Vilvarajah*[13] decided that there should be independent scrutiny of decisions. However the case law develops it will be even more important that good practice models for decision making are utilised to demonstrate fairness, openness and transparency and to support the effectiveness of decisions.

Bunyard (1979) lists two variables that govern the effectiveness of a decision: acceptance and quality. 'Acceptance' is the theory that people are more likely to accept and 'buy into' decisions they have helped to make. The 'quality' of a decision is the extent to which objective facts and not subjective feelings have been used to formulate the decision. Bunyard then suggests that there are four types of decision-making situations:

- Technical problems in which acceptability is not an issue - these can best be made by experts.
- Problems in which there are many alternative solutions, which are of a very similar objective quality, but the key issue is one of fairness – these are best decided by group processes.
- Minor problems in which there are neither important technical nor acceptance issues – these can be made by *laissez faire* methods.

- The most difficult problems in which both quality and acceptance are important. For these, it is suggested that the manager must exercise his or her skills as a discussion leader to arrive at solution that is technically sound but has acceptability.

Taking Bunyard, the Wednesbury judgement and one of the authors' own guides (Beckley, 1999) together it becomes clear that effective decision making needs to take account of the decision making process, the context and the recording and communication of the action. These elements come together in the ACPO human rights tool kit, which has suggested a decision-making model to comply with ECHR:

This model sounds fine for management decisions where time for careful consideration is available. How could this be applied to 'street'

Figure 10.4   Decision making – ACPO in-force audit tool kit (ACPO, 1999a)

Minimum information
1   Defining the aim(s) and objective(s) – evidencing applications of key human rights principles of legality, legitimate aim and proportionality
2   Determining all relevant information
3   Assessing feasible options
4   Documenting decisions reached or actions taken with reasons
5   Reviewing outcomes

Courts will question
- The presence/absence of records
- Whether the decision was audited
- The existence of independent scrutiny
- Transparency
- Accountability
- Whether legal advice was sought.

---

decisions or real time decisions in the midst of an operation? Research by Stewart (1998) emphasised the considerable pressure on police managers to make quick but effective decisions. Schmitt (1994) argued that practice in decision making could aid expertise and reliability. However, operational policing often does not give sufficient opportunity to attain competence nor is it possible to give that practice when life-threatening situations are involved (Lines, 1999). It follows that there is a need for training that simulates incidents. The Scottish Police College recognised this fact many years ago, and there is such a facility now available at the Police Staff College at Bramshill.[14]

In addition to practice in decision-making, there are also models within cases decided under ECHR which demonstrate principles for operational policing decision-making. Cases such as *Osman v UK*[15] provide a 'rehearsed' example of the factors to be taken into account in dealing with a 'clear and obvious risk to the public'. The previously decided cases[16] had held that courts would not intervene with the operational decisions of chief police officers on the grounds of public interest. Whilst *Osman* was based on one specific set of circumstances, it does show how decisions will be tested in the future. It and other cases emphasise that the courts expect a high level of expertise in the management and control of incidents,[17] especially where they involve the use of lethal force[18] or deaths in police custody.[19]

Conclusions

An emphasis on human rights, such as the Human Rights Act provides within British Law, affects police decision making in a number of ways. Firstly, principles such as 'legality', which have been important in judicial reviews of the police, become far more important and will affect day-to-day operational decisions far more directly. In particular, if as has happened in New Zealand,[20] the courts develop a 'tort' of breach of rights, then 'illegality' will increasingly bring not only civil compensation against the police, but also the exclusion of evidence obtained in contravention of the Human Rights Act. Secondly, therefore, decisions by police officers must show not only the rationale for the decision – the 'outcome' – but also the steps taken to secure compliance with human rights standards. Lastly, these steps can most effectively be demonstrated by an organisation whose members are committed to ethical standards which incorporate human rights and interpret them in the language of operational policing.

At a recent conference[21] on human rights, one of the authors made a statement that the introduction of the Human Rights Act would lead to fundamental changes in the way that operational policing is carried out in this country. The changes were characterised as aspirational opportunities and not as threats. Respect for citizens' human rights by police officers will lead to greater professionalism, openness, transparency, accountability, and integrity. Proportionate, sensitive and prudent use of discretion in the operation and use of police powers, policies and procedures will lead to enhanced decision making and greater support from the public we serve. Integral to this message is that ethical behaviour by police officers is essential in all police operations. We have also seen that although police officers will not be personally legally liable for infringements of victims' rights under ECHR, courts will question policing activities closely and hold chief police officers accountable. It is therefore important that police activities are carefully considered and are a measured response to the problem to be solved. The credibility and standing of the police service demands careful, logical thought processes resulting in justifiable decisions and a high standard of service delivery to the public.

There is a golden thread running through our study of police ethics in the preceding chapter; it is that of leadership. Strong leadership on ethics is required to put an ethical code into context within an organisation and act as clear guidance for all its employees. It follows that it is not sufficient to merely condone ethical behaviour by police officers; police leaders must actively encourage it. Furthermore unethical behaviour must be whole-heartedly rejected by the groundswell of opinion of all ranks and employees in police organisations. Chief police officers must actively assume the mantle of ethical behaviour and set an example as role models to which those below aspire. Then we will achieve the objective of ethical policing.

Further reading

A good source of material on ethical codes can be found at the Police Ethics Network (PEN) website www.members.aol.com/Polethnet/page6.htm. The US experience can be found on www.iacp.org. Decision making and operational liability of police officers are discussed thoroughly in Beckley (1997b) *Operational Policing: Liabilities and Entitlements.*

Notes

1 See above at p. 19.
2 See above in Chapter 4.
3 *Govell v UK*, for instance.
4 The date of commencement of the Freedom of Information Act is not known at the time of writing.
5 See the further reading list after the bibliography.
6 BBC2 'Black Britain – Condon answers his critics', Monday 9 November 1998.
7 See the further reading list after the bibliography.
8 Point argued in a presentation at a seminar for practitioners held at County Hall, Worcestershire, 23 March 1999 by Professor Anthony Bradley and Henrietta Hill, Barristers of Cloisters, 1 Pump Court, Temple, London.
9 See Beckley, 1997a.
10 *Associated Provincial Picture Houses Ltd v Wednesbury Corporation* [1947] 2 All ER 680.
11 Richard Wilmot-Smith QC, Barrister speaking at a conference organised by Infolog Training on the Human Rights Act 1998, 16 February 1999, Barbican Centre, London.
12 *R v Min. of Defence ex parte Smith* [1996] 1 All ER 257, QB 157.
13 *Vilvarajah v UK* (1991) 14 EHRR 248.
14 'MINERVA' National Police Training, force training managers conference, 1999.

15 *Osman v UK* (1999) 1 FLR 198.
16 *Hill v Chief Constable of West Yorkshire* [1988] AC53; *R v Chief Constable of Sussex, ex parte International Trader's Ferry Ltd.* [1995] QBD 26 July 1995.
17 *McCann v UK* (1995) 21 EHRR 97.
18 *Aksoy v Turkey* (1996) 23 EHRR 553.
19 *Andronicou and Constantinou v Cyprus* (1997) 25 EHRR 491.
20 This comment is drawn from the communication between ACPO and the New Zealand and Canadian Police prior to the introduction of the Human Rights Act in the UK.
21 Conference on human rights, 'Policing and the Human Rights Act 1998', held at NCVO, Regents Wharf, London N1 on 19 April 2000.

'Auditing' for compliance:
a human rights case study

Introduction

This third chapter on developing 'ethical policing' provides an overview of the role that policy analysis and evaluation can play, by examining the development of the UK police service's response to human rights incorporation, in the period prior to the 2 October 2000. The material is drawn from a twelve month case-study on the Association of Chief Police Officers (ACPO) human rights programme of policy audits and reviews.

The concluding sections of the chapter provide a critique of the approach with specific commentary on the value of the approach in managing change, its transferability to other contexts, views of participating NGOs and academics, and the need for integration of compliance tests into existing performance and inspection regimes including best value.

The UK police service's response to the Human Rights Act 1998

The approach adopted by the Association of Chief Police Officers in preparing for the onset of the Human Rights Act 1998 was informed by European and Canadian human rights experiences, and also drew on the expertise of a wide range of academic, legal and management sources. At the outset there was consensus between ACPO and its partner agencies on the need for a managed programme of work prior to 2 October 2000, which would focus on the development and implementation of a service-wide training and communications strategy.

Early in January 1998 the ACPO human rights sub-committee assumed the role of a 'management board' for the programme with a membership consisting of representatives from the Home Office, ACPO, the Crown

Prosecution Service and legal services. Within the programme, a process of consultation and quality assurance was established which involved service professionals, non-governmental agencies (Liberty and Justice), academics and independent legal opinion.

The focus of the programme was informed by a number of drivers: the recognised need for training and communication strategies and also a perceptible sense of urgency in the need for public authorities, including the police service, to promote human rights compliance in policy management. This was particularly relevant to areas of policy work which directly informed professional and ethical standards in public service management and provision.

A focus on policy management and analysing how reforms within it affect service outcomes has been a key feature of the Labour administration's reform programme. It has been noted in previous chapters that the government's proposals for reform reflect many of the key principles of new public management, as well as the prescription for 're-inventing government' (Osborne and Gaebler, 1992). However, in contrast to previous administrations, the Labour reforms are not distinctly marked by a particular ideological stance, but a drive towards a more citizen-centered collaborative approach to improving public services, in which individual rights are to be reinforced through foreign and domestic policy.

The move towards an active audit of policy was a key consequence of the Human Rights Act. Legal and professional advice was

> that there should be an audit of all practices and procedures, including standing orders, employment practices, disciplinary practices. The audit should consider whether there may be a *prima facie* derogation from a Convention right. Then consider whether it is *prima facie* justified or permitted, and whether it is proportionate to the right abridged.
>
> (Richard Wilmot Smith, 1998)

With this in mind and in recognition of the opportunity that 'policing with human rights' provided to enhance public confidence, the ACPO human rights programme was established under the governance of the ACPO human rights sub-committee. The sub-committee had a service-wide mandate, which included policy analysis and evaluation. The strategic aim of the programme was to ensure that the police service was in a position to respond ethically and effectively to the Human Rights Act.

This aim was developed through three specific objectives focused on policy management:

• To establish the potential degree of risk of non-compliance with the key principles of human rights in specific areas of police policy activity.

- To ensure that there was a process of learning embedded in the development of national policy, whether in making corrective amendments or in future policy creation, which would continuously challenge the level of compliance.
- To establish the key principles of human rights, and lessons from European case law (relating to accountability and decision making), in national policy to inform local policy and practice.

ACPO's approach acknowledged a perceived 'hierarchy of influence' which moves down through legal/social controls, to national policy informing local policy, procedures and ultimately practice. In this context the need was to ensure that ethical and behavioral standards could be directly drawn from HR compliant policy and form a baseline for service, force and ultimately individual performance assessments. For example, through the development and monitoring of relevant HR performance indicators (for example, analysing patterns in stop and search for breaches of Article 14), and identification of core competencies (i.e. HR and ethical behaviours).

ACPO human rights programme – policy audits

In response to ACPO's expressed intentions, a programme of national policy audits and reviews was developed in which it was possible to distinguish and yet integrate approaches to both policy evaluation and analysis. The development of the approach recognised the varied and 'distinct dimensions of policy work' (Geva-May and Pal, 1999) in attempting to embrace an evaluation, analysis and a change focus. As a consequence the programme entered a design phase during January/March 1999 in which a series of policy audit tools were developed for use at national and force level. In addition management processes were defined to assist in handling the referrals/actions arising out of such audit activity (particularly referrals/actions directed to ACPO committees and the Home Office).

The policy evaluation work concentrated the ACPO programme and audit teams on conducting 'evidence-based' audits of existing policy across a range of business processes. These processes had been identified as representing a critical risk of challenge (for example: custody, child protection, firearms, mental health, covert policing, etc). From such audits it was possible to determine levels of 'potential' compliance/non-compliance in national policy against pre-defined criteria, drawn from the human rights principles identified above in Chapter 4. These criteria allowed an assessment of compliance against the core principles of human rights legislation and visibility/accountability in decision making.[1]

The analytical work associated with national policy took two forms. Initially, action centered on the development of a process to handle the audit outcomes or contingency actions (later identified as 'referrals') arising out of the process of audit, which were to be directed to the Home Office, legal advisors and ACPO policy committees for consideration and resolution.

In addition a policy tool (known as a 'generic policy framework') was developed for use by policy units in amending or creating future policy. This activity enabled the programme to meet ACPO's remaining objectives by ensuring that a mechanism was put in place to manage referrals from the current and future policy audits, and also by providing a policy framework against which assessments of practice vis-à-vis policy could be made. The process and tools associated with the national ACPO policy audits and reviews were subsequently evaluated and modified for use by forces and other public authorities.

The guidance to public authorities (forces and partner agencies) took the form of an 'audit guide' which not only challenged all aspects of policy, procedures and practice which had the potential to interfere with an individuals human rights, but also provided a reference guide to key issues in assessing the level of organisational preparedness for the onset of the Human Rights Act.

The 'audit guide' stressed that:

At the heart of the Act lies the challenge of further enhancing the transformation of our Police Service – within a more defined human rights culture. We need to do our business effectively, ethically and as transparently as possible within the confines of operational restrictions. This will be actively reinforced through best value legislation, which focuses on performance in service delivery. Performance in this context will mean the service looking critically at our ability to be compliant with legislative frameworks, of which Human Rights and Freedom of Information will be central in informing all aspects of organisational activity.

(ACPO, 1999a)

The results and reality of policy analysis and evaluation

By June 1999 the first wave of national ACPO policy audits had been completed and the results were reported in a 'Service Wide Impact Assessment'. The areas subject to national audit of policy covered business areas, which had been judged by service professionals and legal advisors as representing both a critical risk of challenge and/or of being in the public interest/safety. The areas identified for the initial round of audits were:

- Child protection
- Complaints
- Covert policing
- Custody
- Domestic violence
- Firearms
- Hate and race crimes
- Major crime investigation
- Mental health
- Personnel – staff appraisal, attendance management, driver training, first aid, substance misuse
- Personnel – grievance procedure
- Public order.

The initial audits gave rise to over 1500 referrals. Referrals in this context were evidence-based issues of 'potential' non-compliance, which the auditors believed required consideration of further action by one or more of the following bodies:

- Home Office (referrals on legislative issues which predominantly focused on interpretation, legal basis of actions, legality of codes of practice etc).
- ACPO Committees (referrals on policy issues, for example highlighting where no national policy existed, or where policy did not include the key tests of legality, proportionality etc).
- Programme team and legal advisors (referrals on professional and/or legal issues, which would be subject to independent professional/legal opinion. These referrals invariably would then be redirected to either the Home Office or ACPO committees as appropriate).

The core themes behind such referrals related to:

- challenges to the legality of powers, authorities or directions given
- application of key principles, for example the test of proportionality in policy
- the adequacy or absence of policy
- the adequacy or absence of mechanisms to give visibility on decision making
- adequacy or absence of procedures for internal and independent review and scrutiny
- public accountability issues (publication of policies, representations and provision of rights).

In order to manage the high volume of referrals and ultimately actions arising out of the audit activity, a formal referral process was initiated in May 2000 between the programme team, ACPO policy committees and nominated Home Office officials. This 'referrals process' was maintained beyond 2 October 2000 to deal with emergent referrals from future policy reviews and audits. In this respect the aim was to ensure that the audit process would continue to be sustained through the ACPO committee structure, with service representatives liaising directly with nominated individuals from the Home Office.

Whilst at national level there was a clear programme and process to effect change to legislation and policy, it was recognised that similar activity was needed to check levels of HR compliance and ethical standards in local policy, procedures and ultimately in practice.

Making the link between ethics and human rights explicit

At this stage in the programme's development, the links between policy audits, training (competencies) and ethics became explicit. The audit programme led into the need for the service to develop and embrace a human rights ethical framework, covering all aspects of decision making and providing a professional code of conduct to promote professional, ethical and human rights-compliant behaviours in the workplace. This message had likewise featured earlier in the recommendations presented by the Chair of the Commission on Policing for Northern Ireland, Christopher Patten, who concluded:

> We recommend a new code of ethics to replace the existing largely procedural code, integrating the European convention on human rights into police practice.
>
> (Patten 1999)

With developments at a national level in terms of ethics and human rights well underway, the 'local' or force perspective to the programme was very much in a formative stage. All UK forces were provided with the audit guide, policy framework and relevant audit training. The human rights programme team reported on the outcomes of a national survey of forces, reporting a 'positive response from forces in recognising the need to audit compliance', concluding that 'all forces had actively considered some or all of the actions recommended in the ACPO Audit Guide' (ACPO HR programme survey, April 2000).

In terms of long-term change, the ACPO human rights programme team felt that the combined impact of national and local training in human rights/ethics, national and local policy audits and the development of ethical standards and codes of conduct would, ultimately, ensure that the service has a secure ethical and HR compliant foundation underpinning the management and delivery of public services. However, it must be noted that predictably the transition at force level (from training and putting policy edicts into practice in order to effect changes in behaviours and values) was still some way off.

Can policy analysis and evaluation promote change?

The value of policy analysis and evaluation as a tool to effect changes in behaviours and values will not be known for some time. The time lapse between identifying a referral and effecting change in legislation, policy and ultimately practice will be measured in years rather than months. In the meantime case law will drive through legal and procedural changes at an accelerating rate.

Given the lessons from European case law, it is clear that in national service policy, which is geared to inform local force policy and practice, there is a need for the service to be more visible and accountable. In this context policy analysis and evaluation can be seen to provide a positive impetus and framework for change.

In assessing the transferability of such a 'policy approach' to other cultural or social settings it is clear that the approach is very much context driven. Whilst such policy tools are founded on principles common to European and international human rights law, their effectiveness in promoting a human rights culture is very much dependent on the existence of a policy framework which informs the actions at strategic, tactical and operational levels. In countries in 'transitional' or chaotic states the integrity of such frameworks can be undermined by any number of influences, not least for example by corruption, racial, social or political tensions.

The real value of adopting a policy management approach to promote change lies in the development of relevant 'challenges'[2] which an organisation can use as tools to promote consistency, transparency and accountability in the management and provision of public services. Relevant challenges in this respect means professional, ethical and/or legal principles which those engaged in public service provision should not only adhere to, but actively promote.

This is not to suggest that a policy approach is a 'model' for performance or change management. It is, in contrast, recognition that cultural or value change is complex and requires significant organisational effort to be able to realise tangible shifts in behaviour at the point of delivery. Change in this context can only be realised through an integrated programme of impacts, which should include both internal and external drivers for change (for example, service-based training, identification of relevant behavioral competencies, effective marketing/communication, internal performance monitoring and measurement, cultural analysis, policy analysis and evaluation, as well as external mechanisms for review and inspection, independent scrutiny, etc).

Integrating human rights into performance management and inspections

At a local level, it has already been noted that forces have been encouraged by ACPO to integrate human rights audits and compliance tests into their existing arrangements for assessing performance, and in particular in service reviews under the best value regime.

The focus on integrating human rights into best value is prompted by a recognition that any assessment of performance (whether at national, regional, organisational or individual level) must actively consider the issue of HR compliance, as all public authorities have a legal obligation to uphold individual human rights when engaged in the provision of public services.

Best value presents public authorities with an ideal opportunity to ensure that, in complying with the legal requirements of the Local Government Act 1998 to review each individual service at least once every five years, they embed HR compliance tests as they assess service performance and apply the rationale behind best value (i.e. challenging whether services should be provided in the first place, consulting on service delivery, making comparisons with other providers and undertaking competitive analysis).

Moving away from the concept of self-regulation within the police service, there is an obvious and pressing need for all key inspection bodies (HMIC, Audit Commission, SSI, Ofsted, etc) to engage with the principles of human rights in development of inspection protocols and methodologies that are focused on public service provision. Whilst there have been limited developments in this area, the human rights programme are currently gearing up to lobby the relevant inspection bodies. This action is being taken in the hope that inspection bodies will adopt an HR perspective in review and inspections of forces and that, ultimately, that they will act as an external driver for change.

This is particularly relevant to those inspection bodies with the legal mandate for best value (notably the HMIC and the Audit Commission's audit and inspection bodies) whose remit is to promote 'continuous improvement' in public services. Whilst in early stages of development, the programme is gearing up to target the recently established joint inspection forums, in the hope that future best value inspection regimes will be grounded in, and focus upon, the key principles of human rights legislation in assessing their own and others performance.

Observations from non-governmental organisations and academics

The value of using independent legal advisors, academics and non-governmental organisations (NGOs) as active participants in the process of quality assurance cannot be underestimated. This form of active consultation and quality assurance has resulted in the development of a set of tools to review and audit policy, procedures and practice which have been acknowledged as having global relevance in the promotion of human rights.

As active participants in the programme, NGO's and academic responses to the police service's preparations for incorporation have been widely supportive. Their comments ranged from acknowledging that the audit toolkit was 'truly a pioneer … from which other public services can and must learn' to welcome for the new 'openness and transparency' that the close involvement of NGOs heralded.[3]

Conclusions: a multiple-impact change programme

It is clear that in seeking to promote change in organisational settings, the ACPO human rights sub-committee has recognised the value of a 'multiple-impact' programme, in order to make a real difference to the professional culture and practice of policing. In moving away from an approach solely focused on training, the programme has sought not only to encourage the service and forces to self-regulate through audits of policy and practice, but also has actively pursued an external and in many respects political agenda – for example in pressing for national developments in the setting of professional/ethical standards and promoting the integration of human rights into mainstream inspection and review processes.

In terms of accountability to the public and service stakeholders, the approach adopted has emphasised the need to take action on a number of professional management issues which, whilst outside the legal parameters of the Human Rights Act, will play a significant part in changing the way the service accounts for its actions. For example, the development of an ethical decision-making framework and tests challenging the adequacy of mechanisms to give greater visibility and accountability in such activity.

The value of the ACPO programme in promoting a professional human rights culture lies in three main areas:

- The diversity and sustainability of its key impacts (encompassing elements of change management, training, marketing, policy analysis/ evaluation etc).

- The strength of the 'informed' strategic leadership of the programme (through service-wide commitment and consultation with NGOs, legal, academic and service professionals).
- The rationale underpinning the programme which was grounded in ACPO's fundamental belief in the 'value added' to policing, by upholding the human rights of individuals in the delivery of public services.

The ACPO human rights programme has in many respects followed a classic model of change intervention or programmatic change. It is marked by a desire to challenge old patterns of behaviour, creating an awareness of the need to change and then seeking to establish and reinforce new patterns of behaviour through training, communication and policy lines (Nicholson, 1993). The complexities and difficulties of 'programmatic change' are significant, not least because of the 'dynamic conservatism' (Nicholson, 1993) of organisations, for example in absorbing or neutralising innovation or resisting change whilst appearing to embrace it.

In preparing for human rights incorporation, ACPO have adopted a 'top down' rather than 'bottom up' approach to intervention, in seeking radical change to organisational culture and behaviour. The danger of such an approach lies in its potential to politicise the change agent (in this context ACPO's HR programme) and, as Mangham interestingly stressed, that such an approach explicitly 'entails an awareness of the levers of power, a willingness to lay hands on them, and securing the committed support of leaders in the organisation' (Mangham, 1979).

The tests of the approach's success will initially lie in the service's ability to be responsive to, and effect, tangible change. Ultimately it will rest in the level of public confidence in the service's ability to ethically and appropriately uphold individual human rights.

Further reading

The ACPO audit guide and links to other human rights materials is on www.cheshire.police.uk/rights. The training programme designed for the ACPO is on www.npt.police.uk.

Notes

1 The audit guide can be found at www.cheshire.police.uk/rights. An extract of the approach can be seen in the previous chapter.
2 Such 'challenges' are illustrated in the ACPO Force Audit Guide and relate to issues of legality, legitimate aim, proportionality, subsidiarity, accountability, review and scrutiny in decision making, etc.
3 Quotations from Dr Geoffrey Hunt, University of Surrey, and John Wadham, Director of Liberty.

Chapter 12

Towards ethical policing

We started this book by arguing that public policing is facing a cycle of continuous crisis, arising from either corruption or incompetence. Most recently there have been the Lawrence investigation and corruption scandals in a number of British forces, and we have also cited a number of international examples, including the Rampart case in the USA (Chapter 9) and the Van Traa inquiry in the Netherlands (Chapter 7). These have in the past led to a cycle of crisis/scandal, proposed changes (usually rule tightening), a shift back to crime fighting and thence back into crisis.

There have been some important attempts to break out of this cycle, most notably the 'reform' and 'community policing' movements that have had some impact in the UK and in the USA. However, there has not been a determined effort to underpin these operational changes by a proper and sustainable professionalism. This has become more and more important as policing faces the challenge of the burgeoning private sector, whose growth has been stimulated by an insatiable desire for 'security' at a time of dislocating international change. The public police are no longer the only, and, in some parts of policing, even the major agency. A demanding public has grown impatient with failure and has shown itself increasingly prepared to seek alternatives.

In the second chapter we reflected on the additional problem that the purpose of the police was unclear and had not been authoritatively scrutinized in the UK since the Royal Commission in 1962. Yet the role has by demand, technology and social change – notably in areas such as the policing of domestic violence, child protection and dangerousness – changed substantially. The shift away from the police as the major agents of social control has been cemented by the new 'Crime and Disorder' strategies and initiatives such as the social exclusion unit's work on neighborhood renewal. As the independent inquiry suggested in 1996, the public police need to renew their mandate and redefine their role. We suggested that this should be as the 'enabling' organisation at the heart of policing, providing key services that demand special skills and regulating others such as neighbourhood patrols.

The enabling role demands a new professionalism, which differentiates a knowledge- and skills-rich public police from the multiplicity of public and private agencies which have emerged to fill gaps in public provision (and to police the growing public–private space). We have discussed four main approaches to ethics that have been used by authors to propose an ethical approach for the police. We have suggested that a 'four track approach' drawing on the ethics of duty, utility, care and virtue may provide a set of principles that could underpin such a new professionalism. Our argument for such a balanced approach reflected our contention that policing is complex and that simple one-line ethical judgements are unable to provide an adequate practical framework for police decision making.

This shift to 'ethical policing' is doubly necessary because of the new international shift to human rights as the *lingua franca* of liberal democracy. In the UK the incorporation of ECHR in 2000 has added urgency to these changes and has added important interpretative principles – legality, proportionality, necessity and remedy – to the principles we have outlined. Police officers in the UK have been used to a system which allowed them to fill the gaps between positive legal provisions by outcome-oriented use of discretion (colloquially known as 'the ways and means act'). The shift to a human rights base in the law has both tightened discretion by requiring officers' actions to be supported by strict legality and at the same time demand that discretion is actively exercised in a justifiable manner – with proportionality firmly in mind. This concentration on both the process and context of decision making as well as the outcomes is a substantial challenge for an organisation whose culture has emphasised outcome and 'utility' based ethics.

We used Part 2 of the book to debate the impact of these challenges and constitutional changes to public policing. We suggested five main implications:

- *The need for a new professional model* which accorded the individual officer greater personal responsibility within an ethical framework. We argued that the hierarchical military model sat uneasily with the personal responsibility and evidenced decision-making that the new human rights regime demanded. We argued that the professional clinician model, which has emerged from the 'community policing' movement, had considerable merits as the core of the new professionalism.

- *There needs to be a new approach to accounting for performance.* Our analysis in Chapter 6 showed that the existing model – partly because of the lack of clarity of the police role, partly because of an overemphasis on quantitative measures – produced a 'ritualistic' and, therefore, ethically problematic system of measurement. We suggested that the system needed to evolve into one that was more values based and linked to processes of negotiation within a differentiated policy network. Such differentiation has become urgent because of the growing differentiation in the levels of policing (Johnston, 2000).

- At an operational level, *police needed to move from a philosophy of justification by results (i.e. ends justify the means) to justification by a balance of compliance and appropriate outcome.* Compliance we suggested was a complex and multi-layered process within which it was possible to discern the principles we outlined in Chapters 3 and 4.

- There were *substantial implications for the operational accountability of the police.* The concept of 'operational independence' needed to be updated. The principle of stewardship requires that the police properly account for their decisions. The human rights provisions mean that police must be able to evidence their decisions and show how they have balanced interests and rights. We suggested that the existing system of accountability in the UK was too top down leaving a substantial deficit at the local level, where the police were too frequently left explaining the limitations on their actions imposed by centrally controlled financial and performance constraints. For the police to be more responsive and accountable there needed to be changes in the role of the very local – district level – bodies, similar to those suggested by Patten in his analysis of the future for policing in Northern Ireland.

- *The policing of diversity and the challenge of corruption and misconduct have caused a huge loss of public confidence.* They require a greater involvement of lay and independent agents in policing. The police, as Bowling has said, should not be a closed agency. Key areas of policy making and service delivery need to be opened to scrutiny by lay advisors and the investigation of misconduct needs to be carried out by an independent agency. This new openness could also be extended to other communities and problems, such as the policing of rural communities, where community confidence has been eroded by rapid social change and rising demand on the police which has forced the replacement of traditional reassurance policing by a combination of response and problem-solving approaches.[1]

The first two parts of the book have, therefore, made out the case for a very different public police, whose broad mission would be supported by ethical principles, whose operational decisions would be evidenced, set within a framework of ethical compliance and open to scrutiny by lay advisors and greater local participation. We have suggested that an 'enabling' style of policing rather than a reliance on the traditional crime-fighting model or the 'social engineering' approach might best allow this new public police to develop and hold the ring of the evolving, diverse economy of 'policing'.

Moving an organisation such as the police, with a well-established occupational culture, towards our proposed model of 'ethical policing' is not a straightforward prospect. In Part 3 we have tried to set out what we feel are some of the major internal drivers of such change. We concentrated on three themes:

- *Recruitment and 'career-long' learning*: many previous strategies have been too focused in change in particular areas such as Community and Race Relations training. These have largely failed because of their narrow focus and lack of congruity with operational realities. We have suggested a broader approach to continuous development of the organization.

- *Ethical codes and developing models of ethical decision-making*: we have not sought to argue that such codes provide a solution in themselves. However, any organization embarking on a long journey needs a route map and sign posts to guide its members. The combination of a code and decision-making tools could provide such guidance. They also convey a strong message to the citizen about the direction and commitment of the police.

- *Compliance auditing of policies, operational practice and partnerships*: we have suggested that this discipline of constant challenge is a vital part of developing the learning capacity of the police and demonstrating the commitment to ethical policing. Some of the lessons can be uncomfortable, particularly in an essentially conservative organization.

The missing element – the fourth theme – that we have touched on many times through the book is *leadership*. With the demand for 'better management' in policing which dominated the 1980s and 1990s, the shift to devolved budgets and the increasing homage paid to 'managerialism', leadership had become a subset of 'management'. Furthermore, management could be learned and taught, whilst leadership could only with difficulty, like good policing, be developed. Yet, as O'Dowd (1999) has stressed, without leadership and, in particular, visible and personal commitment to the values and principles of ethical policing, the Code will remain aspirational, outcomes will continue to hold sway over process and the police will be stuck in the vicious cycle.

Recreating trust in public policing is hard, creating the 'virtuous circle' even harder. In the managerialist vision public confidence will be won through ever-improving performance tables. However, this one-dimensional view of policing, with its often simplistic notions of performance, sits uneasily alongside public perceptions, such as those of rural communities, that public policing, despite improving 'performance' is performing poorly.

Figure 12.1   The virtuous circle and its context

In our last Figure in the book – Figure 12.1 – we represent the elements of the 'virtuous circle' through the arguments presented in this book. The model, which incorporates elements from the 'learning cycle', elements from Ekblom's model of crime prevention and the principles of policing from Chapter 3, has been set out so as to emphasise the context and continuity of the circle. There are a number of elements to the diagram:

- The *distil factors* are shown on the left. These long-term changes in society, such as the political environment and the shift to a human rights culture create the circumstances in which 'ethical policing' can develop.
- The *learning cycle* provides a continuous loop of development. The commitment to such continuous learning is as we have seen in Chapter 9 an integral part of ethics.

219

- The *reinforcing factors* – performance and public confidence – are vital to ensure that public policing continues to maintain the public and political support upon which its continued survival depends.
- In the middle of the learning cycle we have placed *the principles* and some of the major themes that we have drawn out in this chapter. We have sought to relate each of these to a point in the learning cycle.

As this final model seeks to show, good policing in the twenty-first century requires more than 'good performance'. It needs a renewal of the contract between police officer and the citizen, which in turn requires greater openness and scrutiny, continuously improving professional standards and a new commitment to ethics at the core of policing.

Note

1 The authors are particularly drawing on their experience in West Mercia for these comments.

Bibliography

ACPO (1990) Strategic policy document: setting the standards: meeting community expectations. London: ACPO.

ACPO (1995) National guidelines for the management of informants. Unpublished guidelines. London: ACPO.

ACPO (1996a) Report of the Working Group on Patrol. London: ACPO.

ACPO (1996b) *Tackling Crime Effectively: Handbook Vol. II.* London: ACPO, HMIC, Home Office and Audit Commission.

ACPO (1999a) *The Human Rights audit tool.* London: ACPO.

ACPO (1999b) *The Murder Manual.* London: ACPO.

ACPO (1999c) *National Standards for Covert Policing.* London: ACPO

ACPO (2000a) *Keeping the Peace Manual.* London: ACPO.

ACPO (2000b) *National Intelligence Model.* London: National Criminal Intelligence Service.

Adams, D. (1998) 'ACPO pushes for a code of ethics', *Police Review,* 7th August.

Adlam, R. (1997) 'Uncovering the ethical profile of police managers and the moral ethos of police organisations: a preliminary analysis', *International Journal of Police Science and Management*, Vol. 1, No. 2: 162–182.

Alderson, J.C. (1979) *Policing Freedom.* Plymouth: MacDonald and Evans.

Alderson, J.C. (1984) *Law and Disorder.* London: Hamish Hamilton.

Alderson, J.C. (1998) *Principled Policing: Protecting the Public with Integrity.* Winchester: Waterside Press.

Anderson, D., Lait, J. and Marsland, D. (1981) *Breaking the Spell of the Welfare State.* London: Social Affairs Unit.

Argyris, C. (1986) *Change and Defensive Routines.* Boston, Mass.: Pitman.

Ashworth, A. (1994) *The Criminal Process: an evaluative study.* Oxford: Clarendon.

Association of Police Authorities (1998) *Objectives, Indicators, Targets: a Study of Policing Plans and Reports.* London: APA.

Audit Commission (1986). *Improving Performance in Local Government.* London: Audit Commission.

Audit Commission. (1990) *Effective Policing – Performance Review in Police Forces.* Police Paper No. 8. London: Audit Commission.

Audit Commission (1993) *Helping with enquiries.* Police Paper No. 12. London: HMSO.

Audit Commission (1996) *Streetwise: Effective Police Patrol.* London: Audit Commission.

Audit Commission (1997) *Performance Indicators 1995/96: Police services.* London: Audit Commission.

Audit Commission (1998a) *Feedback '98: Results of the Commission's consultation on the local authority performance indicators for 1999/2000.* London: Audit Commission.

Audit Commission (1998b) *Local Authority Performance Indicators 1996/97: Police Services.* London: HMSO.

Audit Commission (1999) *Local Authority Performance Indicators 1997/1998: Police Services.* London: HMSO.

Baier, A. (1985) *Postures of the Mind: Essays on Mind and Morals.* Minneapolis: University of Minnesota Press.

Baldwin, J. and Moloney, J. (1992) *Supervision of Police Investigations in Serious Criminal Cases.* London: HMSO, Royal Commission on Criminal Justice Research Study No. 4.

Barker, T. and Carter, D. (eds.) (1986) *Police Deviance.* Cincinnati, Ohio: Anderson.

Barker, T. (1996) *Police Ethics: a Crisis in Law Enforcement.* Springfield, Illinois: Charles Thomas.

Bauman, Z. (1993) *Post Modern Ethics.* Oxford: Blackwell.

Baron, R.A. and Greenburg, J. (1990) *Behaviour in Organisations.* Third edition. Massachusetts: Allyn and Bacon.

Bayley, D.H. (1994) *Police for the Future.* New York: OUP.

Bayley, D.H. (1996) 'What do the police do?' in Saulsbury, W., Mott, J. and Newbury, T. (eds.) *Themes in Contemporary Policing.* London: Policy Studies Institute.

Bayley, D.H. and Bittner, E. (1994) 'Learning the Skills of Policing', *Law and Contemporary Problems*, Vol. 1, No. 4, 47: 35–60.

Beckley, A (1990) 'In search of a crock of gold – the reflective practitioner?' Quantico, Washington: Federal Bureau of Investigation Library.

Beckley, A. (1997a) 'Futures research – fact or fantasy?' *Police Research and Management*, Vol. 2, No. 1.

Beckley, A. (1997b) *Operational Policing:Liabilities and Entitlements.* London: Police Review Publishing Company.

Beckley, A. (1998) 'Learning for life: the path to job satisfaction? *Police Research and Management*, Volume 3, No. 1.

Beckley, A. (1999) 'Human Rights: the key to police professionalism and better decision making', *Police Research and Management*, Vol. 3, No. 2.

Bellamy, R. (1999) *Liberalism and Pluralism: towards a politics of compromise.* London: Routledge.

Bennett R.R. (1984) 'Becoming Blue: A Longitudinal Study of Police Recruit Occupational Socialisation', *Journal of Police Science and Administration*, Vol. 12, No. 1.

Berkley, S.A. and Giles, F.G. (1999) 'How far can you claim to be reflective practitioners?' Unpublished report, BA in-service Education Studies degree, University College, Worcester.

Bittner, E. (1975) *The Functions of Police in Modern Society.* Chevy Chase: National Institute of Mental Health.

Blair, I. (1999) Speech to the Social Market Foundation, February 1999.

Blair, Tony (1996) *New Britain, a vision of a young country*. London: Fourth Estate.

Boateng, P. (1999) 'Managing Dangerous People with severe personality disorder', *Criminal Justice Matters* No. 37, Autumn: 5–7.

Bok, S. (1989) *Secrets: on the ethics of concealment and revelation*. Vintage: New York.

Bossard, A. (1981) 'Police ethics and international police cooperation' in Schamalleger, F. and Gustafson, R. (eds.), *The Social Basis of Criminal Justice: Ethical Issues for the 1980s*. Washington, D.C.: University Press.

Bottoms, A.E. and Wiles, P. (1996) 'Understanding crime prevention in late modern societies' in T. Bennett (ed.) *Preventing Crime and Disorder: targeting strategies and responsibilities*. Cambridge: Institute of Criminology, University of Cambridge.

Bowling, B. (1999) *Violent Racism*. Oxford: Clarendon Press.

Braithwaite, J. (1989) *Crime, Shame and Reintegration*. Cambridge: Cambridge University Press.

Braswell, M. and Gold, J. (1996) 'Peacemaking, Justice and Ethics' in Braswell, M. and McCarthy, B. (eds.) *Justice, Crime and Ethics*. Cincinnati: Anderson.

Brodeur, J.-P. (1995) 'Undercover policing in Canada: a study of its consequences' in Marx, G.T. and Fijnaut, C. (eds.) *Undercover: police surveillance in comparative perspective*. The Hague: Kluwer Law International.

Brodeur, J.-P. (ed.) (1998) *How to Recognise Good Policing: problems and issues*. Thousand Oaks, California: Sage.

Brown, D. (1997) *PACE Ten Years On: a review of the research*. Home Office Research Study No. 115, London: Home Office.

Bryett, K. and Harrison, A. (1993) *An Introduction to Policing: Volume 3, Policing in the Community*. Sydney: Butterworths.

Bucke, T. (1995) *Policing and the public: findings from the 1994 Crime Survey*, Home Office Research Findings no. 28. London: Home Office.

Bunning, C.R. (1993) 'Continuous improvement through organisational learning'. *Management Update* (Australia), June–July, pp. 20–21.

Bunyard, R.S. (1979) *Police Management Handbook*. London: McGraw-Hill.

Carter, N., Klein, R. and Day, P. (1992). *How Organisations Measure Success: the use of performance indicators in government*. London: Routledge.

Chan, J.B.L. (1997) *Changing Police Culture: policing in a multi-cultural society*. Cambridge: CUP.

Christie, G., Petrie, S. and Timmins, P. (1996) 'Effect on police education, training and socialisation of conservative attitudes', *Australian and New Zealand Journal of Criminology*, Vol. 29, No. 3: 299–314.

Clarke, B. and Francis-Smythe, J. (2000) 'Developing reflective practice in police firearms instruction', *Police Research and Management*, Volume 4 No. 1.

Clutterbuck, R. (1997) *Public Safety and Civil Liberties*. Basingstoke: Macmillan.

Cm 2281 (1992) *Report of the Royal Commission on Criminal Justice*. London: HMSO.

Cm 4162 (1998) *Criminal Statistics: England and Wales 1997*. London: Home Office.

Cm 4181 (1999) *Public Services for the Future: modernisation, reform, accountability – comprehensive spending review: public service agreements 1999–2002*. London: HMSO.

Cohen, H.S. (1991) 'Overstepping police authority', in Braswell, M. and McCarthy, B. (eds.) *Justice, Crime and Ethics*. Cincinnati: Anderson.

Cohen, H.S. and Feldberg, M. (1991) *Power and Restraint: the moral dimension of police work*. New York: Praeger.

Collins, J.C. and Porras, J.I. (1996) 'Building your company's vision', *Harvard Business Review*, September–October.

Commission for Social Justice (1994) *Social Justice: strategies for national renewal*. London: Vintage.

Cooper, R.K. and Sawaf, A. (1996) *Executive EQ*. London: Orion Business Books.

Covey, S.R. (1989) *The Seven Habits of Highly Effective People*. London: Simon & Schuster.

Cramphorn, C. (1999) 'A policing "patten" for the new millennium', *Criminal Justice Matters*, No. 38, 12–13.

Crawshaw, R., Devlin, B. and Williamson, T. (1998) *Human Rights and Policing: standards for good behaviour and a strategy for change*. The Hague: Kluwer Law International.

Critchley, T.A. (1978) *A History of Police in England and Wales*. London: Constable.

Dale, J. and Foster, P. (1986) *Feminists and State Welfare*. London: Routledge.

Davis, K.C. (1975) *Police Discretion*. St. Paul: West.

Davis, M. (1991) 'Do cops really need a code of ethics?' *Criminal Justice Ethics*, Summer/Fall.

Davis, M. (1996) 'Police, discretion and professions' in Kleinig, J. (ed.) *Handled with Discretion: ethical issues in police decision-making*. Lanham, Maryland: Rowman and Littlefield.

Delattre, E.J. (1989) *Character and Cops: ethics in policing*. Washington D.C.: American Enterprise Institute for Public Policy Research.

DETR (Department of the Environment, Transport and the Regions) (1999). *Best Value and Audit Commission Performance Indicators for 2000/2001, Vol. 1.*

DiMaggio, P.J. and Powell, W.W. (1983) 'The iron cage revisited: institutional isomorphism and collective rationality in organisational fields', *American Sociological Review*, Vol. 48: 147–160.

Doerner, W.G. and Nowell, T.M. (1999) 'The reliability of the behaviour-personnel assessment device (B-PAD) in selecting police recruits' *Policing: an International Journal of Police Strategies and Management*, Vol. 22, 3.

Donahue, M.E. (1993) 'Police ethics: a critical perspective' *Journal of Criminal Justice*, Vol. 21: 339–352.

Donziger, S. (ed.) (1996) *The Real War on Crime: The Report of the National Criminal Justice Commission*. New York: Harper Perennial.

Dorn, N., Murji, K. and South, N. (1992) *Traffickers: drug markets and law enforcement*. London and New York: Routledge.

Dunnighan, C. and Norris, C. (1995a) *The detective, the snout and the Audit Commission: the real costs in using informants*, unpublished pamphlet in the National Police Staff College Library.

Dunnighan, C. and Norris, C. (1995b) *Practice, problems and policy: management issues on the police use of informers*, unpublished pamphlet in the National Police Staff College Library.

Durkheim, E. (1959) *On the Division of Labour in Society*. Glencoe, Illinois: Free Press.

Dworkin, R. (1977) *Taking Rights Seriously*. Cambridge, Mass.: Harvard University Press.

Eck, J.E. (1983) *Solving Crimes: the investigation of burglary and robbery*. Washington D.C.: Police Executive Research Forum, National Institute of Justice.

Edwards, S.M. (1989) *Policing 'Domestic' Violence*. London: Sage.

Elliston, F.A. and Feldberg, M. (eds.) (1985) *Moral Issues in Police Work*. Totowa, New Jersey: Rowman and Allenheld.

Ekblom, P. (1999) 'The conjunction of criminal opportunity – a tool for clear, 'joined-up' thinking about community safety and crime reduction' in Pease, K., Ballintyne, S. and McLaren, V. (eds.), *Key Issues in Crime prevention, crime reduction and community safety*, London: IPPR.

Emsley, C. (1991) *The English Police: a political and social history*. Hemel Hempstead: Harvester Wheatsheaf.

Ericson, R.V. (1993) *Making Crime: a study of detective work*. Second edition. Toronto: Toronto University Press.

Ericson, R.V. and Haggerty (1998) *Policing the risk society*. Oxford: Clarendon Press.

Exley, M. (2000) 'First class coach' *Management Today*, May 2000.

Faulkner, D. (1996) *Darkness and Light: justice, crime and management for today*. London: Howard League for Penal Reform.

Feldberg, M. (1985) 'Gratuities, corruption and the democratic ethos of policing' in Elliston, F.A. and Feldberg, M. (eds.), *Moral issues in police work*. Totowa, New Jersey: Rowman & Allenheld.

Feldman, D. (1993) *Civil Liberties and Human Rights in England and Wales*. Oxford: Clarendon Press.

Finger, M. and Brand, S.B. (1999) 'The concept of the "learning organisation" applied to the transformation of the public sector: conceptual contributions for theory development' in Easterby-Smith, M., Burgoyne, J., and Araujo, L. (eds.) *Organizational Learning and the Learning Organization*. London: Sage Publications Ltd.

FIPR (2000) 'The RIPA Bill: briefing paper'. www.fipr.org.uk

Fitzgerald, L., Johnston, R., Brignall, S., Silvestro, R. and Voss, C. (1991) *Performance Measurement in Service Businesses*. London: Chartered Institute of Management Accountants.

Fitzgerald, M. (1999) 'Final Report into Stop and Search'. www.met.police.uk/police/mps/mps/stop.htm

Foster, J. (1989), 'Two Stations: two ethnographic studies of policing in the inner city', in D. Downes (ed.) *Crime and the City*. London: Macmillan.

Francis, P., Davies, P. and Jupp, V. (eds.) (1997) *Policing Futures*. Basingstoke: Macmillan.

Friedson, E. (1983) 'The theory of the professions' in Dingwall, J. and Lewis, P. (eds.) *The Sociology of the Professions*. Oxford: Oxford University Press.

Fyfe, J.J. (1989) 'The split-second syndrome and other determinants of police violence' in Dunham, R.G. and Alpert, G.P. (eds.) *Critical Issues in Policing: contemporary readings*. Prospect Heights, Illinois: Waveland.

Garland, D. (1995) 'Panopticon days: surveillance and society', *Criminal Justice Matters*, No. 20, 3–4.

Garmanikow, E. (1978) 'Sexual division of labour: the case of nursing' in Kuhn, A. and Wolpe, A.M. (eds.) *Feminism and Materialism*. London: Routledge.

Gearty, C. and Tomkins, A. (eds.) (1996) *Understanding Human Rights*. London: Pinter.

Geller, W.A. and Scott, M.S. (1992) *Deadly Force: what we know – a practitioner's desk reference on police-involved shootings*. Washington D.C.: Police Executive Research Forum.

Geller, W.A. and Toch, H. (1996) 'Understanding and controlling police abuse of force' in Geller, W.A. and Toch, H. (eds.) *Police Violence: understanding and controlling police abuse of force*. New Haven and London: Yale University Press.

Gensler, H. (1998) *Ethics: a contemporary introduction*. London: Routledge.

Geva-May, I. and Pal, L.A. (1999) 'Good fences make good neighbours' *Evaluation* Vol. 5, No. 3: 259–277.

Giddens, A. (1990) *The Consequences of Modernity*. Cambridge: Polity Press.

Gilligan, C. (1982) *In a Different Voice*. Cambridge, Mass.: Harvard University Press.

Gillon, R. (1994) 'Medical ethics: four principles plus attention to scope' *British Medical Journal* Vol. 309: 184–8.

Glover, J. (1999) *Humanity, a moral history of the twentieth century*. London: Jonathon Cape.

Goldstein, H. (1975) *Police Corruption: a perspective on its nature and control*. Washington D.C.: Police Foundation.

Goldstein, H. (1977) *Policing a Free Society*. Cambridge, Mass.: Ballinger.

Goldstein, H. (1990) *Problem Oriented Policing*. London, McGraw-Hill.

Goleman, D. (1996) *Emotional Intelligence: why it can matter more than IQ*. London: Bloomsbury Publishing.

Graef R, (1989) *Talking Blues*. London: Collins Harvill.

Green, D. (1982) *Welfare State – for rich or for poor*. London: IEA, Paper 63.

Grubin, D. (1998) *Sex Offending Against Children: understanding the risk*. London: Home Office, Police Research Series, Paper 99.

Haggard, P. (1993) *Police Ethics*. Lewiston: The Edwin Mellen Press.

Hanvey, P. (1995) *Identifying, Recruiting and Handling Informants*. London: Home Office Police Research Group, Special Interest Series, Paper 5.

Hare, R.M. (1981) *Moral Thinking*. Oxford: OUP.

Hebenton, B. and Thomas, T. (1997) *Keeping Track? Observations on Sex Offender Registers in the US*. London: Home Office, Crime Detection and Prevention Series, Paper 83.

Held, V. (1995) *Justice and Care*. Boulder, Colorado: Westview.

HMIC (1997a) *Thematic Inspection Report on Officer Safety*. London: HMIC.

HMIC (1997b) *Winning The Race: thematic inspection report*. London: HMIC.

HMIC (1998a) *What Price Policing? a study of efficiency and value for money in the police service*. London: HMIC.

HMIC (1998b) *Winning the Race: revisited*. London: HMIC.

HMIC (1999a) *Police Integrity: securing and maintaining public confidence*. Report of Her Majesty's Inspectorate of Constabulary. London: Home Office.

HMIC (1999b) *Managing Learning: a study of police training*. Her Majesty's Inspectorate of Constabulary, London. http://www.HomeOffice.gov.uk/HMIC

HMIC (2000) *Policing London: winning consent*. http://www.HomeOffice.gov.uk/HMIC

HMSO (1991) *The Citizen's Charter: running the standard.* (Cm 1599).

Hobbs, D. (1988) *Doing the Business: entrepreneurship, the working class and detectives in the east end of London.* Oxford: Oxford University Press.

Hoddinott, J.C. (1994) 'Public safety and private security' *Policing*, Vol. 10, No. 3: 158–166.

Hofstede, G. (1981) 'Management control of public and not-for-profit activities', *Accounting, Organisations and Society*, Vol. 6, No. 3: 193–211.

Holdaway, S. (1996) *The Racialisation of British Policing.* Basingstoke: Macmillan.

Home Affairs Select Committee (1998) *Inquiry into the Influence of Freemasonry in the Criminal Justice System.* London: HMSO.

Home Office (1983) *Circular 114/83: Manpower, Effectiveness and Efficiency in the Police Service.*

Home Office (1991) *Safer Communities: the local delivery of crime prevention through the partnership approach.* London: HMSO.

Home Office (1993a) *Police reform: a police service for the 21st century.* London: HMSO.

Home Office (1993b) *Circular 17/93: Performance Indicators for the Police.* London: Home Office.

Home Office (1994) *Circular 67/94: Role of HM Inspectorate of Constabulary.* London: Home Office.

Home Office (1995) *Review of Police Core and Ancillary Tasks.* London: HMSO.

Home Office (1996) *Protecting the Public: the government's strategy on crime in England and Wales* (Cm 3190). London: Home Office.

Home Office (1997) *Bringing Rights Home.* White Paper. London: Home Office, Cm. 3782.

Home Office (1998a) *Reducing Offending: an assessment of the research evidence on ways of dealing with offending behaviour.* Home Office Research Study 187. London: Home Office.

Home Office (1998b) *Formula for Police Specific Grant and Police Standard Spending Assessment in 1999/2000.* London: Home Office.

Home Office (1998c) *New Overarching Aims and Objectives take Police Into New Millennium* (Press Release 317/98). London: Home Office.

Home Office (1998d) *Counting Rules for Recordable Offences.* London: Home Office Research and Statistics Directorate.

Home Office (1999a) *The Government's Crime Reduction Strategy.* http://www.Homeoffice.gov.uk/police

Home Office (1999b) *Police Training: a consultation document.* http://www.Homeoffice.gov.uk/police

Home Office (1999c) *Annual Report.* London: Home Office. http://www.Homeoffice.gov.uk/police

Home Office (1999d) *Ministerial priorities, key performance indicators and efficiency planning for 1999/2000.* http://www.Homeoffice.gov.uk/police

Home Office (2000a) *Best Value Performance Indicators.* (Letter to police forces).

Home Office (2000b) *Crime Targets Published Today: driving up performance – driving down crime* (Press Release). http://www.Homeoffice.gov.uk/police

Home Office (2000c) *Home Secretary's Response to the Recorded Crime Statistics October 1998 to September 1999* (press release). http://www.Homeoffice.gov.uk/police

Honderich, T. (ed.) (1995) *The Oxford Companion to Philosophy*. Oxford: OUP.

Hood, C. (1995). 'The "New Public Management" in the 1980s: variations on a theme' *Accounting, Organizations and Society*, Vol. 20, No. 2/3: 93–109.

Hood, R. (1992) *Race and Sentencing*. Oxford: Oxford University Press.

Horsman, M. and Marshall, A. (1994) *After the Nation-State: citizens, tribalism and the new world disorder*. London: Harper Collins.

Hvingtoft-Foster, L. (1993) 'Construing personal and professional development: the case of occupational socialisation in probationer training in the police service', PhD thesis, London Guildhall University.

IACP (1991) *The Law Enforcement Code of Ethics*. Washington D.C.: IACP.

IACP (1999) 'Ethics Training in Law Enforcement'. http://www.theiacp.org/pubinfo/ethicstraining.html

ICJ (1999) *New Europe, Making rights real*. Proceedings of the European Conference of the International Commission of Jurists, Warsaw.

IPPR (1993) *Social Justice in a Changing world*. London: Institute for Public Policy Research.

Jackson, M.W. (1993) 'How can ethics be taught?' in Chapman, R.A. (ed.) *Ethics in Public Service*. Edinburgh: Edinburgh University Press.

Jefferson, T. and Grimshaw, R. (1984) *Controlling the Constable: police accountability in England and Wales*. London: Frederick Muller.

Johnston, L. (1997) 'Policing communities of risk' in Francis, P., Davies, P. and Jupp, V. (eds.) *Policing Futures*. Basingstoke: Macmillan.

Johnston, L. (2000) *Policing Britain: risk, security and governance*. Harlow, Essex: Pearson Education.

Joint Consultative Committee (1990) Operational Policing Review. Surbiton, Surrey: Joint Consultative Committee.

Jones, S., and Silverman, E. (1984) 'What price efficiency? Circular arguments. Financial constraints on the police in Britain', *Policing*, Vol. 1, No. 1: 31–48.

Jones, T., Newburn, T. and Smith, D.J. (1994) *Democracy and Policing*. London: PSI.

Jones, T. and Newburn, T. (1997) *Policing after the Act: police governance after the Police and Magistrates' Courts Act 1994*. London: Policy Studies Institute.

Jowett, P. and Rothwell, M. (1988) *Performance Indicators in the Public Sector*. London: Macmillan.

Justice (1998) *Under Surveillance*. London: Justice.

Justice (2000) 'The Regulation of Investigatory Powers Bill: briefing paper'. London: Justice.

Kakar, S. (1998) 'Self-evaluations of police performance: an analysis of the relationship between police officers' education level and job performance', *Policing: an international journal of police strategies and management*, Vol. 21, No. 4.

Kamenka, E. and Erh-Soon-Tay, A. (eds.) (1978) *Human Rights*. London: Edward Arnold.

Kania, R. (1988) 'Police acceptance of gratuities', *Criminal Justice Ethics*, Vol. 7, No. 2: 37–49.

Kant, I. (1949) *Critique of Practical Reason*, translation by Lewis White Beck. Chicago: University of Chicago Press.

Kaplan, R. S. and Norton, D. P. (1996) 'Using the balanced scorecard as a strategic management system' *Harvard Business Review*, Jan–Feb, 75–85.

Kappeler, V., Sluder, K. and Alpert, G. (1984) *Forces of Deviance: understanding the dark side of policing*. Prospect Heights, Illinois: Waveland.

Kay, J. (1997) 'No plans to govern', *New Statesman*, 16 May 1997.

Keenan, T. (2000) 'Fit for the job?' *People Management*, 25 May 2000: 34–35.

Kenney D.J. and Watson, S. (1990) 'Intelligence and the selection of police recruits' *American Journal of Police*, Vol. 9, No. 4.

Kickert, W. J. M., Klijn, E.-H., and Koppenjan, J.F.M. (eds.) (1997) *Managing Complex Networks: strategies for the public sector*. London: Sage Publications.

Kingshott, B. (1999) 'Cultural ethics and police canteen culture', *Police Research and Management*, Summer: 27–43.

Kleinig, J. (1996) *The Ethics of Policing*. Cambridge: Cambridge University Press.

Kleinig, J. (ed.) (1996a) *Handled with Discretion: ethical issues in police decision-making*. Lanham, Maryland: Rowman and Littlefield.

Klemp, G.O. Jr. (1980) 'The assessment of occupational competence', Report to the National Institute of Education, Washington DC.

Klockars, C.B. (1985) 'The Dirty Harry problem' in Elliston, F.A. and Feldberg, M. (eds.) (1985) *Moral Issues in Police Work*. Totowa, New Jersey: Rowman and Allenheld.

Klockars, C.B. (1996) 'A theory of excessive force and its control' in Geller, W.A. and Toch, H. (eds.), *Policy Violence: Understanding and Controlling Police Abuse of Force*. New Haven and London: Yale University Press.

Knight, P. (1995) *Dedicated Surveillance Operations: a study in effectiveness*. London: Home Office Police Research Group.

Knight, S. (1983) *The Brotherhood: the secret world of the freemasons*. London: Grafton.

KPMG (2000) *Feasability of an Independent System for Investigating Complaints Against the Police*. London: Home Office, Police Research Series, Paper 124.

Lacey, N. (1992) 'The jurisprudence of discretion: escaping the legal paradigm' in Hawkins, K. (ed.) *The Uses of Discretion*. Oxford: Oxford University Press.

Laughlin, R. (1996) 'Principals and higher principals: accounting for accountability in the caring professions' in Munro, R. and Mouritsen, J. (eds.), *Accountability: power, ethos and the technologies of managing*. London: International Thomson Business Press.

Lawrie, L. (1995) 'Preferred policing styles of police probationers after ten months service as a function of the strength of socialisation, volume 1', Ph.D. thesis, University of Kent at Canterbury.

Lawton, A. (1998) *Ethical Management for the Public Services*. Buckingham: Open University Press.

Leadbeater, C. (1996) *The Self-Policing Society*, Arguments 9. London: Demos.

Leadbeater, C. (1999) *Living on thin air: the new economy*. Harmondsworth, Middlesex: Penguin.

Leishman, F., Loveday, B. and Savage, S. (eds.) (1995) *Core Issues in Policing*. London: Longman.

Levinson, S. (1983) 'Undercover: the hidden costs of infiltration', in Caplan, G.M. (ed.) *Abscam Ethics: moral issues and deception in law enforcement*. Cambridge, Mass.: Police Foundation.

Liberty (2000) *An Independent Police Complaints Commission*. London: Liberty

Likierman, A. (1993) 'Performance Indicators: 20 early lessons from managerial use' *Public Money & Management*, Oct–Dec 1993.

Lines, S. (1999) *Information Technology Multi-media Simulator Training: outcomes of critical decision-making exercises*. Bramshill: National Operations Faculty.

Little, R.E. (1990) 'Police academy: towards a typology of anticipatory occupational socialisation among a sample of police recruits' *Police Journal*, Vol. 63, No. 2: 159–167.

Loader, I. (1999) 'Governing policing in the 21st century' *Criminal Justice Matters*, No. 38, Winter: 9–10.

Locke, J. (1960) *Two treatises of government* (edited by P. Laslett). Cambridge: Cambridge University Press.

Mackenzie, I. (1999) 'The dynamics of integrity: managerial and psychological perspectives' in Williams, S. and Williams, G. (eds.) *Policing Integrity*. St. Catherine's House Conference Report, No. 69.

MacIntyre, A. (1981) *After Virtue*. Notre Dame: University of Notre Dame Press.

Macpherson, Sir William (1999) *Report of the the Stephen Lawrence Inquiry*. London: HMSO.

MacLaughlin, E. (1991) 'Police accountability and black people: into the 1990s', in Cashmore, E. and McLaughlin, E. (eds.) *Out of Order? Policing Black People*. London: Routledge.

Maguire, M. and John, T. (1995) *Intelligence, surveillance and informants: integrated approaches*. London: Home Office Police Research Group, Crime Detection and Prevention Series, Paper 64.

Maguire, M. and Norris, C. (1992) *The Conduct and Supervision of Criminal Investigations*. London: HMSO, Royal Commission on Criminal Justice, Research Study No. 5.

Mangham, I. (1979) *The Politics of Organisational Change*. London: Associated Business Press.

Manning, P.K. (1977) *Police Work: the social organisation of policing*. Cambridge, Mass.: MIT Press.

Marx, G. (1988) *Undercover: police surveillance in America*. Berkeley: University of California Press.

Mastrofski, S.D. (1998) 'Community policing and police organisation structure' in Brodeur, J.-P. (ed.) (1998) *How to Recognise Good Policing: problems and issues*. Thousand Oaks, California: Sage Publications.

Matthews, R. (1996) *Armed Robbery: two police responses*. London: Home Office Police Research Group, Crime Detection and Prevention Series, Paper 78.

Mativat, F. and Tremblay, P. (1997) 'Counterfeiting credit cards: displacement effects, suitable offenders and crime wave patterns' *British Journal of Criminology*, Vol. 37, No. 2: 165–183.

Mayhew, P. (1999) *Counting of Detections Obtained by Secondary Methods*. London: Home Office.

Metropolitan Police (1985) *The Principles of Policing and Guidance for Professional Behaviour*. London: Metropolitan Police.

Meyer, C. (1994) 'How the right measures help teams excel', *Harvard Business Review*, May–June 1994: 95–103.

Miller, S., Blackeler, J. and Alexandra, A. (1997) *Police Ethics*. Sydney: Allen and Unwin.

Mirrlees-Black, C., Budd, T., Partridge, S. and Mayhew, P. (1998) *The 1998 British Crime Survey: England and Wales* (Issue 21/98). Home Office Research, Development and Statistics Directorate.

Moore, M.H. (1983) 'Invisible offences: a challenge to minimally intrusive law enforcement', in Caplan, G.M. (ed.) *Abscam Ethics: moral issues and deception in law enforcement*. Cambridge, Mass.: Police Foundation.

Morgan, R. (1989) 'Policing by consent: legitimating the doctrine' in Morgan, R. and Smith, D.J. (eds.) *Coming to Terms with Policing: perspectives on policy*. London: Routledge.

Morgan, R. and Newburn, T. (1997) *The Future of Policing*. Oxford: OUP.

Muir, W.K. (1977) *Police: streetcorner politicians*. Chicago: Chicago University Press.

Mulgan, G. (1997) *Connexity: how to live in a connected world*. London: Chatto and Windus.

NACRO (1997) *Policing Local Communities: the Tottenham experiment*. London: National Association for the Care and Resettlement of Offenders.

Nash, M. (1999) *Probation, Police and Protecting the Public*. London: Blackstone.

Newburn, T. (1999) *Understanding and Preventing Police Corruption: Lessons from the literature*. London: Home Office, Police Research Series, Paper 110.

Newburn, T. and Jones, T. (1997) *Private Security and Public Policing*. Oxford: Oxford University Press.

Neyroud, P.W. (1992) *Multi-agency approaches to tackling racial harassment*. London: Home Office Police Research Group.

Neyroud, P.W. (1993) 'Multi-agency approaches to racial harassment: the lessons of implementing RAG' in Francis, P. and Matthews, R. (eds.) *Tackling Racial Attacks*. Leicester: CSPO, University of Leicester.

Neyroud, P.W. (1998) 'Policing and Privacy: the future of covert policing and human rights in British policing', *Police Research and Management*, Vol. 3: 1.

Neyroud, P.W. (1999) 'Danger signals', *Policing Today*, Volume 5, issue 2, 10–15.

Nicholson, N. (1993) *Managing Change: managing organisational change*. London: Sage Publications.

Nolan Committee (1995) *Standards in Public Life: Vol 1*. First Report of the Committee on Standards in Public Life. London: HMSO.

Norris, C. and Norris, N. (1993) 'Defining good policing: the instrumental and moral approaches to good practice and competence' *Policing and Society*, Vol. 3, No. 3: 205–221.

Norris, N. (1992) 'Problems in police training', *Policing*, Vol. 8, autumn.

O'Connor, L., Evans, R. and Coggans, N. (1999) 'Drug education in schools: identifying the added value of the police service within a model of best practice', *Police Research and Management*, Vol. 3, No. 3: 11–27.

O'Dowd, Sir David (1999) 'Perdition to probity: four steps towards ethical policing'. Presentation to the 8th Annual Internal Affairs Conference, New South Wales.

O'Malley, T.J. (1997) 'Managing for ethics: a mandate for administrators', *FBI Law Enforcement Journal*, April.

Osborne, D. and Gaebler, T. (1992) *Reinventing government*. Reading, Mass.: Addison-Wesley.

Parry, N., Rustin, M. and Satyamurti, C. (1979) *Social Work, Welfare and the State*. London: Arnold.

Patten, C. (1999) *A New Beginning: Policing in Northern Ireland: the report of the Independent Commission on Policing for Northern Ireland*. London: HMSO.

Pedler, M., Burgoyne, J. and Boydell, T. (1991) *The Learning Company: a strategy for sustainable development*. New York: McGraw-Hill.

Peters, T. (1997) *The Circle of Innovation*. London: Hodder and Stoughton.

Police Complaints Authority (1998) *Striking a Balance: the police use of new batons*. London: The Stationery Office Ltd.

Police Complaints Authority (1999) *Deaths in Custody: reducing the risks*. London: The Stationery Office Ltd.

Police Foundation/Policy Studies Institute (1996) *The Independent Committee of Inquiry into the Role and Responsibilities of the Police*. London: Police Foundation/PSI.

Pollock, J.M. (1998) *Ethics in Crime and Justice*. Third edition. Belmont, California: Wadsworth.

Poole, L. (1985) *Police Training: a skills approach*. Harrogate: CPTU.

Popper, K. (1945) *The Open Society and its Enemies*. London: Routledge.

Public Services Productivity Panel (2000) 'Improving police performance: a new approach to measuring police efficiency'. London: HM Treasury.

Puddephatt, A. (1999) 'Human rights: key areas and issues in criminal justice and community safety', *Police Research and Management*, Vol. 3, No. 2.

Punch, M. (1994) 'Rotten barrels: systemic origins of corruption' in Kolthoff, E.W. (ed.) *Strategieen voor corruptie-beheersing bij de politie*. Arnhem: Gouda Quint.

Quinton, P. and Bland, N. (1999) *Modernising the Tactic: improving the use of stop and search*. London: Home Office, Policing and Reducing Crime Unit.

Raghavan, R.K. (1999) *Policing a democracy: a comparative study of India and the US*. New Delhi: Manohar.

Reiman, J. (1996) 'Is police discretion justified in a free society?' in Kleinig, J. (ed.) *Handled with discretion: ethical issues in police decision-making*. Lanham, Maryland: Rowman and Littlefield.

Reiner, R. (1978) *The Blue Coated Worker*. Cambridge: Cambridge University Press.

Reiner, R. (1985) *The Politics of the Police*. Hemel Hempstead: Harvester Wheatsheaf.

Reiner, R. (1991) *Chief Constables: bobbies, bosses or bureaucrats*. Oxford: OUP.

Reiner, R. (1994) 'The dialectics of Dixon: the changing image of the TV. cop' in Stephens, M. and Becker, S. (eds.) *Police Force, Police Service: care and control in Britain*. Basingstoke: Macmillan.

Reiner, R. (1997) 'Policing and the Police' in Maguire, M., Morgan, R. and Reiner, R. (eds.) *The Oxford Handbook of Criminology*. (2nd edition). Oxford: OUP.

Reiss, A.J. Jnr. (1980) 'Controlling police use of deadly force', *Annals of the American Academy of Political and Social Science*, No. 452, November, 122–134.

Reuss-Ianni, E. and Ianni, F. (1983) 'Street cops and management cops: the two cultures of policing', in Punch, M. (ed.) *Control in the Police Organisation*. Cambridge, Mass.: MIT Press.

Richards, S. (1998) 'Cross-cutting issues in public policy and public service'. Report of a research project for DETR by the School of Public Policy, University of Birmingham.

Robbins, S.P. (1990) *Organisation Theory: structure, design and applications*. New Jersey: Prentice Hall International.

Rose, D. (1996) *In the Name of the Law: the collapse of criminal justice*. London: Jonathan Cape.

Rosenbaum, D.P. (ed.) (1994) *The Challenge of Community Policing: Testing the Promises*. Thousand Oaks, California: Sage.

Ross, W.D. (1930) *The Right and the Good*. Oxford: Clarendon.

Rutherford, A. (1993) *Criminal Justice and the Pursuit of Decency*. Oxford: OUP.

Savage, S.P., and Charman, S. (1995) 'Managing change' in Leishman, F., Loveday, B. and Savage, S. (eds.), *Core Issues in Policing*. London: Longman.

Scarman, Lord (1982) *The Scarman Report*. Harmondsworth, Middlesex: Penguin.

Scharf, P. and Binder, A. (1983) *The Badge and the Bullet: police use of deadly force*. New York: Praeger.

Schein, E. (1984) 'Coming to a new awareness of organisational culture'. *Sloan Management Review*, Winter.

Schmitt, J. (1994) *Mastering Tactics: a tactical decisions games workbook*. Quantico: US Marine Corps Association.

Scott, J. (1999) 'Senior women police officers: changing 'monoculture' to managing diversity' *Police Research & Management*, Volume 3 No. 3.

Scott, W.R. (1998) *Organisations: rational, natural, and open systems* (4th edition). London: Prentice Hall International, Inc.

Scott, W.R., and Meyer, J.W. (1991) 'The organisation of societal sectors: propositions and early evidence' in Powell, W.W. and DiMaggio, P.J. (eds.), *The New Institutionalism in Organisational Analysis*. Chicago: University of Chicago Press.

Senge, P.M. (1990) *The Fifth Discipline: the art and practice of the learning organisation*. London: Century Business.

Shapland, J. and Vagg, J. (1988) *Policing by the Public*. London: Routledge.

Sharpe, S. (1994) 'Covert police operations and the discretionary exclusion of evidence', *Criminal Law Review*, November: 793–804.

Shearing, C.D. and Stenning, P.C. (1987) 'Private Policing' in *Sage Criminal Justice System Annuals: Vol. 23*. Newbury Park, California: Sage.

Sheehy, Sir Patrick (1993) *Report of Inquiry into Police responsibilities and Rewards*. London: HMSO.

Sherman, L. (ed.) (1974) *Police Corruption: a sociological perspective*. New York: Doubleday.

Sherman, L. (1985) 'Becoming bent' in Elliston, F.A. and Feldberg, M. (eds.) (1985) *Moral issues in police work*. Totowa, New Jersey: Rowman and Allenheld.

Sherman, L. and Berk, R. (1984) 'The specific deterrent effects of arrest for domestic assault', *American Sociological Review*, Vol. 49, April.

Shipley, P. and Leal, F. (1998) 'The new information technology: salvation or damnation? The place of ethics in this latest faustian bargain' in Shipley, P. (ed.) *Occasional working papers in ethics and critical philosophy*. London: Society for the Furtherance of Critical Philosophy.

Simey, Lady M. (1985) *Democracy Rediscovered: a study in police accountability*. London: Pluto Press.

Singer, P. (1993) *Practical Ethics*. Cambridge: Cambridge University Press.

Skogan, W. and Hartnett, S.M. (1997) *Community Policing: Chicago Style*. New York: Oxford University Press.

Skolnick, J. (1975) *Justice Without Trial*. Second edition. New York: Wiley.

Small, M.W. and Watson, R.C. (1999) 'Police values and police misconduct: the Western Australia Police Service', *The Police Journal*, July: 225–237.

Smart, J.J.C. and Williams, B.A.O. (1973) *Utilitariansim: for and against*. Cambridge: CUP.

Smith, P. (1995a) 'Performance indicators and control in the public sector' in Berry, A.J., Broadbent, J. and Otley, D. (eds.), *Management Control: theories, issues and practices*. Basingstoke: Macmillan.

Smith, P. (1995b) 'Performance indicators and outcome in the public sector', *Public Money & Management*, Oct–Dec 1995: 13–16.

Starmer, K. (1999) *European Human Rights Law: the Human Rights Act 1998 and the European Convention on Human Rights*. London: Legal Action Group.

Stewart, E.M. (1998) 'Operational decision-making' *Police Research and Management*, Summer, Vol. 2, No. 3.

Stockdale, J. (1993) *Management and supervision of police interviews*. London: Home Office Police Department, Police Research Series, Paper 5.

Stoker, G. (1997) *Local Political Participation*. London: Joseph Rowntree Foundation.

Storch, R.D. (1999) 'The old English constabulary' *History Today*, Vol. 49, No. 11: 43–9.

Straw, J. (1999) 'Annual Constitution Unit Lecture', www.homeoffice.go.uk/hract/pr336.htm.

Taylor, R. (1998) *Forty Years of Crime and Criminal Justice Statistics, 1958 to 1997*. Home Office Research, Development and Statistics Directorate.

Toffler, A. (1999) 'Strategies for Survival'. Interview available at www.govtech.net/publications/visions/nov99/toffler

Travis, A. (2000) 'More thought, less populism, to fight crime', *Guardian*, 29 May. www.guardianunlimited.co.uk

Tucker, S. (2000) 'Why babies bug the jet set', *The Times*, 29 May 2000. Times 2: 8.

Turner, B. (1987) *Medical Power and Social Knowledge*. Basingstoke: Macmillan.

UN (United Nations High Commissioner for Human Rights) (2000) *Teaching Human Rights to Police*. New York: United Nations.

Vahlenkamp, W. and Hauer, P. (1996) *Organised Crime – criminal logistics and preventive approaches*. Wiesbaden: Federal Criminal Police Office.

Van Traa, M. (1996) *Report of the Parliamentary Enquiry Committee Concerning Investigation Methods*. Translation of article from the *Nederlands Juristenblad*, 9 February, No. 6.

Verma, A, (1999) 'Cultural roots of police corruption in India', *Policing: An International Journal of Police Strategies and Management*, Vol. 22, No. 3.

Vicchio, S.J. (1997) 'Ethics and police integrity', *FBI Law Enforcement Bulletin*, July.

Villiers, P. (1997) *Better Police Ethics: a practical guide*. London: Kogan Page.

Waddington, P.A.J. (1999) *Policing Citizens: authority and rights*. London: UCL Press.

Waters, I. (1995) 'Quality of service: politics or paradigm shift?' in Leishman, F., Loveday, B. and Savage, S. (eds.), *Core Issues in Policing*. London: Longman.

Westmarland, L. (1999) 'Women managing in the police service' *Police Research and Management*, Volume 3, No. 3.

Westley, W. (1970) *Violence and the police*. Cambridge, Mass.: MIT press.

West Mercia Constabulary (1999) *Four Tracks of Policing: a management handbook*. Worcester: West Mercia Constabulary.

West Mercia Constabulary (2000a) 'Best Value and Policing Plan'. http://www.westmercia.police.uk

West Mercia Constabulary (2000b) 'Evaluation of Beat Management'. Report by University College Worcester for West Mercia Constabulary.

Whitehouse, P. (1997) *Police Ethics in a Democratic Society*. Strasbourg: Council of Europe.

Wiles, P. (1993) 'Policing structures, organisational change and personnel management' in Dingwall, R. and Shapland, J. (eds.) *Reforming British Policing: missions and structures*. Sheffield: Faculty of Law, University of Sheffield.

Wiles, P. (1996) *The Quality of Service of the Sedgefield Community Force: the results of a customer satisfaction survey on the work of the force*. Sheffield: University of Sheffield.

Wilkinson, A. and Willmott, H. (1995) *Making Quality Critical*. London: Thompson International Publishing.

Willis, C. (1983) *The Use, Effectiveness and Impact of Police Stop and Search Powers*. Home Office Research and Planning Unit Paper 15. London: Home Office.

Wilson, J.Q. (1978) *The Investigators*. New York: Basic Books.

Wilson, J.Q. and Kelling, G. (1982) 'Broken windows', *The Atlantic Monthly*, March: 29–38.

Wolff Olins (1988) *A Force for Change: a report on the corporate identity of the Metropolitan Police*. London: Wolff Olins.

Wood, J.R.T. (1997) *Royal Commission into the New South Wales Police Service: Final Report*. Sydney: New South Wales Government Printer.

Wood, R. and Payne, T. (1998) *Competency-Based Recruitment and Selection*. Chichester, UK: John Wiley & Sons.

Woodcock, Sir J. (1991) 'Overturning police culture', *Policing*, Vol. 7, 172–182.

Wright, A., Waymont, A. and Gregory, F. (1993) *Drugs Squads*. London: Police Foundation.

Young, J. (1999) *The Exclusive Society*. London: Sage Publications.

Zander, M. (1994) 'Ethics and crime investigation', *Policing*, Vol. 10, No. 1: 39–48.

Index

Accountability of the police 69–70, 75, 129, 146–154, 217
  interactionists' view of 150
  managerialist view of 147
  radical view of 147, 150
  to government 150
Actions against public authorities 59
Association of Chief Police Officers 96, 107, 110, 190–191, 198, 212–213
  Human Rights Programme 206–214
  policy audits 207–210
  Working Group on Policing and Human Rights 198, 205–211
Association of Police Authorities 97, 107
Audit 67
Audit Commission 94, 97, 99, 107, 112, 127
Australia
  Aborigine community 13
  corruption 12
  policing 9

Belgium
  paedophiles 12
'Best value' 16, 26, 30, 95, 111
British Crime Survey 105–106, 114
Brixton disturbances 7, 10
Budget 29
  cost benefits 33
  fiscal restraint 31
Burglaries 118, 127, 128

Canada
  Charter of Rights 4, 54, 63
  control of policing 9
Care, duty of 68
  ethics of 45
CCTV 33
Characteristics of human rights 58
Chief Constables 96, 99
Child protection 23, 59, 209
Children, actions on behalf of 59
Citizen and policing 21
  rights 9
Citizens' Charter 106, 112–113
Civilianisation 16
Civil rights 56–57
Code of Conduct for Law Enforcement Officials 81–62, 189, 192, 197
Commission for Racial Equality 99
Commission on Social Justice 30
Communities, diversity of 34
Community policing 8, 31, 78, 84, 215
Complaints 67, 143, 146, 153, 154–159, 209
  independent investigation of 154–155
  learning from 154–155
Comprehensive spending review 17, 26
Computers 15
Comradeship in the police 80–81
Conflict resolution model 141
Consequentialism 41–42

Corruption 4–7, 12, 38, 42, 81, 130,
        154–159, 170
    causes of 156
    prevention 157–159
Council of Europe 54, 55, 56
    Declaration on the Police 61–62, 190
Court escorting 24
Covert policing 6, 13–14, 124–135, 209
    ACPO code on 131
    and human rights 131
    control of 125–131, 133–135
    deception 125–126
    intrusion into privacy 126–131
Crime and Disorder Act 25
Crime and Disorder Partnerships 26
Crime audit 84
    expenditure on control of 28–29
    fighting 4, 24, 26, 28, 30–31, 33
    figures 105–106
    police role 25
    prevention 22,–23, 31
    recording 106
    reduction strategy 26, 28
Criminal statistics 114
Crown Prosecution Service 110, 205–206

Dangerousness 124, 135–137
    management of 15
Deaths in custody 12, 67
Decision making 198–203
Declaration on the Police 61–62, 190
Definition of human rights 58
Demand management 34
Democracy and policing 21–22, 66
Demonstrations 84
Deontological ethics 41–42
Desborough reforms 22–23
Detection rates 106
Discretion 5, 38, 65–66, 73, 75, 78, 82–86
Discrimination, in British justice 45–46
    in the police 77, 86
District Policing Partnership Board 152
Domestic violence 83, 85, 209
Drugs 129–130, 131
Duty 41–42
Duty of police 38

Eastern Europe 10, 13

Effectiveness of policing 120–121
Efficiency of police 121
Egoism 41
Encounters, phases of 139
Equal Opportunities Commission 99
Ethical standards 189–198, 218
    content of 194–195
    need for 193–194
Ethical theories 40–47
Ethics and policing 4, 47–50, 75, 77
European Convention on Human Rights 8,
        54, 56, 59, 60, 61–68
European Court of Human Rights 8, 11,
        56, 61, 87
European Union 54
'Evidence-based policing' 16
Expenditure on police 116, 119

Financial Management Initiative 106
Firearms, use of 66, 140, 176, 209
Force, use of 28–29, 68, 124, 137–143
    avoidance of 139
    justification 137–138
    lethal force 202
'Four tracks of ethics' 49, 61, 67, 91
'Four tracks of policing' 35–36, 49
Funding of the police 113–115

Globalisation 3, 13
Government and policing 19–22

Hard policing 7
Health and Safety Executive 99
Her Majesty's Inspector of Constabulary
        97, 99, 107, 110, 112, 196–197
History of policing 22–26
Holland 12
    drug dealing 12
    Van Traa Commission 12
Home Affairs Select Committee (1998)
        87
Home Office 97, 107, 132, 205
Home Secretary 96–97, 99, 113–114
Human Rights Act (1998) 4, 26, 198
Human rights, history of 55–56

Independence of the police 22–23
Independent Advisory Groups 153

India
   corruption 182–183
   integrity 13
   policing 9
Information technology 15, 33, 34
Informers 40, 43, 44, 45, 125, 127, 129
Integrity of police 38
Interdependence 23–24, 26, 32, 216
International Association of Chiefs of
      Police 183, 198
International Commission of Jurists 55
Internationalisation 13–14, 55, 150–151,
   153
Intrusion by police 38

Joint performance management 112
Judgement in policing 38
Judicial review 199–200

Kidnapping 39–40, 42

Landlords 84
Leadership 218
Local Government Act (1999) 111
Localisation 14, 55

Macpherson report 12, 50, 146, 159
Management control systems 101–105
   behaviour controls 101
   input controls 101
   outcome controls 102
   output controls 101
   public demand 102
   ritual controls 102
Management reforms 95
Managerialism 16, 77, 218
Managers 5, 6
Media 15
Medical services, ethics for 47–48
Medicine compared with policing 78
Megan's Law 136
Mental health 136, 209
Metropolitan police 22–23, 96, 161, 189,
   190
Miner's strike 23
Minority communities 13, 146, 151, 154,
   159–164, 197
Miscarriages of justice 4, 8

Misconduct 154–159
Mission of policing 20, 22–26, 42, 47, 51,
   79
Morality 38, 46
Morgan Report 24
Murder investigation 118

National Crime Management model 33
National Criminal Justice Commission
   11
National Police Staff College 76
National priorities in policing 107
New Zealand
   breach of rights 202
   Charter of Rights 4, 54, 63
Nolan report 50, 87
Numbers of police 116–117

Oath of Office 192
Offender profiling 135
Open society and policing 20
Operational police review 23, 29
Optimal policing 21, 35
Organisational learning 119–122, 184–185
Organisational theories of policing
   agency theory 98–99
   organisational field theory 99–100
   policy networks theory 100
Organisation, development of 34
Organisation of policing in Britain 96–98
Osman case 15, 136, 202
Outcome of policing 19–36
Overarching Aims and Objectives 26–27,
   36, 51, 105, 112

Patrols 24, 29, 30, 32, 34, 77, 114, 153
Patten Report 3, 4, 50, 63, 68, 87–88,
   145–147, 151–152, 190, 192, 210
Performance and Development Reviews
   118
Performance indicators 95–96, 106–109
   judgement of 115–117, 217
   management of 105–122
Pledge, The 189
Police and Community Consultative
   Groups 98–99
Police and Criminal Evidence Act 23, 134,
   151

Police and Magistrates' Court Act (1995) 96–97
Police Authorities 96–97, 99, 186
Police Code of Conduct 189
Police Complaints Authority 99, 153, 155
Police culture 7, 73, 78–82, 92, 179
Police officers
  as demonstrators 88
  as freemasons 87–88
  ethnic minority officers 77
  gifts and benefits 90–91
  misconduct 138
  religion 87–88
  rights of 87–90
  second jobs 88
  sexuality 88–89
  sponsorship 89
  women 77
Police Reform White Paper 96
Police Service Statement of Common Purpose 190
Police training 39, 141, 175–181
  competency based 39
  decision making 201–202
  ethics 40, 170, 182
  personal development of staff 183
  Personal Development review 179–180, 197
  Probationer Training Programme 177
  reflective practice 176–177
  socialisation 177–178
  tutor constables 177
Policing as a profession 74–78
Policing of privacy 6
'Policy networks' 95
Political rights 56–57
Postmodern ethics 46
Postmodernism 55
Principles of policing 50–51, 67
Private policing 24–25, 59, 77, 215
Private sector competition 31
Privatisation of policing 3, 16
Proactive policing 4, 7
Professionalism 5, 81, 86
Protection of human rights 4
  of minority groups 38
Protests
  miners strike 23

roads 25
Public concerns 97–98
  demand on police 29
  priorities in policing 29
Public Interest Disclosure Act (1998) 186
Public policing 4, 16, 24
Public service role 26, 38, 74–75
  ethics in 39
Public space, policing of 14–15
  privatisation of 24
Purposes of the police 19–36

Queen's peace 22

Racial harassment 23
Racial prejudice 79
Racism in the police 160–161
Rampart Study 169–170, 178, 181
Ransoms 39–40, 42
Recorded crime 119
Recruitment of police 6, 170–175, 218
  competence 172–174
  desired character traits 176
  education 75, 174
  gender issues 175
  minority communities 175
  psychological testing 174
  screening candidates 171–172
  values-based recruitment 174
Reform, 82
  opportunities for 10
Relativism 41
Rights and democracy 60
  and justice 60
  and law 60
  and legality of police action 64
  balancing 64, 65–66
  conflicting 64
  development of 63
  links between 63
  overlapping 64
  types of 63
Risk 44
  assessment 15, 135
  avoidance 80
  communicating 15, 28
  managing 28
  policing 15, 29

Role of the police 19–36
    future 29–36
Royal Commission on Criminal Justice 8,
    145
Rusher Report 170

Scarman report 7, 22, 28, 151, 159
Security services 14
    private agencies 14–15
Sex Offenders Act (1997) 136–137
Sexual offenders 40, 136–137
Sheehy report 24, 76, 96
Skills in policing 76
Social contract 20, 85
Social control and policing 21
Society and policing 20
South Africa
    human rights 54
Stakeholders in the police 97, 102, 115
Standard for law enforcement officials 55
Stop and search 12, 31, 161–164, 207
Structure of the police 82
Subjectivism 41
Surveillance 15, 60, 125, 127, 129, 134

Technology 3, 15, 31, 33
Teleological ethics 42
Telephone interception 65, 128
Tenants 84
Traditional policing 4
Trainers 5

Treasury 97, 99
Trespass 24
Trust 16

Uncertainty and ethics 45–47
United Nations 54, 58
    Code of Conduct for Law Enforcement
        Officials 61–62, 189
    Universal Declaration on Human
        Rights 56
USA
    confidence in police 11
    New York 25
    O. J. Simpson trial 11
    police 7
    Waco siege 11
Utilitarianism 42–44

Vehicle search 31
Vehicle theft 118
'Vicious cycles' 9–10, 14, 31, 95
Virtue, ethics of 44–45
'Virtuous cycle' 10–11, 219
Violence 5, 14, 43

Wednesbury judgement 200–201
Willink Royal Commission 22–23

Youth Offending Teams 25

Zero tolerance 4, 25, 31